THE SPECTRUM OF TEACHING STYLES

THE SPECTRUM OF TEACHING STYLES

FROM COMMAND TO DISCOVERY

MUSKA MOSSTON

SARA ASHWORTH

Longman

New York & London

The Spectrum of Teaching Styles: From Command to Discovery

Longman, 95 Church Street, White Plains, N.Y. 10601

Associated companies:
Longman Group Ltd., London
Longman Cheshire Pty., Melbourne
Longman Paul Pty., Auckland
Copp Clark Pitman, Toronto

The following figures and text were originally published in TEACHING
PHYSICAL EDUCATION, Third Edition, by Muska Mosston and Sara
Ashworth. Copyright © 1986 by Merrill Publishing Company, Columbus, Ohio.
Reprinted with generous permission of the Merrill Publishing Company.

Figures 4.3, 4.4, 4.5, 5.1, 8.13, 8.14, 8.17, 10.6, and 17.4; material appearing on
pages 34–36, 47, 59, 118, 122, 157, 205–7, 207–8, 273–4, and 283.

Executive editor: Raymond T. O'Connell
Production editor: Dee A. Josephson
Cover design and cover illustration: Anne Li
Production supervisor: Kathleen Ryan

Library of Congress Cataloging in Publication Data
Mosston, Muska.
    The spectrum of teaching styles: from command to discovery /
Muska Mosston, Sara Ashworth.
        p.   cm.
    Bibliography: p.
    Includes index.
    ISBN 0-8013-0350-8
    1. Teaching.   I. Ashworth, Sara.   II. Title.
LB1025.2.M639   1989
371.1′02—dc20   89-12274
                                                          CIP

ABCDEFGHIJ-MA-99 98 97 96 95 94 93 92 91 90

- To Richard C. Anderson; to Evelyn Ogden.

M.M.

- To all the teachers who helped us grow.

S.A.

- To Bob Ward, in memoriam.

M.M. S.A.

Contents

CHAPTER 7   STYLE D: THE SELF-CHECK STYLE   115

CHAPTER 8   STYLE E: THE INCLUSION STYLE   128

CHAPTER 9   ABOUT STYLES A–E   161

CHAPTER 10   STYLE F: THE GUIDED DISCOVERY STYLE   193

Preface

The Spectrum of Teaching Styles was conceived in 1964, when I was teaching at Rutgers University. I was struck by the tug-o-war that existed in education. It became clear to me that the hallmark of education (and of teaching) was *fragmentation*. Individualized instruction versus group experiences, cognitive versus affective education, creativity versus conformity, the teacher's idiosyncratic preferences versus teaching models of all sorts. This fragmentation continues to exist and to dominate the educational scene even today, as evidenced by the two prominent movements identified as Teaching Effectiveness and Thinking Skills. The former is rich in principles and techniques, backed by voluminous research that points toward improvement of classroom performance (Berliner, 1976, 1984; Joyce, 1981; Good and Brophy, 1987; Roeche and Baker, 1986; Burke Guild and Garger, 1987). The latter is rich in analysis of thinking processes, models of cognitive behavior, metacognition, critical thinking, creativity, problem solving, task analyses, questioning, and programs for the teaching of thinking (Halpern, 1984; Presseisen, 1987; Costa, 1984; Oxman, 1984; Lipman, 1984, 1985; Rothenberg and Hausman, 1976; Whimbey and Lochhead, 1986; Doyle, 1983; Dillon, 1984; Nickerson et al. 1985).

This fragmentation posed a dilemma that prompted me to search for a conceptualization of teaching that would show and emphasize the *relationships and connections* among such aspects, rather than the isolation and disparity among them. The result of the search was the formulation of The Spectrum of Teaching Styles, an integrated structure for teaching that provides the contextual framework for the various movements that have contributed to the improvement of teaching.

The early exploration of these teaching styles was conducted in the public schools in the vicinity of Rutgers University. These explorations brought forth many issues, questions, and insights concerning the development of theoretical structures, transforming theoretical models into classroom practices, reaching students who march to a different drummer, identifying what was going on in classes, and experimenting with what could be occurring in classrooms. The first book describing the essentials of the Spectrum was published during those early days of exploration (Mosston, 1966). In 1972, with the aid of a Title III federal grant, the Center On Teaching was established under my direction. It provided the opportunity for me and my colleague, Sara Ashworth, to continue the study of the Spectrum and its implementation in a variety of classes in schools throughout New Jersey. Many teachers in scores of schools, who chose to participate in the training, joined us in the refinement of the styles and their practical application in all grade levels accross the curriculum. The empirical data from analyzing thousands of teaching episodes evolved into a network of insights and connections embodied in the Spectrum. The Spectrum became the framework for the confluence of ideas about teaching, while it demonstrated respect for their diversity and uniqueness. Indeed, we are grateful to all the teachers who joined us in the challenges of exploration and the joys of the results. The teachers who were willing to examine their own teaching behavior, and were able to endure the awkward phase of learning new behaviors, reaped the results of their labor. The results included the expansion of their teaching repertoire, expansion of the students' decision-making ability, the reduction of discipline problems, and widening of social interaction among students. After successfully crossing the milestone of the United States Office of Education's validation process that was conducted by Richard C. Anderson (Pichert et al, 1976), we continued teaching the Spectrum to teachers in schools, and to colleagues in universities in the United States, Canada, and many European countries. Additional insights, questions, and data that shed more light on the nature of the Spectrum have been accumulating (L. White-Stevens, 1977; Shirey et al, 1978; Chamberlin, 1979; Oxman and Michelli, 1981, Goldberger et. al, 1982; Ashworth, 1983; Mosston and Ashworth, 1985, 1986).

Think of the Spectrum as you would a map. It is a map that shows the relationship among the variety of styles and the relationship among the teaching elements within each style. The Spectrum, then, provides simultaneously a macro-conceptualization of the teaching act as a whole, and micro-insights into the specific instances that comprise the teaching act. The Spectrum is a map that shows patterns within seemingly random teaching behaviors, and shows the connections among these patterns, connections that form a unified structure of teaching. *The Spectrum of Teaching Styles: From Command to Discovery* represents the search for an expanded pedagogy. It represents the wish to join hands with those who seek the integration of knowledge (Fergusen, 1980; Bohm and Peat, 1987).

Here is a preview of the *key features* of the Spectrum:

1. The identification of an axiom that states: "teaching behavior is a chain of decision making" (Mosston, 1966). This axiom serves as the unifying principle that governs all teaching. (This notion has also been expressed by Shavelson, 1976; Hunter, 1979; Berliner, 1984).
2. The formulation of the "anatomy of any style" (Chapter 3). The anatomy establishes a structure for the decision categories that are made in any teaching-learning episode. The "anatomy of any style" provides the *basis* for answering the question: who makes which decision, about what, when - and for what purpose?
3. Each of the landmark styles on the Spectrum answers this question in a different way. Each style delineates specific roles for the teacher and for the learner in making specific clusters of decisions. This *distribution* of decisions between the teacher and the learner defines the structure of each style, its operation, and its outcomes.
4. The structure of the Spectrum identifies two clusters of styles: styles A–E are used when the objectives of the teaching episodes are the *reproduction* and replication of past knowledge. Styles F–K are used when the objectives of the teaching episodes are the *production,* the discovery, the creation of new knowledge.
5. The Spectrum provides a formulation for thinking processes and cognitive operations (Chapter 2) that go hand in hand with the structure of the styles.
6. The Spectrum provides the teacher with the awareness and the knowledge of the teaching styles (options), and provides a practical guide for implementation and the shifting from one style to another.
7. The Spectrum provides a comprehensive framework (a unified structure) that shows the relationship between the styles and their place on the Spectrum.

The goal of the Spectrum is to invite each teacher to internalize and use as many styles as possible and thus create new realities in the classroom. These new realities will provide greater opportunities for expanded learning.

ACKNOWLEDGMENTS

We would like to thank Nesher, Phyllis, and James Ashworth, Ben and Miki Bragman, Risto and Tuula Telama. Many thanks to our editors, Elaine Luthy Brennan and Dee Josephson.

M.M. and S.A.

Special thanks to Sheila Gallanter, Steve and Laney Sokolow, Lewis and Elaine Fromkin, Sel Lederman, Bill and Jeanne Cantor, Frank and Gail Rubin.

S.A.

THE SPECTRUM OF TEACHING STYLES

CHAPTER 1

An Overview

WHAT IS TEACHING

This book is about teaching. It is about the relationships between teacher and learner—relationships that are, at the same time, both ubiquitous and uniquely personal. It is a book about the mastery of this pervasive human behavior.

When teaching takes place a special human connection evolves, a connection of many dimensions that simultaneously affect the learner and the teacher. Both are subjected to a tacit agreement to share information, to deliver and receive accumulated knowledge, to replicate and reproduce portions of the past, to acquire and discover new information, and to construct and create pathways for the yet unknown. This connection, inevitably, invites feelings for one another—feelings of cooperation or discord, acceptance or rejection, anger or joy. It invites both the teacher and the learner to participate in a unique social context, with its special hierarchies, rules, and network of responsibilities. It inspires aesthetic sensations and seeks to expand the very boundaries of the self. It triggers the brain, stimulates the emotions and, at its best, uplifts the human spirit. The evolution of this connection is an inescapable process that is at the very core of human development. All cultures provide for it, all humans participate in it, and all educational processes and goals rely on it.

How, then, does a teacher translate these educational processes and goals—lofty as some may sound—into daily procedures, daily activities, daily behaviors? What are the practical issues and questions that face *every* teacher, every day? The following are some categorical questions that persist in the mind of every teacher—novice or veteran—when preparing to enter the classroom:

1. What do I want my students to accomplish? What are the objectives of the lesson?
2. What methodology will I choose in order to reach the objectives? What will be my teaching behavior?
3. What is the sequence of the lesson? How do I arrange the materials?
4. How do I organize the class for optional learning? In groups? In pairs? By providing individual activities?
5. How do I motivate my class? How do I offer appropriate feedback?
6. How do I create a climate conducive to thinking, social interaction, and good feelings?
7. How do I know that my students and I have reached the objectives? Have we reached all of them? Some?
8. How will I know that the *action* that took place during the lesson was congruent with my prelesson *intent*?

In the course of answering these questions—and, indeed, many others —the teacher must make *decisions* (choices). There are many different ways to answer these questions and there are many ways of teaching. However, the many options and the many idiosyncratic variations in teaching all stem from several universal patterns that reflect the *decisions* that are made by the teacher and by the learner during any given episode. Teaching and learning episodes differ from one another because of the decision patterns that take place in the given episode. The decisions made by the teacher define his/her teaching behavior and the decisions made by the learner define the learning behavior. The teaching-learning process is a continuous interaction between the behavior of the teacher and the behavior of the learner.

Teaching Behavior

↕

Learning Behavior

This book describes the options that are available in the interaction between teaching behavior and learning behavior. It offers some answers to the categorical questions listed above by:

1. Identifying the various decision patterns
2. Identifying the specific decisions within each pattern
3. Describing a framework that shows the relationships among the various patterns

The decision patterns are called *teaching styles,* and the framework that holds them together is called the *Spectrum of Teaching Styles.*[1] The Spectrum identifies the structure of *each style* by delineating the decisions that are made by the teacher and those made by the learner. It describes how to shift appropriate decisions from the teacher to the learner as both move from style to style. It describes the influence of *each* style on the learner in the cognitive, affective, social, physical, and moral domains.

What is teaching? It is the ability to be aware of and utilize the possible connections with the learner—in all domains.

It is the ability to behave, in a *deliberate* manner, using a style that is most appropriate for reaching the objectives of a given episode. Skillful teaching is the ability to move deliberately from style to style as the objectives change from one teaching episode to another.

AN OVERVIEW OF THE SPECTRUM OF TEACHING STYLES

The fundamental proposition of the Spectrum is that *teaching is governed by a single unifying process: decision making.* Every act of deliberate teaching is a consequence of a prior decision. Decision making is the central or primary behavior that governs all the behaviors that follow: how we organize students; how we organize the subject matter; how we manage time, space, and equipment; how we interact with students; how we choose our verbal behavior; how we construct the social-affective climate in the classroom; and how we create and conduct the cognitive connections with the learners. All these are secondary behaviors; all emanate from prior decisions, and all are governed by those decisions.

Identifying primary decisions and understanding the possible combinations of decisions opens up a wide vista for looking at the teacher-learner relationships. Each option in the teacher-learner relationship has a particular structure of decisions that are made by the teacher and by the learner. The Spectrum of Teaching Styles defines the available options or styles, their decision structures, the specific roles of the teacher and the learner in each style, and the objectives best reached by each style.

---

[1] The term *Spectrum of Teaching Styles* was coined in the mid-1960s to designate this particular framework for teaching (Mosston 1966). The term *teaching style* was selected to differentiate the descriptions of specific teaching behavior from contemporary terms of that time. Terms like *methods, approaches, models,* and *strategies* were used and are still being used in many different ways by different writers. Recently, the term *style* has been used by others in reference to personal style. In this book, as in recent publications by the authors (Mosston and Ashworth 1986), the term *teaching style* refers to a structure that is independent of one's idiosyncrasies.

Six Premises of the Spectrum

Figure 1.1 is a schematic overview of the structure of the Spectrum of Teaching Styles. This structure is based on six underlying premises, each of which is described below.

1. The Axiom. The entire structure of the Spectrum stems from the initial premise that teaching behavior is a chain of decision making. Every *deliberate* act of teaching is a result of a previously made decision.

2. The Anatomy of Any Style. The anatomy is composed of the conceivable categories of decisions that must be made in any teaching-learning transaction. These categories (which will be described in detail in Chapter 3) are grouped into three sets: the *preimpact set,* the *impact set,* and the *postimpact set.* The preimpact set includes all decisions that must be made prior to the teaching-learning transaction; the impact set includes decisions related to the actual teaching-learning transaction; and the postimpact set identifies decisions concerning evaluation of the teacher-learner transaction. The anatomy delineates *which* decisions must be made in each set.

3. The Decision Makers. Both teacher and learner can make decisions in any of the categories delineated in the anatomy. When most or all of the decisions in a category are the responsibility of one decision maker (e.g., the teacher), that person's decision-making responsibility is at "maximum" and the other's is at "minimum."

4. The Spectrum. By establishing *who* makes *which* decisions, about *what* and *when,* it is possible to identify the structure of eleven *landmark styles* as well as alternative styles that lie between them on the Spectrum.[2]

In the first style (Style A), which has as its overriding objective precise replication, the teacher makes all the decisions; the learner responds by adhering to all the teacher's decisions. In the second style (Style B), nine specific decisions are shifted from the teacher to the learner, and thus a new set of objectives can be reached. In every subsequent style, specific decisions are systematically shifted from teacher to learner—thereby allowing new objectives to be reached—until the full Spectrum of Teaching Styles is delineated.

5. The Clusters. The structure of the Spectrum of Teaching Styles reflects two basic human capacities: the capacity for *reproduction* and the capacity for *production.* All human beings have, in varying degrees, the capacity to *reproduce* known knowledge, replicate models, and practice skills. All

---

[2] The concept of landmark styles and alternative or *canopy* styles will be discussed in more detail in Chapter 9.

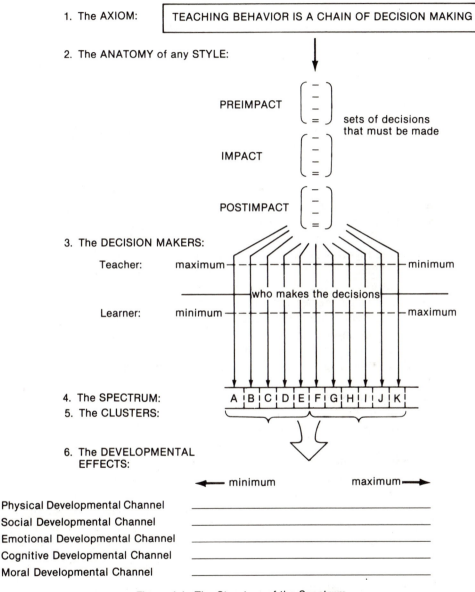

1. The AXIOM: | TEACHING BEHAVIOR IS A CHAIN OF DECISION MAKING |

2. The ANATOMY of any STYLE:

PREIMPACT

sets of decisions
that must be made

IMPACT

POSTIMPACT

3. The DECISION MAKERS:

Teacher: maximum — minimum

who makes the decisions

Learner: minimum — maximum

4. The SPECTRUM: A B C D E F G H I J K
5. The CLUSTERS:

6. The DEVELOPMENTAL
   EFFECTS:

◄— minimum   maximum —►

Physical Developmental Channel
Social Developmental Channel
Emotional Developmental Channel
Cognitive Developmental Channel
Moral Developmental Channel

Figure 1.1. The Structure of the Spectrum

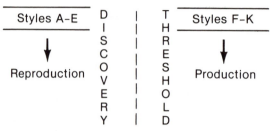

Figure 1.2. The Clusters of Styles

human beings have the capacity to *produce* a range of ideas and a range of things; all have the capacity to venture into the new and tap the yet unknown.

The cluster of Styles A–E represents the teaching options that foster *reproduction* of past knowledge; the cluster of Styles F–K represents options that invite *production* of new knowledge—that is, knowledge that is new to the learner, new to the teacher, and—at times—new to society. The line of demarcation between these two clusters is called the *discovery threshold* (see Figure 1.2). It identifies the boundaries of each cluster. Styles A–E are designed for the acquisition of basic skills, the replication of models and procedures, and the maintenance of cultural traditions. Activities in Styles A–E engage the learner primarily in cognitive operations such as memory and recall, identification, and sorting—operations that deal with past and present knowledge. This knowledge includes factual data, events, dates, names, computation procedures, rules, and the use of tools. It also includes the knowledge that is required to perform in music, dance, and sports.

The cluster of Styles F–G represents the teaching options that foster the *discovery* of single correct concepts. The cluster of Styles H–K is designed for the development of *discovery* and *creativity* of alternatives and new concepts. Styles F–K engage the learner in problem solving, reasoning, inventing; they invite the learner to go beyond the given data.

The clusters and each of the styles within them are integral parts of our humanity. Each style contributes to our development and none seeks, nor merits, supremacy over the others. For teacher and student alike, the Spectrum serves as a guide for selecting the style appropriate for a particular purpose, and for developing deliberate mobility in moving from one style to another.

6. The Developmental Effects. Since *decisions* always influence what happens to people, each style affects the developing learner in unique ways. The Spectrum provides a framework for studying the influence of each style on the learner in the cognitive, affective, social, physical, and moral domains.

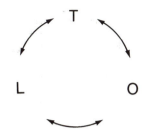

Figure 1.3. The T–L–O Relationship

THE O–T–L–O RELATIONSHIPS

The previous section presented an overview of the Spectrum and offered the large picture of the entire structure. This section describes the elements that constitute any given episode.

The interaction between teacher and learner always reflects a particular teaching behavior, a particular learning behavior, and particular sets of objectives to be reached. The bond among teaching behavior (T), learning behavior (L), and objectives (O) is inextricable. The T-L-O always exists as a unit, conceived as the *pedagogical unit*. This relationship is diagrammed in Figure 1.3.

Each style is defined by the particular behavior of the teacher (the decisions made by the teacher), the particular behavior of the learner (the decisions made by the learner), and the objectives that this relationship reaches. Hence, each style has its own distinct T–L–O.

There are always two sets of objectives to be reached in any teacher-learner interaction: *subject matter objectives* and *behavior objectives* (Figure 1.4). The first set contains specific objectives that pertain to the particular content of the episode (e.g., citing the capitals of European countries, using the quadratic equation, translating a speech to another language, dribbling the basketball, writing a poem). The second set contains specific objectives of human behavior (e.g., cooperation, accuracy of performance, self-assessment, honesty, replication, creating).

Subject matter objectives and behavior objectives always exist in teaching. The T-L relationship determines the kind of objectives that can be reached in the subject matter and in the behavior, and conversely the particular objectives (both in subject matter and in behavior) determine which teaching behavior and learning behavior are more likely to achieve them.

One more aspect needs to be considered in this context. *Objectives* are an a priori statement of what is to be achieved in a given episode; at the end of an episode, however, there are always *outcomes*—again, both subject matter outcomes and behavior outcomes. The entire process of any episode,

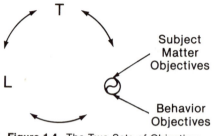

Figure 1.4. The Two Sets of Objectives

therefore, constitutes a flow and an interaction of objectives, teaching behavior, learning behavior, and outcomes. This flow is diagrammed in Figure 1.5.

The objectives of an episode (O_B) affect the teaching behavior (T), which in turn influences the interaction with the learning behavior (L). This interaction culminates with the particular outcomes (O_U), outcomes in subject matter and in behavior. Logically, then, in a successful teaching-learning episode, the outcomes are congruent with the objectives ($O_B \cong O_U$). Stated differently, in a successful episode the intent and the action are congruent:

$$INTENT \cong ACTION$$

TEACHING AND THINKING

The multiple goals of schooling reflect the wish (and the philosophy) to educate the learner in all the domains of development. It is, indeed, commonly accepted that the educational experiences in schools—in all subject areas—affects the learners' growth and involvement in the physical, affective, social, cognitive, and moral domains.

These domains constantly intertwine and it is quite difficult to claim the dominance of one over the others in any given episode. All human experiences involve some physiological activity or dexterity, all experiences evoke or reflect some feelings, all experiences occur within some social context (from isolation to crowds), and all experiences, in one way or another, touch moral standards.

However, these four domains seem to be influenced and guided—if not governed—by the cognitive domain. Thinking processes, yet unfathomed and mysterious, seem to control many of our functions and actions (both on the conscious and the unconscious levels). Thinking is involved in every task we do. It is involved in every task that teachers design for their students—and in the decision making that goes into designing and carrying out those tasks. Since thinking is such an essential part of the teaching-

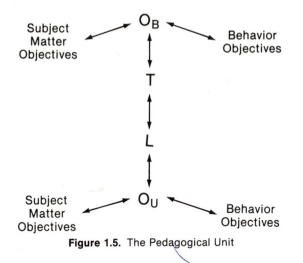

Figure 1.5. The Pedagogical Unit

learning experience, we need to make clear the assumptions and theories about thinking and the teaching of thinking that underlie the Spectrum of Teaching Styles.

Therefore, before we begin to delineate and develop the details of each style, we present in Chapter 2 a formulation and terminology of thinking that can facilitate the decision making that is the focus of the Spectrum. In Chapter 3 we will examine the nature of the various categories of decisions.

CHAPTER 2

On Thinking

The ability to think is pervasive. All humans use their thinking ability at different times and for different purposes. They may display different degrees of skillfulness in their thinking, and the thinking may vary in its speed, variety, or depth, but the underlying process is the same in all humans.

The professional literature on thinking is vast. It contains treatises on the nature of thinking, research on specific aspects of thinking, and proposals for the teaching of thinking. The proliferation of ideas has, inevitably, produced a rich terminology that often conflicts in meaning and in usage. This chapter presents a formulation of the processes and operations of the complex phenomenon of human thinking as it relates to the Spectrum of Teaching Styles. This formulation is an attempt to identify a framework for the relationships that seem to exist among the various thinking processes and cognitive operations that characterize the teaching-learning experience. Several new terms were coined in conjunction with the new formulation, and are kept consistent throughout the chapter and the rest of the book.

THE PREMISE

The formulation presented here identifies three basic processes of conscious thinking: memory, discovery, and creativity.

The *memory process* enables the *reproduction* aspect of learning by recalling and replicating past knowledge. This knowledge commonly includes facts, dates, names, events, routines, procedures, rules, and previous models.

The *discovery process* enables the learner to find out about knowledge that already exists, but was unknown to the learner. This knowledge can include concepts, relationships between or among entities, principles, and

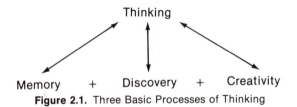

Figure 2.1. Three Basic Processes of Thinking

theorems. The discovery process, unlike memory, engages the learner in *production* of knowledge that was previously unknown to him/her.

The *creative process* is manifested by the *production* of something that is entirely new—new to the learner and new to others as well. This could be a new idea, a new formulation, a new arrangement of previous models, a new tool, a new poem, or a new product. Although the notion of differentiating discovery from creativity is quite reasonable, based on our operational definitions, the line of demarcation between the two is often quite subtle and even blurred. The interaction of the three processes, however, is fundamental to the very structure of thinking (Figure 2.1).

A GENERAL MODEL FOR THE FLOW OF CONSCIOUS THINKING

Thinking occurs when something or somebody triggers the brain to engage in memory, discovery, or creativity. The trigger is always in a form of a particular *stimulus* (S) that induces a state of unrest in the brain and evokes the need to know. The stimulus moves the person into a state of *cognitive dissonance* (D) (Festinger 1957). The need to know motivates the brain to start a search for an answer, a solution, or a response that will reduce the dissonance. The search, regardless of how long it takes, engages the *memory process* and/or the *discovery process* and/or the *creative process*. This phase in the flow of thinking is designated as *mediation* (M).

When the search is completed, a *response* (R) is produced in a form of an answer, a solution, a new idea, or a new product. In summary, the phases and sequence in the flow of conscious thinking are

    S = The stimulus (the trigger)
    D = The state of cognitive dissonance (the need to know)
    M = Mediation (the search)
    R = The response (the answer or solution)

Schematically, the general model for the flow of Conscious Thinking looks like this:

$$S \rightarrow D \rightarrow M \rightarrow R$$

THE STIMULUS (S)

Many kinds of stimuli trigger thinking: a task to be done, a social situation, an emotional problem, a game, a creative endeavor. In fact, any life event can serve as a stimulus. But regardless of the event, the stimulus always raises a *question* in the mind of the person, a question that induces cognitive dissonance and thereby arouses the need to search for an answer. All questions, whether they are asked by others or by oneself, can therefore be assigned to one of three categories which correspond to the three basic thinking processes used in searching or mediating. Some questions trigger the memory, some questions trigger discovery, and some questions invite creativity.

When did the Olympic Games take place in Paris? Who was the first signer of the Constitution of the United States? Name the Scandinavian countries. (This command is converted in the mind to the question: What are the names of the Scandinavian countries?) State Newton's laws. How many symphonies did Beethoven compose? Which muscles raise the arm laterally? These questions and a thousand others in this category can be answered by resorting to memory. Questions in this category serve as *specific stimuli* that instantly trigger the brain to engage in a search via memory, if the learner had previously known these facts.

Another category of questions (and another category of tasks) will engage the brain in discovery. For example: How can any set of five objects be arranged into two groups where the objects in one group share one common attribute that the other group of objects does not have? Repeat this task ten times, using a different attribute each time.

This set of tasks obviously calls for the cognitive operation of categorizing. The ten different categorization attempts will, in all likelihood, be successful if one can *discover* some of the possible categories. Although memory may come into play, the dominant cognitive operation is categorizing.

Yet another category of questions would invite the person to engage in creativity. For example: How can the same five objects be arranged or used so that they will form a toy that was not known before?

As previously stated, the line of demarcation between discovery episodes and creativity episodes (and sometimes between these and memory episodes) can be subtle due to a possible overlap between the two processes. For example, the nine-dots problem shown in Figure 2.2 could be solved by memory, by discovery, or by creativity. If you have previously solved this problem, then you can solve it again by memory (replication). If, however, this example is new to you, you will have to discover the solution by continuously asking yourself the question: How do I connect the dots? Suppose a further question is presented to you after you have discovered the known solution: What are two additional solutions that are possible? This question may trigger the creative process to embark on a different search.

Using no more than four
straight lines and without
lifting your pen from the
paper, draw a line through
all nine dots

Figure 2.2. The Nine-Dots Problem

Still another example: What would be some changes in our lives if the clock had 25 hours instead of 24? How might this exercise in hypothesizing and extrapolating make use of memory? How would it induce discovery? How would it invite creativity?

As we have seen in this section, the stimulus is transformed in the mind by a triggering question (Q), and the questions available to us fall into three categories or clusters that correspond to the three basic processes of thinking (Figure 2.3).

Q_M represents the cluster of questions that trigger the memory process, Q_D represents the cluster of questions that trigger the discovery process and Q_C represents the cluster of questions that invite creativity. In teaching, it is necessary, therefore, to select and design questions that are appropriate for each of the three processes—questions that will produce congruity between action and intent.

COGNITIVE DISSONANCE (D)

Dissonance is a state of unrest, a condition manifested by the need to find an answer. A learner enters the state of cognitive dissonance when the stimulus (the question) is relevant to his/her interest, need, and level of knowledge.

The dissonance motivates the learner to act upon the need to know, and moves him/her to the next phase: mediation. If the stimulus is not relevant to the learner, he/she will ignore it and will not enter the state of cognitive dissonance. This is manifested by a lack of the need to know and the need to search.

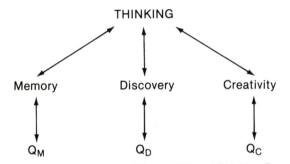

Figure 2.3. Different Questions Trigger Different Thinking Processes.

MEDIATION (M) AND THE ROLE OF COGNITIVE OPERATIONS

Human thinking capacities span a large variety of cognitive operations. For example, all humans can engage, with varying degrees of proficiency and speed, in the following *specific* operations:

- Comparing
- Contrasting
- Categorizing
- Analyzing
- Synthesizing
- Inferring
- Hypothesizing
- Extrapolating

Mediation involves the engagement in a *specific* cognitive operation that is triggered by the specificity of the stimulus (the question). One will engage, for example, in *comparing* only if a stimulus calls for this operation; otherwise, there is no need to compare. The need to compare may arise from different sources: a question posed by a social situation, the need to choose between or among options, a question that arises in one's mind, a question

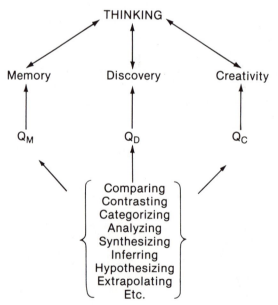

Figure 2.4. The Role of the Cognitive Operations

presented by another person, and so on. Only when the question is specifically directed at comparing will this cognitive operation be activated. Otherwise, it will lie dormant waiting to be called upon. The same is true for all the other cognitive operations. The brain will engage in contrasting, categorizing, hypothesizing, and so on, *only* when there is a need to do so, and that need is triggered by the specific stimulus.

Now, each one of the cognitive operations can be activated by any of the three basic thinking processes: memory, discovery, and creativity. It is possible, for example, to *remember* how to categorize a set of objects (or a set of events, etc.) based on previous experience. It is also possible to *discover* previously unknown options in categorizing the same set of objects. And it is also possible to *create* entirely new categories. The activation of the particular cognitive operation and its use—via memory, discovery, or creativity—during the mediation period depends on the nature of the stimulus or the question. It is as if the cognitive operations stand poised to be recruited to bring to fruition any of the three thinking processes. This is shown schematically in Figure 2.4.

Dominant and Supportive Cognitive Operations

During the mediation period, the specific cognitive operations can serve two functions:

1. A dominant function
2. A supportive function

Let's engage in an exercise. Stop reading now, and assemble a collection of objects: a pencil, a paper clip, an eraser, a rubber band, a pebble, a coin, and so forth. Your task is to arrange these objects in two groups, so that the objects in one group will share a common attribute. The objects in the other group will *not* possess this attribute. When you finish the task, mix the objects and do it again, grouping the objects by another attribute. Repeat this exercise six times.

Now, let's identify what you have just experienced. First, the task was designed in such a way that it moved you to a state of cognitive dissonance; you asked yourself the questions: How do I group these objects? What do they share in common?

Second, the dissonance invited inquiry and moved you into the mediation phase. During this phase your brain was engaged in the act of categorizing the objects. Categorizing, for this episode, became the *dominant* cognitive operation because it was congruent with the purpose of the task. It ceased to function when you completed the categorizing activity.

Third, in order to engage in categorizing you needed to identify a common attribute; to do that, you had to engage in comparing the objects. Comparing, in this case, served as a *supporting* cognitive operation. It is virtually impossible to engage in categorizing without, first, engaging in comparing. The act of comparing—functioning here as the supporting operation—identified the common attribute shared by the objects and fed this information to the dominant operation, so that it could "do its job" of organizing the objects into specific categories. At every step of the process, comparing preceded categorizing.

Finally, in order to compare, the brain was engaged in memory, which fed the comparing operation with prior knowledge of shape, color, texture, and other attributes. Memory, in this case, served as a *supporting* operation for the act of comparing.

The Minihierarchy of Operations

In the episode just described, the interacting cognitive operations formed a temporary bond—a *minihierarchy*—for the purpose of answering the question that governed the episode: How can I categorize the objects? The three interacting operations (memory, comparing, categorizing) functioned in *sequence* or in *reciprocation,* moving back and forth between any two operations when additional information was needed (memory ↔ comparing; comparing ↔ categorizing). They *did not* function simultaneously. The information, however, always flowed in the direction of the dominant operation, in this case, categorizing.

The minihierarchy is formed during the mediation phase to serve as a bridge between the question (stimulus) and the solution (response). The minihierarchy is formed in order to provide the information needed at that time, and it will be sustained as long as the learner is in the state of cognitive dissonance.

When a solution is found, the minihierarchy is dissolved, the learner returns to a state of cognitive consonance, and the episode is over. The minihierarchy is a formation of *temporary* relationships. When another stimulus is aimed at another dominant cognitive operation, a different minihierarchy will be formed. The supportive operations will be recruited as needed during the mediation time, in order to serve the purpose of the new episode.

To test your understanding of the concept of minihierarchies, you might ask yourself questions such as these: What would a minihierarchy look like when a task in social studies calls for hypothesizing? For synthesizing? When a task in physics calls for reasoning? For extrapolation? You can discover and formulate similar questions in virtually any subject matter.

THE RESPONSE (R)

The interplay between the dominant and the supporting cognitive operations sooner or later results in a response. The mediation phase, regardless of the length of time it requires, ends when a response is available. The response can be a consequence of memory, discovery, or creativity, but it is always within the domain of the dominant cognitive operation. The speed, the quantity, and the quality of the response depend on the learner's experience in the given cognitive operation, his/her prior knowledge of the particular subject matter area, and perhaps on his/her unique ability or talent.

CONVERGENT AND DIVERGENT THINKING

The flow of thinking in the three basic processes—memory, discovery, and creativity—can follow one of two paths:

1. Convergent thinking
2. Divergent thinking

It is possible to engage in memory via a convergent path that requires the learner to remember a single correct answer to a question. Examples of this process are answers to questions such as these: What is the capital of Italy? Which Beethoven symphony is called *Pastoral*? In a right-angle triangle, $a^2 + b^2 =$ what? What is the name of the major muscle that extends the arm at the elbow joint? In order to answer these questions, the learner's search converges on one correct answer.

It is also possible to engage in memory via a divergent path that requires the learner to remember several correct answers to a single question. For example: What are the names of some New England states? Name six red items that you saw in the library. What are the three processes you learned to prove that $a^2 + b^2 = c^2$? Name some of Beethoven's symphonies that have names. What were three of the reasons for the French Revolution, as explained in your textbook? In order to answer these questions, the learner's search diverges and seeks to remember the multiple answers to the question.

When engaging in the discovery process, it is possible to follow a convergent path that leads the learner to discover a single solution or a single concept (see Chapters 10 and 11). It is also possible to take a divergent path in which the learner discovers multiple solutions to the same problem (see Chapter 12). Similarly, creativity can converge and result in the creation of a single product, or it can flow in divergent paths by creating a variety of new products connected by the same general concept or, indeed, create totally different products.

All the options—convergent and divergent memory, discovery, and creativity—adhere to the phases described in the general model for the flow of conscious thinking: S→D→M→R.

The stimulus triggers the dissonance that, in turn, determines which path will be taken during mediation—will it be a convergent or a divergent path? At the end of mediation, the result emerges in a form of a single

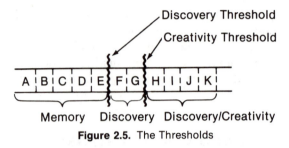

Figure 2.5. The Thresholds

response or multiple responses—emanating from memory, discovery, or creativity.

THE THRESHOLDS

What separates the sets of conditions and teaching styles that evoke memory, discovery, and creativity? Between the cluster of styles that trigger memory and the styles that evoke discovery there is a theoretical, invisible line called the *discovery threshold* (see Figure 2.5).

In the memory cluster of teaching styles, the teacher may be actively engaged in various cognitive operations, but his/her role is to "deliver" acquired knowledge or skills. The role of the learner is to be a "receiver" who reproduces the knowledge or skills. Throughout the cluster of Styles A–E, the learner remains in a relative *state of cognitive acquiescence* with regard to *active* engagement in cognitive operations other than memory. Any engagement by the learner in comparing, contrasting, categorizing, solving, or other cognitive operations is done by *remembering* how to compare, how to categorize, how to solve—the learner does it by replicating what the teacher has done.

For example, the teacher explains the criteria for comparing two poems, and demonstrates how to do it. The learner, then, replicates the comparing process by doing similar exercises. Or, the teacher shows an example of how to solve a geometry problem by using particular steps, and then the learner practices by solving similar problems.

Staying in a relative state of cognitive acquiescence ensures the success of episodes designed for the engagement in memory and reproduction.

When the objective of an episode shifts to *discovery* (Styles F–H), the teacher and the learner must cross the *discovery threshold* by changing their behaviors. The teaching behavior shifts by introducing different stimuli (questions) that move the learner across the threshold and engage him/her in the discovery process. The learning behavior shifts to *active* engagement in discovering—by comparing data, by categorizing information, by actively engaging in the cognitive operation in focus.

Between the discovery styles (F–G) and the creativity styles (H–K)

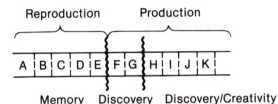

Figure 2.6. Human Capacities, Thinking Processes, and the Spectrum of Teaching Styles

there is another theoretical, invisible line called the *creativity threshold* (Figure 2.5). In order to cross this threshold the teacher and the learner must change their behaviors once again. The teaching behavior shifts by introducing different stimuli (questions) that move the learner to engage in the creative process, or the learner himself/herself asks the questions that stimulate the creative process.

Since the line of demarcation between discovery and creativity is sometimes blurred (despite the operational definitions) it is impossible, at times, to know whether the learner is discovering or creating. Therefore, Styles H–K are under the designation of both processes. In each of these styles the learner can engage in discovering preexisting knowledge or engage in creating new solutions or products.

In summary, the Spectrum describes the cluster of styles (A–E) that serve the human capacity for *reproduction* and the clusters of styles (F–K) that serve the human capacity for *production* (Figure 2.6).

In Chapter 3 we will examine the decisions that constitute the anatomy of each style along this Spectrum.

CHAPTER 3

The Anatomy of
Any Teaching Style

The single unifying principle (the Axiom) that governs the theoretical structure of the Spectrum of Teaching Styles states that *teaching is a chain of decision making*. Every act of teaching is a result of a previously made decision, and every decision affects the people involved. It affects their thinking, their feelings, and their behavior.

Understanding the decisions, who makes them, how they are made, and for what purpose, provides us with insights into the *structure* of the possible relationships between teacher and learner and the consequences of these relationships.

The Anatomy of Any Style (Table 3.1) is a model that delineates the categories of decisions that must be made (and are being made) in any teaching-learning relationship. The decisions are identified and organized in three sets:

1. *The preimpact set,* which includes all the decisions that must be made prior to the face-to-face transaction. These decisions define the *intent*.
2. *The impact set,* which includes decisions related to the actual transaction and the performance of the tasks. These decisions define the *action*.
3. *The postimpact set,* which includes decisions concerning the evaluation of the performance during the impact set and the *congruity* between the intent and the action.

The three sets together constitute the Anatomy of Any Style. Let us, now, delineate the specific decision categories in each set.

TABLE 3.1. THE ANATOMY OF ANY STYLE

Decision Sets	Decision Categories

Preimpact
(Content:
Preparation)
	1. Objective of the episode
	2. Selection of a teaching style
	3. Anticipated learning style
	4. Whom to teach
	5. Subject matter
	6. When to teach (time):
	    a. Starting time d. Stopping time
	    b. Pace and rhythm e. Interval
	    c. Duration f. Termination
	7. Modes of communication
	8. Treatment of questions
	9. Organizational arrangements
	10. Where to teach (location)
	11. Posture
	12. Attire and appearance
	13. Parameters
	14. Class climate
	15. Evaluative procedures and materials
	16. Other

Impact (Content: Execution and Performance)	1. Implementing and adhering to the preimpact decisions (1–14) 2. Adjustment decisions 3. Other

Postimpact
(Content:
Evaluation)
	1. Gathering information about the performance in the impact set
	   (by observing, listening, touching, smelling, etc.)
	2. Assessing the information against criteria (instrumentation,
	   procedures, materials, norms, values, etc.)
	3. Providing feedback to the learner:

About subject matter	a. Value statements b. Corrective statements c. Neutral statements d. Ambiguous statements	About roles
Immediate		Delayed

4. Treatment of questions
5. Assessing the selected teaching style
6. Assessing the anticipated learning style
7. Adjustment decisions
8. Other

THE PREIMPACT SET

1. *Objective of the episode.* This decision identifies the episode's goal. It answers the teacher's questions: Where am I going? Where is the learner going? What are the specific expectations for this episode? (O–T–L)
2. *Selection of a teaching style.* This decision identifies the teaching

behavior that will evoke the learning behavior leading the learner to the objective(s) of the episode. (T–L–O)

3. *Anticipated learning style.* This decision can be approached in two ways:
   a. If the selection of a teaching style serves as an entry point for the conduct of the episode, then the learning style anticipated is a reflection of the teaching style in operation.
   b. If the needs of the learner, at a given time, serve as an entry point, these needs determine the selection of the teaching style. (L–T–O)

   This dual approach means that, at times, the learner is invited to behave in correspondence to the teaching style. This approach is based on the "non-versus" foundation of the Spectrum—that is, no style is in competition with any other as the "best" or "most effective" style. Each style has its own assets and liabilities; the goal is for teachers and learners to be able to move from one style to another in accordance with the decided-upon objectives of each episode. The assumption here is that every learner should have the opportunity to participate in a variety of behaviors. In the context of the Spectrum, a learning style is conceived in terms of the learner's ability to make decisions. Therefore, in a given episode, when the teacher is in Style X, the learner is also in Style X.

   At other times, the learning style of the learner invites the teacher to select the teaching style that will correspond to "where the learner is." The interplay between these two approaches, each used for the purpose of an entry point to an episode, represents the most crucial decision determining the success of an episode. (For a detailed discussion of this issue, see "Selecting a Style" in Chapter 17.)

4. *Whom to teach.* A decision must be made about the participants in a given episode. In any given class a teacher can address the entire class, part of it, or individuals. (This decision is separate from the institutional decision concerning who shall attend school, how many will enroll in a given class, etc.)

5. *Subject matter.* This category involves decisions about what to teach and what not to teach. It involves decisions about:
   a. *Type* of subject matter. This decision takes into account the reasons—philosophical or practical—for the use of a given subject matter or task. It answers the questions: Is this subject matter appropriate for the learners? Relevant? Congruent with the objective?
   b. *Quantity* of task(s). There is no human activity devoid of quantity; therefore, a quantity decision must be made that answers the questions: How much? How many?
   c. *Quality* of performance. This decision answers the question: How well? What is expected of the performance in the given task? (See

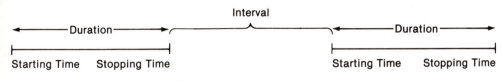

Figure 3.1. The Interval Decision

Chapter 8 for a detailed discussion of quantity and quality of subject matter.)

   d. *Order* of performance. This decision answers the question: In what order—sequential or random—will tasks or parts of tasks be performed?

6. *When to teach.* Time decisions must be made about:
   a. Starting time of each specific task.
   b. Pace and rhythm of the activity—the speed of performing the task.
   c. Duration—the length of time per task.
   d. Stopping time per task.
   e. Interval—the time between any two tasks, parts of a task, and/or the time between episodes (see Figure 3.1).
   f. Termination of the entire episode or the lesson.

7. *Modes of communication.* These decisions concern the modes of communication that will be used in the teaching episode. (Details will follow in "The Classroom Communication Model" in Chapter 9.)

8. *Treatment of questions.* In varying situations, people ask different kinds of questions, and questions can be dealt with in multiple ways. Decisions, therefore, must be made about how to treat these questions.

9. *Organizational arrangements.* These are the decisions about various logistical needs and classroom management.

10. *Where to teach.* This decision identifies the exact spot where the task will be done.

11. *Posture.* This decision refers to the relationship among the positions of body parts during the performance of the task.

12. *Attire and appearance.* A decision must be made about clothing, arrangement of hair, makeup, wearing glasses for safety, and so on.

13. *Parameters.* These decisions refer to limits, particularly in conjunction with the categories of location, time, posture, and attire·and appearance.[1]

---

[1] We are fully aware that a *parameter* is "a constant whose value may vary." However, in this context we'll use the more common meaning of "limits." For discussion on the uses of this word, see William Safire's column "On Language" in the *New York Times Sunday Magazine,* May 13, 1979.

14. *Class climate*. Class climate refers to the affective and social conditions that evolve in a classroom. These conditions result from the sum total of the decisions in categories 1–13.
15. *Evaluation procedures and materials*. Decisions must be made in reference to evaluation that will take place in the postimpact set. What kind of evaluation? What evaluation materials and criteria will be used? How do they relate to the objectives? What is the quality of the performance?
16. *Other*. The Anatomy is an open-ended structure. If another exclusive category is identified, it can be included here.

THE IMPACT SET

1. *Implementing and adhering to the preimpact decisions*. This category includes decisions about how to act on the decisions in categories 1–14 above.
2. *Adjustment decisions*. Since planning cannot always be perfect—nor can the performance be perfect at all times—mishaps do occur. When that happens adjustment decisions must be made. There are two options:
   a. Identify the decision that caused the problem, correct it, and continue the teaching episode.
   b. If the problem is severe, terminate the episode and for the time being move on to another activity.
3. *Other*. The model is open-ended.

THE POSTIMPACT SET

The postimpact set includes decisions that deal with evaluating the performance of the tasks done during the impact set and the selection of the appropriate feedback offered to the learner. This set also includes decisions about evaluating the congruence between the preimpact and the impact sets (intent ≅ action). This evaluation determines whether or not adjustments are needed in the following episode. These decisions are made in the following sequence, a sequence that is intrinsic to any evaluative procedure.

1. *Gathering information about the performance in the impact set*. This can be done by observing, listening, touching, smelling, and so on.
2. *Assessing the information against criteria*. Decisions are made in the course of comparing and contrasting the performance against the criteria, the standard, or the model.
3. *Providing feedback to the learner*. Decisions must be made about how

to provide feedback, which is the information and/or judgment given to the learner about the performance of the task, and about the role of the learner in making his/her decisions. Feedback can be either immediate or delayed, and it can be offered by gesture, symbols, or verbal behavior. Regardless of the mode of communication, *all* feedback is presented in one of four forms:

a. *Value statements*. This form of feedback always includes a word (or symbol) that projects a value or a feeling about the performance. For example: "You wrote a beautiful poem." "The assignment is poorly done." "The experiment was well done."

b. *Corrective statements*. This form of feedback is used whenever an error is evident and the learner's response is incorrect. Corrective feedback includes one or both of the following:
  i. A statement that identifies the error.
  ii. A statement about how to correct it. For example: "The second and fifth words in this column were spelled incorrectly." "Five times 7 is not 36, it is 35."

c. *Neutral statements*. This form of feedback is descriptive and factual. It does not correct nor judge the performance; it acknowledges what the learner has done. For example: "I see that you have completed the assignment." "You have followed the criteria for writing the. . . ."

d. *Ambiguous statements*. Phrases like "not bad," "pretty good," or "do it again" can be used for feedback. These words do not convey to the learner precise information about the performance—too much is left to guessing. This kind of feedback is ambiguous.

In addition to being aware of these four forms of feedback and their meanings, one must be aware of the connotation of the tone, as well as the cultural inclination and the idiosyncracies of the persons giving and receiving the feedback. (For a detailed analysis of the structure of feedback and its impact on teaching and learning behaviors, see Chapter 9.)

4. *Treatment of questions*. Decisions about how to treat questions are made here.

5. *Assessing the selected teaching style*. Decisions are made about the effectiveness of the teaching style used in the completed episode, and its impact on the learner.

6. *Assessing the anticipated learning style*. In connection with the decisions made in the previous category (5), a decision is made about whether or not the learner has reached the objectives of the episode. Together, categories 5 and 6 provide the information concerning the congruity between intent and action.

7. *Adjustments*. Based on the assessments of the episode, decisions are made about any adjustments needed for subsequent episodes.

8. *Other*. The model is open-ended.

To reiterate, these three sets of decisions—the preimpact, impact, and postimpact sets—comprise the Anatomy of Any Style. These are the decisions that are always made in any teaching-learning relationship and that govern the operation of any teaching. At times these decisions are made deliberately; at other times they seem to represent habits; at still other times some of the decisions are omitted or are made by default. Regardless of the condition, the primary behavior in teaching is the act of making decisions in the sequential three sets of the Anatomy. The Anatomy of Any Style, therefore, is a universal model that is at the foundation of all teaching. It describes *what* decisions must be made in any teaching model, strategy, or educational game.

Several fundamental questions arise now: From this Anatomy how do we identify a specific style? How many styles are there? How do we differentiate one style from the other? And how are all the styles related to one another to form a comprehensive framework for all teaching?

CHAPTER 4

Style A: The Command Style

Do you remember the last time you attended a concert performed by an orchestra? Do you remember watching a shell gliding through the water powered by eight people pulling their oars? Have you participated in any ritual lately? Have you attended an aerobics class? A beginners' class in another language? What is common among these diverse experiences?

The common element is the particular relationship that exists between the participants and the conductor of the activity. In all of these examples the participants behave in correspondence with the behavior of the conductor of the orchestra, the coxswain, the master of ceremonies, or the teacher. All the participants respond in particular ways that are directly related to the stimuli, cues, and models presented by the conductors of these activities.

These behaviors are the results of repetitions, routines, and habits. All are behaviors that are needed for achievement, security, sense of aesthetics, and—at times—survival.

In order to accomplish certain tasks and certain objectives, we learn to behave in this manner. It becomes one of many alternatives in our repertoire of behaviors—one of many alternatives in our repertoire of teaching-learning transactions.

The following are more examples that represent this behavior, this relationship:

- Dancing in a classical ballet
- Doing school figures in ice skating
- Synchronized swimming
- Crew (rowing)
- Doing group calisthenics

- Performing in an orchestra during a concert
- Working on an assembly line in a factory
- Square dancing
- Folk dancing
- Singing in a choir
- Pronouncing words in another language
- Performing surgery in an operating room
- Acting in theater productions
- Doing martial arts
- Cheerleading
- Performing in a drill team
- Doing other drills
- Marching in a band
- Dancing with the Radio City Rockettes
- Marching in certain parades
- Performing choral responses

Diverse as these activities may be, they share some or all of the following objectives, objectives that can be grouped into clusters that represent social objectives, performance and production objectives, artistic objectives, safety objectives, and so on.

OBJECTIVES OF STYLE A

The specific objectives that these activities reach fall into the two main categories of objectives cited in Chapter 1: subject matter objectives and behavior objectives.

Subject Matter Objectives

To reproduce a model by immediate performance

To achieve accuracy and precision of performance

To use time efficiently

To achieve immediate results

To cover more material

To master subject matter skills

To perpetuate traditional rituals

Behavior Objectives

To socialize the individual into the norms of the group

To achieve conformity

To achieve uniformity

To build group identity and pride—belonging

To follow directions on cue

To adhere to a particular kind of discipline (Style A discipline; each style has its own form of discipline)

To develop habits and routines

To control groups (or individuals)

To maintain safety

To achieve specific aesthetic standards

If any of these objectives are included in your educational goals, then episodes in Style A will get you there.

THE ESSENCE OF STYLE A

All learning occurs as a response (or responses) to some stimulus (or stimuli). People learn because something or somebody stimulates them. People are intrigued, motivated, challenged, inspired, or forced to learn. Regardless of the source or the purpose, the *response* (R) is always related to the *stimulus* (S).

Now Style A represents a particular form of this S-R relationship, which is highly visible and recognizable. The following characteristics constitute the *essence* of this style.

1. The S-R relationship is on a one-to-one basis. This means that each specific response is produced in correspondence to a specific stimulus. For example, each single note produced by the orchestra is a specific response to a specific movement by the conductor. Each movement of a dancer is a specific response to a specific cue (stimulus) projected by the music, the command words, or the drum beat. This specificity is a major characteristic of Style A.
2. This bond or relationship between the stimulus and the response is *known in advance*. A particular response—not just *any* response—is expected to come forth in relationship to a particular stimulus. This predictability is a major characteristic of Style A.
3. The expected response follows the stimulus within the shortest possible amount of time. This immediacy is a major characteristic of Style A.
4. The learner is engaged in doing the task most or all of the time. The percent of the learner's time-on-task is high in this style, resulting in efficient production and learning. This productivity is a major characteristic of Style A.
5. This kind of relationship between the stimulus and the response calls upon memory and recall as the dominant cognitive operation. It does not permit nor does it deliberately invite the intervention of other cognitive operations. This engagement of memory is a major characteristic of Style A.
6. In all subject matter areas, only a portion of the subject matter (names, dates, terms, basic facts) can comply with the requirements of the elements just cited. Hence, Style A can be used only for selected purposes. This selectivity is a major characteristic of Style A.
7. Most learners, if not all, can learn and accomplish certain tasks in a relatively short period of time. This time efficiency is a major characteristic of Style A.

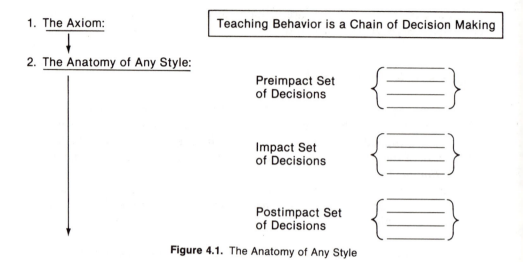

1. The Axiom:

Teaching Behavior is a Chain of Decision Making

2. The Anatomy of Any Style:

Preimpact Set
of Decisions

Impact Set
of Decisions

Postimpact Set
of Decisions

Figure 4.1. The Anatomy of Any Style

THE ANATOMY OF STYLE A

Let us see how these characteristics, the essence of this style, are expressed in the decisions that are intrinsic to the behavior of Style A—the command style.

We have identified so far the Axiom and the Anatomy of Any Style (see Figure 4.1). From this Anatomy how can we derive the specific structures of teaching styles? How many teaching styles are there? What *differentiates* one from the other?

The identification of the specific styles and the differentiation among the styles occur when we identify *who* makes the decisions. In any teaching-learning relationship there are two decision makers: the teacher and the learner. Each can make the minimum to the maximum number of decisions delineated in the Anatomy. This minimum-to-maximum continuum in decision making constitutes the *theoretical limits* that can be applied to the Anatomy of Any Style. Thus, each option in the teacher-learner relationship can be expressed by a rather precise identification of who makes which decisions, about what, and when.

Style A emerges when the teacher makes the maximum number and the learner makes the minimum number of decisions. This kind of teaching-learning relationship (style) is responsible for the experiences (episodes) described in the beginning of this chapter.

Let us follow the schematic representation (Figure 4.2) that describes the flow from the Axiom to the emergence of the specific structure of Style A.

- *Step 1:* Identifies the Axiom.

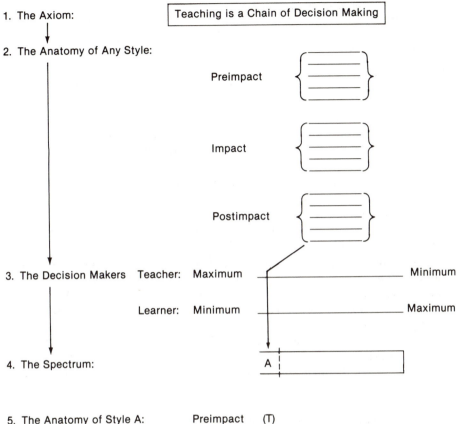

Figure 4.2. The Emergence of Style A

- *Step 2:* Identifies the Anatomy of Any Style. It describes *what* decisions must be made.
- *Step 3:* Identifies the first condition on the Spectrum, a condition where the teacher makes the maximum number of decisions and the learner makes the minimum number.
- *Step 4:* Identifies the relationship between the teacher and the learner that is designated as Style A, the beginning of the Spectrum.
- *Step 5:* Identifies the role of the teacher as one who, in the specific anatomy of this style, makes *all* the decisions in the preimpact, impact, and postimpact sets, designated as (T)/(T)/(T). The role of the learner is to perform—that is, to follow the decisions made by the teacher in the given episode.

TABLE 4.1. DECISION STRUCTURE OF STYLE A

	Teacher	Learner
Theoretically	All	None
Operationally	All − 1	One

The designation (L), therefore, does not appear in the anatomy of Style A. It will appear in later styles when the learner actually makes decisions in specific sets. In Style A, the *only* decision the learner is making is the decision concerning the choice between "yes" or "no," "I'll do it" or "I will not do it." Once a "yes" decision is made, the learner proceeds to follow every decision made by the teacher. If a "no" decision is made by the learner, there is *no transaction* between the teacher and learner as anticipated in the preimpact set. (The "no" decision and alternative ways for dealing with it will be discussed in Chapter 16.)

Note that in theory the teacher makes all the decisions and the learner therefore makes none. Operationally, however, the learner always makes one decision, and that is the choice between "yes" and "no," to obey or not to obey, to follow or not to follow. And therefore, the teacher under this condition makes all decisions minus one (see Table 4.1).

Since a learner *can* invoke the "no" decision at any time and in any style, the designation "all − 1" (read as "all minus one") is a constant and is not entered in the anatomy of Style A, nor those of other styles.

IMPLEMENTATION OF STYLE A

The questions that confront a teacher who wishes to implement episodes in Style A are: What is the "picture" of such episodes? How do I do it? What subject matter is conducive to this style? The following three sections address these questions.

Description of an Episode

The following descriptions of Style A episodes are presented in order to offer a visual image of this style.[1] Let's start with the familiar: a choir. When students enter the room, each sits in a prescribed chair (location decision) in order to accommodate the different voice range requirements of the choir. They sit in a particular posture to accommodate the proper breathing and the visual contact with the teacher. The teacher then announces the task, and often demonstrates it by playing the piano, by singing the musical phrase, or

---

[1] The word *episode* in Spectrum terminology means "a period of time within which the teacher and the learner are engaged in the same style, going toward the same objective(s)."

both. The sounds of the piano and the vocal examples by the teacher serve as the model—the precise notes and tones to be reproduced.

Next the teacher uses the *preparatory* signal (raising the baton, etc.) to call the choir to readiness, and then the teacher exhibits the *command signal* or cue (a hand motion, a head nod), which elicits an *immediate* response from the participants. The responses represent the learners' attempts to perform the task by singing the particular notes and by emulating the model presented by the teacher.

At the end of the task performance (at the end of a note or a cluster of notes), the teacher offers feedback to the singers. The feedback offered is in any one or a combination of the three forms: value, corrective, or neutral. It all depends on the performance and its proximity to the model. The teacher signals to continue and the choir sings the next phrase or, if necessary, repeats the previous one. And thus the teacher and the learners move on until the entire musical piece is performed accurately both technically and musically. This kind of episode is efficient and productive. The objective is clear, the tasks are clear, and the expected behavior is clear. It represents high level of fidelity to the structure of Style A, and hence will reap the benefits of its objectives—in this case, the objectives of precision of sound, unison, synchronization, and projection of the composer's musical intent.

The next example is an episode in teaching pronunciation of words and phrases in another language. The objective in this episode is *precision*. When one studies another language, one of the objectives is to be able to communicate in the new language. Precision in pronunciation is mandatory for effective and proper communication. Operationally, it means that the learner must go through a series of experiences reproducing the sounds of words and phrases as closely as possible to sounds of the native speaker. First the teacher announces the objective for the given episode, and immediately proceeds with the exercises of sounding and saying the words. The teacher pronounces the word or phrase; then after a very short pause, he/she might say "Ready?" and then emit the command signal that will elicit the response from the learners—the reproduction of the word or phrase. The teacher can call upon the entire class to respond in unison, then invite groups within the class to respond, and then go back to the entire class. In between, the teacher can call upon individuals to respond so that he/she can verify the precise pronunciation of individual students. Periodically the teacher provides feedback appropriate to the situation.

This process is productive and efficient because it enables all the learners to participate in hearing and speaking the words and to do so with considerable frequency.

How to Do It

The following steps describe the use of the anatomy of the command style as guidelines for implementation. This process involves the preimpact, impact, and postimpact decisions.

The Preimpact Set. The purpose of the preimpact set of decisions is to plan the interaction between the teacher and the learner. The teacher's role is to make decisions about the categories delineated in the preimpact of the anatomy of Style A.

The Impact Set. This is the "doing" time. The purpose of the impact set of decisions is to engage the learners in active participation and to follow through with the preimpact decisions. It is putting the intent into action. In the command style (as in all other styles), it is imperative that the learners know and understand the expectations of the episode. They must know the expectations of the task performance and of the teacher-learner relationship (i.e., the roles of the teacher and the learner). When expectations are known, both teacher and learner can be held accountable for their behaviors. Therefore, the teacher must make a sequence of decisions to set the scene for an episode in the command style.

Setting the scene includes these components:

1. Explanation of the roles (the teacher's and the learner's)
2. Delivery of the subject matter
3. Explanation of the logistical procedures

These three components are constants in any episode in the impact set, and they appear in this order. Explaining the roles sets expectations for the behaviors of the teacher and the learners; delivery of the subject matter establishes what is to be done; and the logistical procedures define the parameters of the task environment.

Explanation of the Roles. In the initial stages (the first two or three episodes in this style), the teacher explains the following things to the students:

1. When a teacher and student are in a face-to-face situation, a variety of decisions can be made by the teacher and/or the learner.
2. These decisions can be distributed between the teacher and the learners in a variety of ways depending on the relationship's purpose at the particular time and the particular episode.
3. One of these particular arrangements is a relationship where the teacher's role is to make all the decisions and the learner's role is to follow, perform, and respond to each decision.
4. The purpose of such a relationship (called Style A or the command style) is to accommodate an immediate response so that certain tasks can be learned accurately and quickly.
5. A series of episodes in this style facilitates the accomplishment of objectives such as replication of a model, precision and accuracy of performance, and synchronized performance. (See the list of objectives cited earlier in this chapter.)

Experience with the Spectrum styles indicates that most students can internalize the structure and operation of a given style within two or three frequent episodes when the introduction to the styles covers points 1–5. Therefore, to set the expectations in subsequent episodes, the teacher announces the name of the style and moves on to the delivery of the subject matter.

Delivery of the Subject Matter. Since in Style A the role of the learner is to replicate a model, the teacher's role is to present the model of the task as accurately and succinctly as possible. Tasks can be presented by various modes (visual, audio, etc.) depending on the subject matter, the nature of the task, the learner, and the objective of the episode. (See "The Classroom Communication Model" in Chapter 9.)

Two aspects concerning the task delivery always exist in this style: (1) demonstration of what is to be done, and (2) explanation of how to do it. The practical steps are as follows:

1. The teacher demonstrates the whole task and/or its parts.
2. The demonstration can be relegated to a film, videotape, pictures, or to a student who can perform the task according to the model. (For the analysis of the demonstration, see Chapter 9).
3. The teacher explains the necessary details to enhance the understanding of the task. This includes the use of the appropriate terminology. This explanation step reflects the teacher's knowledge of the subject matter, its intricacies, and its techniques.
4. Different tasks may require varying ratios of demonstration/ explanation and a decision about which comes first.

Explanation of the Logistical Procedures.

1. The teacher establishes the preparatory and command signals for the episode. These may change during the episode to accommodate different aspects of the subject matter.
2. The teacher establishes managerial procedures concerning equipment, materials, and so forth.

At this point the teacher and the learners are ready to begin the activity, which is the essence of the impact set. The learners behave according to the command signals and the rhythm support procedures conducted by the teacher.

The Postimpact Set. In the postimpact set of decisions, the teacher offers feedback to the learner about the performance of the task and about the learner's role in following the teacher's decisions. (See the section on feedback forms in Chapter 9.)

The command style experience is one of action. The repetition in performing each task and replicating the model brings about the contribution of this style to learning and development. Passivity is incongruent with this style. In any given episode, a maximum amount of time is used by the learners in active participation. A minimum amount of time is used by the teacher for demonstration and explanation. Talking time by the teacher is minimal. Time-on-task in this style is very high.

Examples of Style A Episodes

Episode 1: Introducing Style A to Young Children. Let's examine the sequence of an episode when the teacher introduces this style to young children. The subject matter objective of the episode is to recognize the number facts by reading them from the board. The following are the steps in the *impact* set:

Setting the Scene: Role Identification

1. State the objective of this style: "The purpose of this style is to learn to do the task accurately and quickly."
2. Describe the roles of the teacher and the learner: "The role of the teacher is to make all the decisions; your role is to follow, to do the task."
3. Explain that a command signal will precede every action by the learner. (The specific signal is not stated here.)
4. Explain that time will be allotted for asking questions for clarification.

These steps, which are needed only in the first two or three episodes in this style, clearly set the expectations for the behaviors of the teacher and the learner in this relationship.

Setting the Scene: Subject Matter Identification

1. Describe the task to be done.
2. Select and establish the parameters necessary for the performance of the task:
   a. Posture
   b. Location
   c. Attire and appearance
   d. Quantity
   e. Identify the command signal
   f. Other
3. Explain the time decisions:
   a. Starting time. Explain the starting time signals: "The preparatory

phrase will be the word 'Ready?' The signal to start will be my pointing at the board.''

   b. Pace and rhythm. Explain the technique you will use to maintain the pace (your voice, pointing to words on the board, etc.)

   c. Stopping time. Explain the stopping time signal.

Again, these steps are necessary to set the expectation about the process of the interaction between the teacher and the learner. Going through them may initially seem cumbersome, but it takes only minutes to establish these clear expectations.

When this is done, the actual task performance begins.

Episode 2: Teaching the Multiplication Table. The following steps are a possible model for an episode with young learners:

1. The teacher announces that the objective is to read each exercise and the answer from the board.
2. The teacher tells the learners that in the next episode the answers will be covered and their task will be to compute and remember the answer.
3. The teacher reads the first exercise, $1 \times 1 = 1$, and says: "One times one is one." This demonstrates to the class the specific way of doing the task (recognizing the number facts by reading) and the expected pace and rhythm.
4. The teacher says: "When I point at the exercises, you will read them as I demonstrated."
5. The teacher asks: "Are there any questions for clarification? If so, indicate by raising your hand now." If there are any questions for clarification, the teacher answers them and then proceeds. (In Style A the learner may ask questions for clarification only when the teacher allots time for this purpose.)
6. The teacher says: "Ready?" (pause).
7. The teacher points to each part of the first exercise; the learners respond: "One times one is one."
8. The teacher says: "Correct!" The teacher then points to the next exercise and the learners respond: "One times two is two."
9. The teacher moves on, as swiftly as the class can follow with precision, until all the exercises have been performed.
10. There is no need to stop after every response and give feedback; the learners know that they are performing correctly.
11. If errors are heard, the teacher has two options:
   a. To stop the process and read the exercise for the class, then say: "Ready?" (pause) and give the command signal (i.e., point to the exercise on the board).
   b. To point *again* at the part of the exercise that needs to be repeated without stopping to read it. This is a more efficient and comfortable way. There is no need to stop the whole process at every error. It

gets to be tedious. The opportunity for immediate repetition will provide for the correct response.

Note that the word "Ready?," followed by a brief pause, is used in two circumstances. It is used before the first response and followed by the command signal. It is also used when starting up again after a *stop* for corrections or redemonstration. When the flow of the performance has been broken, use of the word "Ready?" or its equivalent helps recruit the learners and ensures more accurate performance.

Note, too, that a major potential problem in Style A is the maintenance of pace and rhythm. Whenever the class gets out of synchronization, stop the process, offer corrective feedback *about* pace and rhythm, and proceed.

Episode 3: Memorizing the Multiplication Table. A second set of exercises can be carried out after the previous one. In this case the teacher announces the new objective for the subject matter: "To compute the exercises from memory and utter the results." The steps are as follows:

1. The teacher covers the answer on the board or chart and explains that he/she will point to the blank space next to each exercise, and the learner will provide the answer.
2. The teacher says "Ready?" and points at the blank space next to the first exercise. The learner says: "One."
3. The teacher pauses for a couple of seconds as the learner computes the second exercise.
4. The teacher points to the blank space next to the second exercise; the learner says: "Two." This step is repeated until all the exercises are completed.
5. After doing the exercises in sequence, the teacher randomly points at the blank spaces. This will challenge the learner's memory (the cognitive operation in this episode).
6. At the end of the episode, the teacher offers the learners feedback about the performance of the task and their participation in Style A—their role in following the teacher's decisions.

In the same manner, initial episodes can be introduced to learners at *any* age and for any tasks suitable for Style A. Style A provides the teacher with opportunities to employ a wide variety of activities and techniques of presentation. The limits of episodes in this style depend only on the teacher's experience and imagination.

The Lesson Plan

When several episodes are combined to comprise a lesson, a lesson plan can serve as a useful tool for planning the sequence and the organization of the episodes. The lesson plan is the statement of intent; it describes what the teacher intends to do and accomplish during the ensuing lesson. The chart in Figure 4.3, page 40, is a proposed model for a lesson plan. Let us examine each of its parts:

1. *Subject matter.* Identifies the subject matter (i.e., algebra: the quadratic equation; social studies: the migration West; music: the scales; etc.).
2. *The overall objective of the lesson.* States in broad terms the overall lesson objectives. What is the expected outcome to be achieved by the end of the lesson?
3. *Episode number.* An episode is a unit of time in which the teacher and the learner are in the same style, heading toward the same objective. A lesson can be composed of one or more episodes, each one planned in terms of the style (the T–L–O), the activity, and the supporting logistical arrangements. (See Figures 4.4 and 4.5.)[2]
4. *Specific tasks.* Identifies and describes the specific tasks that the learners will engage in to accomplish the overall objective of the episode.
5. *Objectives.* The objective of an episode is, in a sense, the reason for selecting the particular task. These objectives, or reasons, can be stated in terms of the subject matter (what will be accomplished in the particular subject matter) and in terms of the learner's role in engaging and developing various qualities such as socialization, cooperation, competition, honesty, and so on. In the lesson plan, the learner's role is stated when such objectives are the episode's focus. Otherwise, the role is implicit in the decisions and the identification of the style. (You are invited to review the section on the T–L–O in Chapter 1, where the objective (O) of an episode is described *both* in terms of the subject matter and the behavior (role) of the learner).

    Note that the order of steps 4 and 5 may be interchangeable. Logically, the ''Objective'' column should precede the ''Specific Tasks'' column. At times, however, one can proceed from the selected task and then identify the objective.
6. *Style.* Identifies the style that will accomplish the objectives.
7. *Logistics.* To reach the objectives of the selected activity in the selected style, several decisions must be made about the logistics of the episode. These decisions concern two major aspects:
    a. The organization of the learners. In the classroom there are many options for organizing learners. They can be organized in a variety of random ways, or they can be organized in specific geometric patterns (lines, circles, etc.). The guiding principle is: Organize learners so that they may efficiently participate in the activity and interact with the teacher.

---

[2] This section is adapted from Muska Mosston and Sara Ashworth, *Teaching Physical Education*, 3rd ed. (Columbus, Ohio: Charles E. Merrill Publishing Co., 1986).

Subject Matter _____

The overall objective of the lesson _____

| Episode No. | SUBJECT MATTER | OBJECTIVES | | LOGISTICS | | |
	Specific Tasks	Subject Matter and/or Role	Style	Organization of Learners; Equipment; Task Sheet; etc.	Time	Comments
1						
2						
3						
4						
5						
6						
7						

Figure 4.3. A Lesson Plan

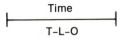

Figure 4.4. An Episode

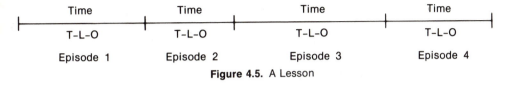

Figure 4.5. A Lesson

b. The organization of equipment. Use the same principle as in (a), adding the consideration of maximum participation by each learner. It cannot be emphasized enough that equipment must be organized to facilitate maximum learning for each student if the objectives of the episode are to be reached.

8. *Time.* Identifies a reasonable length for the episode so that all (or most) learners can reach the objectives. The time decisions depend on the task, the capability of the learners, and the objectives.

9. *Comments.* This column is used for statements, questions, or suggestions made after the lesson is done (in the postimpact phase). These can include statements about what went well and what needs adjustment for next time, or questions that need to be resolved.

SELECTING AND DESIGNING THE SUBJECT MATTER

The next central questions in Style A are:

- What subject matter areas are conducive to the use of this style?
- Within a given subject matter area, what kind of tasks are conducive to the use of this style?
- Is there a connection between the structure of the task and the way it ought to be taught and learned?

Every subject matter has tasks that activate one of the two fundamental human capacities: (1) reproduction of the known and (2) production and discovery of the unknown, the new. (See the section on "The Clusters" in Chapter 1.) Tasks that call for reproduction can be taught by any of Styles A–E, but tasks that are conducive to Style A must have the following characteristics:

1. They represent the S-R relationship where each single stimulus evokes a predetermined single response.

2. The response is produced immediately after the stimulus is presented. The time lapse between the stimulus and the response is as short as possible.
3. The final result is as precise a replication of the model as possible.
4. The task can be done individually or in a group with a high level of synchronization.
5. The task can be controlled by decisions made by a teacher (or surrogate) about starting time, pace and rhythm, stopping time, quantity, and quality. Some examples of tasks that meet these criteria and are quite common in the school curricula are listed below. These tasks are sorted into two categories based on whether they demand (1) instant recall and recognition, or (2) repetition.

Instant Recall and Recognition
Learning notes in music
Identifying colors and shapes
Identifying nouns and verbs
Learning the multiplication table
Learning names and dates
Learning locations and names of
  states and their capitals
Learning the names of other
  countries
Learning vocabulary in any
  language
Learning scientific terms

Repetition
Singing songs or reciting poems
Reciting lines in a play
Doing exercises and aerobics
Giving dance performances
Practicing safety procedures
Giving concerts (orchestra, band)

All of these tasks when taught by Style A reach the learning outcomes previously cited and become a part of a particular O–T–L–O, a particular classroom reality.

IMPLICATIONS OF STYLE A

Each style on the Spectrum affects a network of implications for a number of educational variables. Understanding these implications will increase the teacher's insights into the contribution and consequences of each style. The following sections offer analyses concerning verbal behavior, rewards and reprimands, and feelings.

Verbal Behavior

Human communication is rich in its possibilities and options; the glance of the eyes, the touch, the movement of the body, the word. The meanings are many, the symbols are varied. In the classroom one of the most pervasive and powerful modes of communication between teacher and learner is verbal behavior. Verbal behavior is used in every aspect of the interaction: in delivering the task, in conveying ideas, in offering feedback, in eliciting the learner's ideas and feelings, in dealing with behavior deviations, and in ordinary discourse. Succinctly stated, our verbal behavior reflects the decisions we make; and the decisions we make always represent a particular style. Therefore, each style intrinsically suggests a particular verbal behavior with certain "dos" and "don'ts." When a given style is in use, a certain degree of precision in verbal behavior is necessary in order to reach the objectives of the style and the episode. In Style A the verbal behavior used instantly conveys the intent and the meaning of this style; it establishes the teacher as the one who makes all the decisions in *this* episode.

The linguistic format of this style requires attention to two aspects of speech:

1. The teacher may use the pronoun "I" or phrases that reflect the "I" ("I want you to. . . ."; "Cite for me the list of. . . ."; "When I point to the syllable you will repeat its sound.") However, since Style A represents the teacher's "I," constant reference to the "I" is not necessary.
2. The teacher should use the imperative (verbs such as "cite," "state," "start," "go," etc.) as the command signal. This emphasizes the role of the teacher as the decision maker.

Note that the use of Style A can represent extremes in the intent of the teacher; it can be used to evoke high-level performance of tasks in appropriate subject matter, or it can be used to control people in negative ways and with negative consequences. The use of verbal behavior and the projected mood clearly convey the intended message.

One more thought about verbal behavior: Teachers develop their own patterns of verbal behavior, and their verbal behavior often represents their value system and educational philosophy. Since each style calls for a different relationship between the teacher and the learner, in essence each style reflects a different value system. Therefore the awareness of the different styles invites the teacher to examine his/her verbal behavior patterns and the value system they represent. To have maximum mobility along the Spectrum of Teaching Styles, teachers must be willing to develop flexibility in their verbal behavior.

Systems of Reward and Reprimand

Style A also has implications for the system of reward and reprimand that is used.

Users of the command style are often very clear about the reward and reprimand system that will be employed when the style is in use. Standards are set, rules and regulations are established, procedures are fixed, and the expectations are explicit. Hierarchies are designed and conditions for mobility are specified. Reprimands and their relationship to the potential violations are stated orally, on posters, or in rule books. The coveted rewards are publicly announced, presented, and displayed. Highly organized command-style institutions have devised ways for external manifestations of their reward systems: uniforms, rank, insignia, medals and decorations, trophies, certificates, and public ceremonies.

In this style, rewards and reprimands are always imposed from the "outside." If the command style is used all the time, then it functions as the value system that governs the reality, and its systems of reward and reprimand are the essential motivators. If, however, the teacher accepts the "non-versus" notion of the Spectrum and understands the command style not as a dominating style but as a partner with other styles, then the teacher must ask questions such as: Are the rewards I use appropriate? Is it clear to my students that these rewards are in relationship to the command style only and are not necessarily the only rewards that will exist in my class all the time? Have I scrutinized the various rewards I have been using? Have I thought about their consequences, that is, their impact, immediate or long range? Have I done the same analysis with the reprimand system I have been using?

The Command Style and Feelings

The command style has a unique impact on people. Some feel very comfortable in the role of receivers—receivers of decisions made for them by others. Yet others feel a sense of resistance, dissonance, and at times resentment. In varying degrees, Style A represents to many people the tug-of-war between control and freedom. It is therefore necessary for teachers to become sensitive and alert to the state of the learner and to learn when and how to use Style A most effectively and appropriately.

The teacher must be aware of the emotional context of this style. There are at least two possibilities that can develop in this style. One is the abuse of power by the teacher, who may use this style for control and reprimand purposes. (When we reprimand someone, we usually take away decisions.) When this kind of teaching behavior prevails, negative feelings often result and the learner will reject the teaching style, the teacher, and the subject matter. The second possibility is that the teacher will use Style A with affection, warmth, and care. Style A doesn't mean "being mean"; this style can be used to motivate learners, elevate their self-concept, and develop *esprit de corps*.

Many people have experienced the command style during emotionally adverse conditions, mainly during moments of anger. When teachers, parents, and other adults feel angry, often their behavior toward others takes the shape of the command style. Those who have experienced this may have developed negative feelings about the command style and those who use it. The very act of the teacher's making all the decisions may trigger the memories of harsh reprimands, put-downs, and harassment.

Therefore perhaps the most difficult aspect of using Style A is to refrain from using it as a punitive measure—either as a threat for potential misconduct or as an actual punishment when anger intercedes. (We have a task for you: The next time you get angry, try not to do it in Style A!)

There are teachers using the command style who feel that public admonition, put-downs, and exclusions are appropriate techniques to be used with this style. There are others who use this style with affection and care. Each approach has its consequences in the way learners feel about the teacher, about themselves, and about schooling. The skill of using this style is, indeed, a major challenge for the teacher.

There is another aspect to the feelings that are generated in this style, and that is the experience itself—the experience of participating in activities that are designed and structured for Style A behaviors. These experiences evoke joy, excitement, motivation to excel, and an inner sense of beauty.

Young children, for example, enjoy many Style A activities such as Simon Says and Follow the Leader. All represent *imitating behaviors.* Emulating, repeating, copying, and responding to directions seem to be necessary ingredients of the early years. Learning to do a task is a part of growing and of becoming socialized into a group. Obeying and responding to directions are important behaviors for the young.

In every culture children participate in games composed of songs that are accompanied by clapping and body movements, all experienced in unison to a particular pace and rhythm. The laughter, enjoyment, and sense of belonging are quite evident.

Older learners choose to participate in Style A experiences for a variety of reasons: personal development, social engagement in a subculture's activities and rituals, enjoyment of cultural/aesthetic experiences, testing the limits, competition, and various combinations of these.

An example of such an experience is aerobics sessions, which illustrate all the components and objectives of Style A: high time-on-task, repetition, high degree of uniformity, and precision. It is reasonable to assume that the primary purpose and motivation for participating in aerobics are not these components, but the sense of development (fitness, being in shape, losing weight). An equally powerful reason for participating in aerobics is the sense of participating in a socially accepted environment and manner.

Another example of a Style A experience is karate, primarily the training time. Many of the participants in these activities accept not only the Style A behaviors, but the manners and rituals that may not have been a part of their culture or personal conduct.

A third type of Style A experience is participation in high-risk sports. Acquiring some of the necessary skills requires Style A relationships and discipline. When safety is paramount, Style A is mandatory during training and often during the experience itself. Some of these activities are parachuting, mountaineering, and scuba diving. In such activities, Style A episodes focus on the particular physical responses and the appropriate and precise use of equipment and accessories. In addition, deliberate and controlled episodes are designed to teach management of stress and panic. Only when these aspects are learned and integrated (mostly by Style A experiences) can participants move on to the real experience of participating in and enjoying the sport.

A fourth type of Style A activity is participation in cultural/aesthetic experiences. The command style is often used to teach various dance techniques. Examples can be found in ballet, certain aspects of modern dance, and in folk dance. In these diverse forms of dance, precise performance and adherence to a predetermined model are important. The dance forms themselves project aesthetic values and the continuity of cultural standards. These values and standards are also evident in orchestral performances, choir concerts, certain theatrical performances, and formal social events.

A fifth type of Style A activity is found in many competitive sports. Synchronized swimming may represent the epitome of Style A because of its high-level precision, synchronization, and projection of a particular set of aesthetic values. The compulsory part of competitive gymnastics is another example, and rowing cannot be successful without group synchronization and high-level precision. It is fascinating to realize that such diverse activities, which represent different purposes, share the same teaching-learning process—the command style—which generates joy, excitement, motivation to excel, and an inner sense of beauty.

STYLE-SPECIFIC COMMENTS

This section contains some comments about the operation of Style A—some "dos" and "don'ts," warnings about common pitfalls, and special thoughts —that could help the teacher further understand the essence of this style, and at times prevent mishaps that might reduce the possibility of reaching the objectives of a given episode.

The teacher must be aware that following all the decisions constitutes only a portion of the teaching-learning experience. A successful Style A episode is a result of integrating the decisions with proper selection of subject matter, high time-on-task, appropriate verbal behavior, accommodating logistics, and sensitivity to the state of the learner in this style. When these components are integrated *within* the structure of the command style, it becomes possible to judge the merits of the episode in terms of the congruence between the intent and the action.

When an episode is not reaching its objectives it may be for one or more of the following reasons, each of which is a pitfall to avoid:

1. Excessive amount of teacher-talk and too little time for active learner's participation.
2. Lack of class synchronization in the performance of the task. The teacher needs to adjust the selected pace and rhythm for the given subject matter.
3. Excessive repetition of the same task. This may cause boredom and, in some subject areas, fatigue.
4. Excessive interruption of the episode. Stopping the action of the entire class because one or two learners are having difficulty will stop the flow of the activity and divert the class's attention to the inadequacies of the individuals.
5. Lack of teacher movement. In this style the teacher does not have to stay in one fixed position when conducting the episode. Moving about (e.g., using rhythm-support techniques other than counting) provides the teacher an opportunity for individual and private feedback without stopping the action.

There are two characteristics that lend Style A its uniqueness: (1) the *model,* and (2) the *presenter* of the model. The model is the real or aspired image of performance in any area. It is the form to be attained, the standard to be emulated. It calls for a decision about the *quality* of the performance. A model embodies the cumulative knowledge in a given area or in part of it; it represents the state of the art as agreed upon by experts. It may reflect the unique vision and artistry of the maverick, or it may project the daring thinking of the scientist.

The people who design or present the model are those who have acquired the knowledge and the experience; they are the people who possess the vision, the artistry, and the scientific spirit. They are the people who have the ability, the power, and perhaps even the right to invite others to reach for the model. They are the *masters.*

It is rather difficult to question the role of the Olympic gymnastics coach in presenting the best of aspired-to models to the participants, and insisting and persisting in the demands of reaching for the models. Renowned architects struggle to make sure that the reality of their buildings is as close as possible in profile and detail to the fantasy charted on paper. Choreographers strive to translate their vision of aesthetics into high levels of performance. These masters *defy* the status quo; they design and create new models. They offer humanity new levels of aspiration. But when they teach others or when they translate fantasies into reality, they often make all or almost all the decisions for their pupils—dancers, football players, builders, musicians—who want to "receive" and participate in the knowledge, the experience, the inspiration. Indeed, the command style is prevalent in some of the most esteemed cultural and social events. One is reminded of a television program on Jascha Heifetz in which this master of the violin was engaged in teaching aspiring young violinists. The episode focused on how Heifetz shows and tells his pupil every detail, every nuance. Fascinating. Ingenious. Great precision, great insights, great inspiration. In a moment of impatience he picked up his violin and began to play, and—with his eyebrow—motioned his pupil to follow, as if to say: "Come, follow my performance, reach for my model."

And then there is another kind of master. These are the people who have accumulated knowledge and experience and have reached positions where their major role is to *maintain the status quo*. These are people who are engaged in many vital jobs and responsibilities that *at times* require them to make all decisions for others. These are the managers of various establishments, the supervisors on the assembly lines, drill sergeants, assistant coaches, writers of etiquette books, some religious leaders, and many others.

Teachers, too, must perform this role of carrying *a portion* of the past into the present. It is imperative to convey vital facts of various fields, to uphold some traditions and rituals, to enforce rules of safety, and to maintain some modicum of social conduct. All these require previous models. All these invite the command style.

The charts shown in Figure 4.6 (page 49) and Table 4.2 (page 50) can serve as summaries for the teacher and/or reminders for the learners. They can be given out as aid materials, or presented as wall charts.

STYLE A AND
THE DEVELOPMENTAL CHANNELS

Perhaps the ultimate question in education and teaching is: What really happens to people when they participate in one kind of an educational experience or another? In a broad sense this question is often answered by various philosophical treatises. The specific connection between an educational experience and its outcome is being studied by a multitude of research activities. The questions of *why* and *what for* are paramount in our minds. With the development of the Spectrum of Teaching Styles, these questions are vital in understanding the contributions and boundaries of each style. Since the Spectrum delineates specific and differentiated styles, it is worthwhile to hypothesize, to inquire, and to verify the possible relationships between the experiences in a given style and the place of the learner on various developmental channels.

This section offers a schema for identifying these relationships—for determining what happens to a person along a particular channel when he/she is experiencing a given style. The schema examines five channels: (1) the physical developmental channel, (2) the social developmental channel, (3) the emotional developmental channel, (4) the cognitive developmental channel, and (5) the moral developmental channel.

Each individual can move along these channels from minimum to maximum development (see Figure 4.7). An individual can also be placed at a given point on a channel; this point represents only a relative position between minimum and maximum.

In order to make a reasonable assumption about the relationship between a style and the developmental channels, certain criteria must be used. These criteria can be degree of independence, the degree of depen-

---

COMMAND STYLE

The purpose of this style is to learn to do the task(s) accurately and within a short period of time, following all decisions by the teacher.

ROLE OF TEACHER

o   To make subject matter decisions

o   To make all impact decisions:

    Subject matter

    Order of task

    Starting time

    Pace and rhythm

    Stopping time

    Interval

    Attire and appearance

    Initiating questions for clarification

o   To provide feedback to learner about role and subject matter

ROLE OF LEARNER

o   To follow and perform the task when and as described

Figure 4.6. Style A Classroom Chart

TABLE 4.2. THE ANATOMY OF STYLE A: THE COMMAND STYLE

Decision Sets	Teacher's Decision Categories	Learner's Decision Categories
Preimpact (Content: Preparation)	1. Objective of the episode	Not involved
	2. Selection of a teaching style	Not involved
	3. Anticipated learning style	Not involved
	4. Whom to teach	Not involved
	5. Subject matter	Not involved

	6. When to teach (time):
	  a. Starting time d. Stopping time
	  b. Pace and rhythm e. Interval
	  c. Duration f. Termination
		Not involved

	7. Modes of communication	Not involved
	8. Treatment of questions	Not involved
	9. Organizational arrangements	Not involved
	10. Where to teach (location)	Not involved
	11. Posture	Not involved
	12. Attire and appearance	Not involved
	13. Parameters	Not involved
	14. Class climate	Not involved
	15. Evaluative procedures and materials	Not involved
	16. Other	Not involved
Impact (Content: Execution and Performance)	1. Implementing and adhering to the preimpact decisions (1–14)	Responds as prescribed
	2. Adjustment decisions	Not involved
	3. Other	Not involved
Postimpact (Content: Evaluation)	1. Gathering information about the performance in the impact set (by observing, listening, touching, smelling, etc.)	Not involved
	2. Assessing the information against criteria (instrumentation, procedures, materials, norms, values, etc.)	Not involved
	3. Providing feedback to the learner:	Not involved

	4. Treatment of questions	Not involved
	5. Assessing the selected teaching style	Not involved
	6. Assessing the anticipated learning style	Not involved
	7. Adjustment decisions	Not involved
	8. Other	Not involved

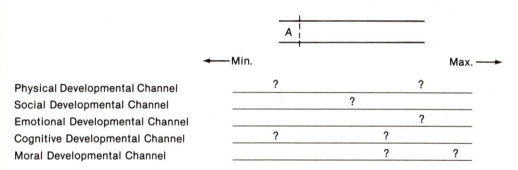

Figure 4.7. The Developmental Channels

dence, creativity, group participation, or others. When a different criterion is used, the individual's placement on the channels will change.

Therefore, before we can determine the relative position of a person on any of the channels, we must take two steps. First, we must identify the criterion by which we will study the relationships between the style and each of the channels. Second, we must define the channel involved in the relationship. This two-step procedure heightens the objectivity of the analysis and reduces the idiosyncratic interpretations of this relationship.

Placement Using the Criterion *Independence*

Let us begin with the criterion of *independence* and ask: When Style A is in operation *how independent* is the learner in making decisions *about* his/her . . . ? (see Figure 4.8.)

The Physical Developmental Channel. The physical developmental channel refers to the psychomotor development of the learner—the development of strength, agility, balance, coordination, skill in performing tasks in various sports, physical dexterity, and so on.

Since the teacher makes all the decisions in Style A, the learner is *not* independent in making decisions *about* his/her physical development. Therefore the learner is placed toward "minimum" on this channel. Note that we are not talking about physical development per se. Most of the physical attributes can be highly developed by the use of Style A. We are focusing here on the independence of the learner in making decisions *about* physical development.

The Social Developmental Channel. The social developmental channel refers to development of social skills during the interaction with other people. These include verbal behavior skills, communication, manners, the ability to listen, and so on.

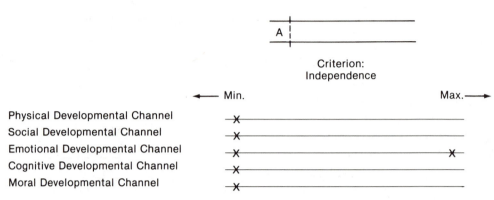

Figure 4.8. Style A Criterion: Independence

Since the teacher makes all the decisions in Style A, the learner is *not* independent in making decisions about these social skills. The learner follows the models set by the teacher. Therefore he/she is placed toward "minimum" on this channel.

The Emotional Developmental Channel. The analysis of the relationship between Style A and the emotional developmental channel is most intriguing. It is quite difficult to identify with certainty how independent a person is in his/her emotional structure. Nevertheless we'll proceed with the following suggested analysis. As a general definition, this channel refers to:

1. The *trust* that evolves between the teacher and the learner
2. The degree of security the learner feels about him/herself
3. The degree of security the learner feels during interaction with others

Now since feelings are always in reaction to someone or something, it is necessary to specify the conditions that trigger the feelings. When we identify these conditions, the possible position on this channel is bifurcated:

Placement toward "Minimum"
When Style A is used as punishment.
When Style A is used in anger.
When Style A is used to oppress the learner rather than teach subject matter.
When the teacher's idiosyncracies rule and violate the integrity of the learner.
Under this set of conditions the

Placement toward "Maximum"
When the use of Style A is appropriate in reaching the objective.
When the learners see improvement in their performance and begin to understand the purposes of Style A.
When the teaching behavior is consistent in mood.

learners cannot feel independent about their emotional state.

When teaching is done with pleasantness.

When the teacher's idiosyncracies do not violate the integrity of the learner.

Under this set of conditions the learners can feel independent about their emotional state.

The Cognitive Developmental Channel. The cognitive developmental channel refers to the engagement and development of the learner in various cognitive operations, such as memory and recall, comparing, contrasting, hypothesizing, and problem solving.

Since the teacher makes all the decisions in Style A and the role of the learner is to *reproduce* what the teacher has said or shown, the learner is primarily engaged in memory and recall. Because Style A does not invite the participation in other cognitive operations, the learner is *not* independent in making decisions about *exhibiting* the engagement in these operations. Hence, the learner is placed toward "minimum" on this channel when *independence* is used as criterion. If, however, the criterion used is the outcome of reproduction learning, the placement of the learner is toward "maximum"; the engagement in memory in Style A, indeed, brings about maximum reproductive learning.

The schematic representation in Figure 4.9 might be useful in this kind of investigation. It suggests different relationships between the style (Style A in this case) and various operations of the cognitive domain.

The Moral Developmental Channel. The moral developmental channel refers to developing a sense of right and wrong and acting upon it.

Differently stated, moral development involves identifying, clarifying, and developing a value system.

Since the teacher makes all the decisions in this style, he/she has a major part in establishing the moral climate in the episode. Standards of behavior are a result of the decisions made by the teacher, and the learner has very little to do with establishing the standards. This does not mean that the learner will necessarily abide by the standards, but the learner is *not* independent in establishing the rules that govern the episode. Therefore the placement of the learner on this channel is toward "minimum."

It must be emphasized that being placed toward "minimum" on this channel is not synonymous with "minimum moral development" or "low morals." It merely indicates that the learner *does not* make the decisions *about* the rules of conduct.

Placement Using the Criterion
Perfection of Performance

The analysis based on the criterion of independence offers a particular picture of what happens to the learner. A different criterion will produce a

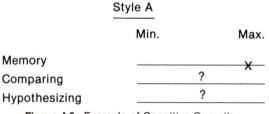

Figure 4.9. Example of Cognitive Operations

different picture. If, for example, we select *perfection of performance* as a criterion, we might find the learner placed on each channel as shown in Figure 4.10. As you can see the picture here is different. The reasons for this are explained below.

The Physical Developmental Channel. The question here is: How perfect can the performance be in the physical domain when Style A is used? It is quite apparent that when this style is used in activities requiring physical skills and dexterity the performance can reach high standards. The repetition, the emulation of the model, the persistence—all contribute toward reaching perfection; hence, the placement is toward "maximum" on the physical developmental channel.

The Social Developmental Channel. The placement on the social developmental channel bifurcates. From one perspective, it is toward "minimum" because Style A does not call for social interaction. However, perfection of performance evokes social status and peer acceptance and, at times, admiration. From this perspective, the placement is toward "maximum."

The Emotional Developmental Channel. The placement on the emotional developmental channel also bifurcates. The analysis offered for the criterion of independence applies to the present criterion as well.

The Cognitive Developmental Channel. Reaching toward perfection in Style A means that the learner has reached for the model and has achieved the expected performance. Cognitively this is a result of being maximally engaged in memory and recall. Hence, the learner is placed toward "maximum" on the cognitive developmental channel insofar as the memory and replication operations are involved.

The Moral Developmental Channel. People who accept the Style A conditions or the institutions can follow and live by the moral standards promulgated by these institutions and, therefore, are placed toward "maximum" on the moral developmental channel. On the other hand, people who cannot accept the morality of Style A institutions cannot live by the value system they represent. Under this condition, the placement is toward

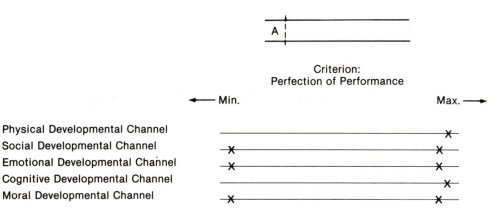

Figure 4.10. Style A and the Developmental Channels (Criterion: Perfection of Performance)

"minimum." Again, we see the possibility of dual positions emanating from the command style.

To sum up this section, the analysis of relationships between a given style and the developmental channels has two purposes. First, it helps us understand the boundaries of each style. Each style can make only finite contributions to the development of the learner. Each style has its limits and it is imperative to know what it can do and what it cannot do.

Second, our analysis provides a schema for generating hypotheses about the development of the learner under a given set of conditions. It proposes some thoughts about the impact of particular teaching behaviors on the learner, an impact that goes beyond the mere acquisition of knowledge. Studying and researching this vast network of relationships will provide some answers to the question posed at the beginning of the section on the developmental channel: What really happens to people when they participate in one kind of an educational experience or another?

We are ready to move on to the next style.

CHAPTER 5

Style B: The Practice Style

Style B, the practice style, is akin to the command style, yet significantly different. What does the new relationship look like? Consider, for example, an episode when a parent shows a young child how to tie the shoes: The parent shows the child how to do it, the child follows by trying the knot, and when it's done the parent either approves of the knot or offers corrections. Or consider an episode when a mechanic assigns a task to an apprentice: While the apprentice works, the mechanic watches and corrects errors or approves the performance. Or an episode when a golf pro is teaching a stroke to a novice: The pro demonstrates the stroke, the novice does it, and the pro watches and offers feedback and corrections. In the classroom it is a familiar procedure: The teacher explains (or demonstrates) the task, then the students practice it. When they are done (or sometimes while they are practicing) the teacher offers feedback about the performance. These kinds of episodes are very common on all educational levels (elementary, middle, high school, and college) and in many subject matter areas—for example, conversational exercises for learning a language, science labs, seat work doing written tasks in arithmetic, practicing a task in a given sport, practicing a particular melody on the violin, and so on.

The common element of these experiences is the following sequence of events: The teacher assigns the task, the learner practices it with *some* degree of independence, and the teacher offers individual feedback. The differences between Style B, the practice style, and style A, the command style, are in the specific behaviors of the teacher and the learner in the impact and the postimpact sets of decisions.

THE ANATOMY OF STYLE B

Style B evolves by shifting some decisions from the teacher to the learner (Figure 5.1). This shift occurs in the impact set. In this set *nine* decisions are shifted from the teacher to the learner. The other decisions remain the same as in Style A and the teacher makes all the decisions in the preimpact and in the postimpact sets.

The nine decisions shifted to the learner in the impact set are:

1. Posture
2. Location
3. Order of tasks
4. Starting time per task
5. Pace and rhythm
6. Stopping time per task
7. Interval
8. Attire and appearance
9. Initiating questions for clarification

All the episodes described at the beginning of this chapter represent the anatomy of the practice style: The teacher (or surrogate) makes the decisions about the subject matter task (preimpact), the learner performs and practices the task while making the nine decisions (impact), and the teacher has the time to observe the performance and offer individual and private feedback (postimpact).

Style B as a Landmark Style

It is interesting to note that in the development of the Spectrum a question arose about which decisions should be shifted in order to identify the next style that is akin to—yet significantly different from—Style A. It is theoretically possible to shift one decision at a time, and thus identify a great number of styles. If a different single decision were shifted at different times, the number of styles would be virtually endless. In reality, however, we are

	A	B

Preimpact	(T)	(T)
Impact	(T) ⟶	(L)
Postimpact	(T)	(T)

Figure 5.1. The Shift from Style A to Style B

seeking to identify the *cluster* of decisions that will constitute a significantly new O–T–L–O. The nine decisions that are shifted in Style B constitute such a *cluster*. All nine are within the physical domain (location, posture, pace and rhythm, etc.). The *doing* (performance) of any task requires making decisions in the physical domain. Moreover, all nine of the shifted decisions occur in the impact set, so that the student learns first how to make decisions about *doing* the task. At this point the learner is not making decisions about the subject matter (preimpact) nor about evaluating the performance (postimpact).

Because each of the styles on the Spectrum involves shifting significant decisions, they are identified as *landmark styles*. The options that occur between the landmark styles are known as *canopy styles* and will be discussed in Chapter 9.

OBJECTIVES OF STYLE B

In Style A the central theme is immediacy in the performance of the task by adhering to every decision made by the teacher. In Style B the overarching objective (and outcome) is the beginning of a weaning process in which the learner gradually becomes more independent of the teacher. The structure of this style provides the special time for the learners to practice, to interact with the task by themselves, and to learn to make the nine decisions. The specific subject matter objectives and behavior objectives are as follows:

Subject Matter Objectives	*Behavior Objectives*
To reproduce the model after practicing by oneself	To experience the beginning of independence by making the nine decisions
	To learn to be accountable for the consequences of each decision
	To learn to respect others' rights to make decisions
	To initiate an individual and private relationship between the teacher and the learner

IMPLEMENTATION OF STYLE B

Description of an Episode

The initial two or three episodes in Style B begin with the teacher's explanation of the style. This explanation includes a short statement about the difference between the practice style and the command style, the objectives of the new style, an identification of the roles, and a delineation of the decisions that are shifted to the learner. This explanation establishes the *expectations* for the ensuing episode. The teacher continues with the explanation and/or demonstration of the subject matter at hand and presents the task. At this point the learners begin to make the decisions that are being shifted to them. The teacher can actually observe the decisions made one by one—location, posture, starting time, and so on. Learners will pick up the necessary materials, task sheets, or lab equipment; establish their location for doing the task; and within a reasonably short time will settle into the performance of the task. Calm climate sets in and learning is in process. The teacher observes all this for a few moments and then begins to move about from learner to learner. Time is available for individual contact and private feedback. The teacher stays with a learner for a moment or two, observes the performance of the task, asks questions about it, listens to the learner's questions, offers feedback, and moves on to the next learner. When learners know this style and understand its purposes, this process usually proceeds smoothly and with productive use of time.

At the end of the episode the teacher offers feedback to the entire class about their participation in making decisions and working independently on the task. The teacher and the learner can move on to the next episode.

How to Do It

The following steps describe the use of the anatomy of the practice style as the guidelines for implementation. This process involves making the decisions in the preimpact, impact, and postimpact sets.

The Preimpact Set. As in Style A, the teacher's role in Style B is to make all the decisions in the preimpact set. The three major differences are (1) the awareness of the deliberate shift of decisions that will occur in the impact set, (2) the selection of tasks conducive to this style, and (3) the decisions about the logistics and parameters.

The Impact Set. Since the structure of Style B defines different roles for the teacher and the learner, the spirit of this style and the shift of the nine decisions must be explained to the learners during the first two or three episodes. After that only the designation of the style (by name or letter) is needed to picture the ensuing episode because the expectations will be clear.

The following is the sequence of events for the episode:

1. The teacher sets the scene by stating that a new style will be used in the next episode.
2. The teacher states the style's objectives:
   a. To offer time for each learner to work individually and privately.
   b. To provide time for the teacher to offer individual and private feedback to learners.
3. The teacher describes the role of the learner and the shift in decision

making. Initially, the teacher actually names the nine decisions (or points to a chart). This procedure clearly identifies the specific decisions shifted to the learner.

4. The teacher describes the role of the teacher:
   a. To observe the performances and offer individual and private feedback.
   b. To be available to answer questions by the learner.
5. The teacher presents the task. The way in which the task is presented will depend on two factors:
   a. The teacher's decisions regarding the following components of communication and the options within each component:[1]
      i. Content. Each task has a particular content in terms of what is to be done.
      ii. Mode. Each task can be presented through different modes: audio, visual, audiovisual, or tactile. The teacher needs to decide which mode is best for a given task.
      iii. Action. Each mode has its own form of action; the teacher has a choice of speaking about the task, demonstrating it, or using a combination of both. Each choice depends on the task, on the situation at hand, and on the purpose of the communication. At times a demonstration of the task conveys a clear image of what's to be done; at other times, a few words are needed to clarify the task.
      iv. Medium. Various media can deliver the task: the teacher, a film, a video, or a task sheet. A decision must be made about which option to choose.
   b. The teacher's decisions about the quantity of each task (the number of repetitions per task, or the length of time for the task to be performed), and the order of tasks (sequence or random).
6. At this point the learners know the expectations of the roles and the subject matter tasks. The teacher then establishes the parameters for the episode. Parameter decisions here would apply to the categories of location, time, posture, and attire:
   a. *Location parameters* must be established by the teacher for the following reasons:
      i. Safety. ("You may do your task anywhere in the room except on the windowsills" or " . . . except in front of the door.")
      ii. Clear communication. This particularly applies in the gymnasium or in outdoor activities (sports, nature studies, etc.). Without clear location parameters, the learners might make a decision to choose a location outside the visual and audio communication

---

[1] For a detailed analysis, see the section on "The Classroom Communication Model" in Chapter 9.

range. This interferes with the teacher's capacity for individual feedback.

iii. Teachers' idiosyncrasies. The teacher may have particular feelings concerning "off-boundaries" areas.

b. *Time parameters*. These parameters are mandatory. The teacher may say something like this: "You have 20 minutes to complete your tasks." Within the time parameters the learners make the decisions about starting time, pace and rhythm, interval and stopping time *per task*. Time parameters teach most people to perform a task within a reasonable amount of time. In most jobs things have to be done on time and within a certain amount of time. This does not imply rigidity and a fanatic approach to time. It merely states that it is important to teach students the relationship between task performance and time.

c. *Posture parameters*. In a typical class one rarely thinks about posture; however in subject areas such as choir, typewriting, or practicing handwriting it is necessary to establish some reasonable posture for successful performance of the task. Posture, in these subject areas, accommodates the performance. It is interesting to note that in physical education the posture decision is a part of the task itself.

d. *Attire parameters*. Sometimes it is necessary for the teacher to establish attire parameters. This will occur mainly for safety, cleanliness, health reasons, or institutional preferences. These situations are quite prevalent in art, shop, home economics and physical education. A decision about attire parameters is also made for the band, the cheerleaders, the drama class, and athletic teams. In these instances the decision is made for aesthetic values, social norms or *esprit de corps*.

From these four categories the teacher selects those that apply directly to the upcoming episode. If parameters in a given category are not relevant to the conduct of the episode, there is no need to mention them. Time parameters, however, apply to almost all episodes. At times, some learners will exhibit "testing behavior" by pushing beyond the stated parameters. This behavior may occur in order to test any and all four categories of parameters. This testing behavior is usually exhibited soon after the introduction of a new style. Learners need time to learn the new decisions and need to be reminded of the parameters with a high degree of consistency.

7. The teacher announces procedures concerning logistics—for example, pickup and dropoff of lab equipment, materials, task sheets, sports equipment, and so forth.

8. Once the scene has been set, the teacher may say: "Are there any questions for clarification?" "You may begin when you are ready."

9. The learners start making the decisions that were shifted to them in the impact set. The class will disperse, each learner making his or her

location decision, and will proceed with practicing the task and making the rest of the decisions.

10. The teacher observes the initial moments of the episode and then moves about to initiate individual contact with the learners.

The Postimpact Set. The purpose of the postimpact time is to offer feedback to all learners. To accomplish this the teacher moves about from learner to learner observing both the performance of the task and the decision-making process, then offers feedback and moves on to the next learner. During this process, the teacher needs to do the following:

1. Identify, as quickly as possible, the learners who are making errors in the performance of the task and/or the decision-making process.
2. Offer corrective feedback to the individual learner.
3. Stay with the learner to verify the corrected behavior. (In many cases a few seconds are sufficient for this step.)
4. Move on to the next learner.
5. Visit, observe, and offer feedback to those who perform correctly and make the nine decisions appropriately. These students also need the teacher's time. (Often teachers offer feedback only to those who make errors.)
6. Remember that for some tasks it may take two or three episodes to observe every learner in the class. Learners usually develop the patience needed for such cycles.
7. Be aware of the options available in choosing the feedback form and consider the impact of each form on the learner in a given instance. (Corrective, value, neutral, and ambiguous forms of feedback are described in Chapter 3 and discussed in detail in Chapter 9.)

The value of one-to-one contact and individual, private feedback has been expounded by educators and researchers for quite some time, and the practice style provides for such behavior. The teacher has time to provide this attention, and the cumulative positive effects on the learner and the class climate are quite visible. However, there are times in Style B when group feedback is necessary and desirable. For example, when the teacher realizes that a number of learners exhibit the same error, it is efficient to stop the whole class or a part of the class, demonstrate the task again, reexplain the specifics, and then continue with the episode. The structure and the climate of Style B, however, must maintain the process of individual and private feedback.

At the end of the lesson, the teacher should assemble the class for a closure. A *closure* is a one-minute "ceremony" for ending the lesson. This can take many forms such as a quick review of the learned content, general feedback to the class, or a statement about the next lesson. A moment of closure provides the teacher and students with a sense of completion.

SELECTING AND DESIGNING THE SUBJECT MATTER

Task Description

In order to achieve the objectives and purposes of Style B, the task description must be congruent with its structure and intent. Any deviation or any inappropriate use of verbal behavior will abort the style and will lead the learner to exhibit behavior that is a reflection of another style.

The following are the characteristics of a Style B task:

1. It calls for and reflects a *single standard* in design and performance (no alternatives should be evoked). There is only one correct response, one correct factual answer.
2. It contains specific descriptions of *what* to do.
3. It contains specific descriptions of *how* to do it (no options are available to the learner). This prescribes the *quality* of the performance.
4. It prescribes the *quantity* of the task.
5. It facilitates the learner in making only the *nine decisions*.
6. It elicits the cognitive operations of *memory* and *recall*.

The following are examples of Style B tasks:

- Your task is to read the following 20 sentences. Underline the subject once and the predicate twice.
- Your task is to complete all the addition and subtraction exercises on page ___.
- Write the names of all the states and their capitals in the appropriate spaces on the maps provided.
- In our textbook, based on the chapter called "The Civil War," list the five advantages the Union had and the three advantages the Confederacy had in 1861.
- Using the negative in the enlarger (in our photography lab), your task is to make one 8×10 enlargement on polycontrast paper, exposing for 20 seconds, developing for 70 seconds, stopping for 30 seconds, fixing for 5 minutes and washing for 30 minutes.
- Practice the hook shot, as demonstrated, 20 times from the designated spots on the floor.
- Your task is to pin the jacket pattern to the material provided, as just demonstrated.
- Combine $Be + Cl$, $Li + O$, and $B + O$; and disassociate MgF_2 and KCl following the demonstrated procedure.
- Prepare a wet mount of onion cells for microscopic observation, following the steps on page 35 of your manual.

• Play the first page of the Mozart Violin Concerto no. 5, following the interpretation I offered you.

There are many, many tasks in each subject matter area that are most conducive to teaching by Style B. These are tasks that require practice or review of specific skills that have been demonstrated by the teacher, by a book, by a chart, or by a computer. The precision of these skills may be necessary for the accurate functioning of instruments, safety of people, standards of production, aesthetic levels in the arts, progress in scientific research, and success in sports.

Let us now examine some tasks as written by teachers during training, and see if they are appropriate for Style B. You are invited to participate in the analysis of the examples below. Your task is to:

1. Read each example.
2. Compare and contrast against the criteria for task description (the characteristics of Style B tasks).
3. Identify whether or not the example is congruent with the style.
4. Circle the word or words that indicate a deviation from the style.
5. Identify the decision category in which the deviation occurred.

Tasks

a. "After you read Chapter 10, write a paragraph describing how you feel about the main character."
b. "What are some ways to solve the problem of . . . ?"
c. "What do you think happened when . . . ?"
d. "Write a poem describing what you saw at sunset."
e. "Perform a forward roll."
f. "Design three different plans for organizing the school's parking lot."
g. "Identify and circle the personal nouns on the task sheet. When you complete the task, get a 'key' at my desk and check your answers."
h. "Work in your SRA workbook following the directions, and then check your work."
i. "Identify as many minerals as you can from the rocks on the table."
j. "Do _____ the best you can."
k. "In a two-minute period do as many correct sit-ups as possible."

Although each of these is a legitimate task, none is appropriate for Style B. The following analysis identifies the *verbal behavior* that causes the task to deviate from the style, explains why the deviation occurs, and shows which characteristics of a Style B task are not complied with.

Analysis of Tasks That Deviate from Style B

a. "After you read chapter 10, write a paragraph describing **how you feel** about the main character."

The flaw: The words "how you feel" invite the learner to make subject matter decisions. It is inappropriate for Style B.

Does not comply with:
Characteristics 1–6:
1. Single standard
2. Specific description of what to do
3. Specific description of how to do it
4. Prescribed quantity
5. The 9 decisions
6. Only memory

b. "What are **some ways to solve** the problem of . . . ?"

The flaw: The words "some ways to solve" invite the learners to make subject matter decisions and will produce alternative responses. It violates the principle of single standard.

Characteristics 1–6

c. "What do **you think** happened when . . . ?"

The flaw: The personal thoughts of the learner will be evoked, which is inappropriate for this style. In addition, responses by learners will vary. The word "think" is a general term for cognitive involvement. Learners may engage in cognitive operations other than memory and recall.

Characteristics 1–6

d. "Write a poem describing what **you saw** at sunset."

The flaw: Again, this verbal behavior invites divergent personal interpretations, which is inappropriate for this style.

Characteristics 1–6

e. "Perform **a** forward roll."

The flaw: Which forward roll is meant? There are many kinds. The specifics of what to do and how to do it are missing. It leaves the task too open to alternative performances.

Characteristics 1–6

Analysis of Tasks That Deviate from Style B, continued

f. **"Design three different** plans for organizing   Characteristics 1–6
    the school's parking lot.''

The flaw: There are two deficiencies here.
The words "three different" obviously call
for divergent production rather than adhering
to the single standard. The word "design"
may elicit the learner's own ideas concerning
the issue at hand.

As you can see, these examples all cause the same kind of deviation despite the diversity in the verbal behavior. It is, indeed, fascinating to observe the power of verbal behavior. Seemingly innocent words are used, yet they take the student out of the intended behavior. Let's continue with the analysis:

Does not comply with:

g. "Identify and circle the personal nouns on   Characteristic 5
    the task sheet. When you complete the task,
    get a 'key' at my desk and **check your an-
    swers.**"

The flaw: The task shifts more than nine decisions to the learner. It shifts decisions in the
postimpact phase. The clue for the deviation
is in the words "check your answers." (This
task design places it in a different style.)

h. "Work in the SRA workbook following the   Characteristic 5
    directions, and then **check your work.**"

The flaw: Same as in example g.

i. "Identify **as many** minerals **as you can** from   Characteristics 4 & 5
    the rocks on the table."

The flaw: The task shifts quantity decisions to
the learner, which is inappropriate for Style B.
In addition the phrase "as many . . . as you
can" makes it legitimate to do *only one* and
then stop.

Analysis of Tasks That Deviate from Style B, continued

j. "Do _____ the **best you can.**"   Characteristics 3 & 4

The flaw: This task shifts the decisions about
the standard of performance to the learner. In
Style B the learner must be asked to perform
the task as described.

k. "In a two-minute period do **as many correct**   Characteristics 4 & 5
sit-ups **as possible.**"

The flaw: This shifts the quantity decision to
the learner. It makes it legitimate to do only
one sit-up and stop. Note, too, that there is
no need to include the word "correct" in the
description of a task. It is obvious that a
teacher expects the learner to perform a task
correctly.

To conclude this section, whenever you describe a task in Style B,
ascertain that it meets the criteria of this style. Then and only then can you
ensure that the action will be congruent with the intent.

Task Sheets

One of the most useful aids for accommodating the learner's practice of a
task (or a series of tasks) is the *task sheet* (sometimes called a work sheet or
a ditto). Its purposes are as follows:

1. To start weaning the learners and provide them with the opportunity
   to do the task on their own.
2. To present the learners with the tasks to be done (to remind the
   learners *what* to do and *how* to do it).
3. To increase the efficiency of time-on-task and teacher-learner communication.
4. To cut down the number of repeated explanations by the teacher.
5. To teach the learners to listen to the initial explanation and/or observe
   the demonstration.
6. To teach the learners to follow specific written instructions.
7. To record the progress of the learners (optional).

Using a task sheet makes clear to learners that part of schooling is
listening and observing. It is the learner's role to listen to the explanation
and observe the demonstration. Then, during practice time, the task sheet

becomes the source of information. This puts the focus on the learner. The learner becomes responsible for following up by using the information on the task sheet.

This technique reduces the learner's manipulation of the teacher. Students who have learned to manipulate ignore the teacher during the initial demonstration and/or explanation. Then, while the class is engaged in doing the task, they call the teacher over for another private explanation and thus dominate the teacher's time. When this behavior occurs it reverses the control in the class and reduces the teacher's available time to move about and offer feedback. For example, the manipulative learner may say: "I forgot what you said we should do with. . . ." The teacher cannot ignore the request to repeat the explanation nor can the teacher hold the learner accountable for the initial explanation. When this occurs half a dozen times during the performance of any given task, a good portion of the teacher's time is used up and the teacher cannot move about and offer feedback.

When task sheets are used, however, a learner who requests additional explanation may be asked by the teacher: "What is the description on the task sheet?" The teacher thereby initiates a different relationship with the learner. The learner now must resort to the information available on the task sheet. The teacher continues: "Is the description clear?" (The teacher has taken the second step in initiative.) The learner must focus on the description of the task. The learner now has only two options. One is to say: "Yes, it is clear." The teacher then says: "Let me see you perform it," offers the appropriate feedback, and moves on to the next learner.

The learner's second option is to say "No." The teacher then says: "Which *specific* phrase or word is not clear?" (Again, the teacher initiates.) This question invites the learner to focus on the description of the task and be specific or *accountable*. The teacher offers the explanation, waits to see the performance, offers feedback, and moves on.

This is a different teacher-learner relationship than the one previously described because it is based on verbal behavior that decreases manipulation by learners. It reestablishes the teacher in the appropriate role during the postimpact phase—the role of inviting the learner to participate in understanding and performing the task and of being available for feedback.

The following guidelines will help ensure an effective, well-designed task sheet:

1. The task sheet should contain the necessary information about what to do. It may include the actual exercises to be done (in subject areas like math, grammar, social studies, music, or language vocabulary), describe the exercises (e.g., physical activities), or tell where the exercises can be found (e.g., on page 211 of the textbook).
2. If necessary, it can include a section on how to do the task. It may include an example of the process (long division), and/or the procedure to follow

(chemistry lab). This establishes the standard to be attained, the model. Often, however, only a sentence or two will tell the learner how to do the task. This approach is useful if the teacher has offered an oral explanation and/or a demonstration on the board (or via other visual techniques).

3. If necessary, it will specify the quantity of the task. For example: "Repeat the measurement five times and calculate the average result." "Practice the second page of the music score three times." "Dribble the ball around the cones four times the width of the gymnasium." Obviously some tasks do not require such quantity specification.
4. It should use one of two verbal behavior forms:
   a. Infinitive: "Your task is *to answer* the questions about the migration movements found on pages 85–87. These questions are about factual information in your textbook."
   b. Imperative: "*Complete* the missing parts in the mathematical statements to make them true."

Figure 5.2 is a general format for a task sheet. Note that this format provides for the following information:

1. Identifying information (name, class, date).
2. Designation of the teaching style that will be used. In this case it is Style B (circled). The same task sheet can also be used for Styles C and D.
3. The task sheet number, indicating the order or sequence of the sheets. This helps keep the sheets organized and available for future use.
4. The general subject matter or activity (e.g., algebra, Spanish, gymnastics).
5. The specific topic or the particular aspect of the subject matter that will be practiced (e.g., quadratic equations, identifying verbs, handstand).
6. Comments "to the student," describing the purpose of the activity and any logistical or other relevant information the student might need.
7. A description of the tasks and their parts. The task description, when necessary, should also include an illustration of the tasks and/or their parts.
8. If needed, quantity specifications for the task, using units that are relevant to the prescribed task (e.g., the number of repetitions, the length of time for doing the particular task, the number of successful trials out of total number of attempts).
9. Feedback. Space is available for feedback comments that, depending on the style, may be provided by different people. In Style B, the feedback is provided by the teacher (optional).

Name _____		Style A Ⓑ C D
Class _____		Task Sheet # _____
Date _____		Subject Matter (topic) _____
		_____

To the student _____

_____

Task Descriptions	Feedback and Progress notations (optional)
1.	
2.	
3.	
a.	
b.	
4.	
5.	
a.	
b.	
c.	

Figure 5.2. A General Format for a Task Sheet

10. Progress notation. This column can be used by the student and the teacher to mark the completed task, to indicate incompletion, to comment on the next session, and so forth (optional).

These are the essential parts of a task sheet for Styles B, C, and D. They can be arranged in various formats and in different order, depending on the subject matter demands, the learner's reading level, and the creative ideas of the teacher. One thing must be maintained: adherence to the characteristics of task design for Style B.

Name _____   Style Ⓑ C D C

Class _____   Task Sheet # _____

Date _____   Alphabetizing _____

To the student: Rewrite the following words in alphabetical order.

red _____

vitamin _____

peach _____

timid _____

scale _____

undercoat _____

pearl _____

officer _____

told _____

understand _____

scarf _____

official _____

record _____

ninth _____

headlight _____

instant _____

degree _____

heat _____

nurse _____

note _____

deport _____

intake _____

magnetic _____

exhaust _____

Figure 5.3. A Task Sheet for an Episode in Language Arts

Figures 5.3, 5.4, and 5.5. are examples of task sheets in three different subject matter areas.

Planning a Lesson

A lesson is a period of time in which the teacher and the learners are engaged in activities that lead to predetermined and identified objectives. Some lessons can be composed of one episode; however, many lessons are usually composed of several episodes, each with its specific objective and specific task (activity). When these episodes are well connected and sequenced, they directly contribute to the *overall objective* of the lesson. This can only occur with thorough and systematic planning (preimpact). Random and spontaneous lessons are fine on occasion. They add spice but they cannot serve as steady diet.

If a successful lesson is one where intent is congruent with action (intent $\cong$ action), then the more we plan the intent, the greater the chances of congruent action. A thoroughly worked-out lesson plan helps in the following ways:

1. It specifies the intent of each episode. It answers the question: Where am I going and why?
2. It provides guidelines for checking the lesson's progress and answering the question: Am I on the right track? If adjustments are needed, corrections can be made.
3. At the end of the lesson when it becomes possible to assess the results, the lesson plan makes it possible to determine whether or not the objectives were reached. Was the action congruent with the intent?

Especially for the novice teacher, the more meticulous the planning, the greater the chances of identifying discrepancies that may be corrected in the next episode or lesson. The more experienced teacher uses the planning to visualize the process and to anticipate and orchestrate the events in the lesson.

Planning a lesson, therefore, is a rational activity. It is based on a particular sequence of decisions that are related to the teacher's knowledge of the subject matter, the teacher's conception of teaching, and his/her awareness of the learners. The lesson plan transforms the preimpact decisions into action (impact).

The following comments are related to the model lesson plan (exemplified in Figure 5.6) used in conjunction with the Spectrum of Teaching Styles. The main principle of this lesson plan is the steps that identify the sequence of decisions throughout the planning; these steps ascertain that each decision is connected with its antecedent.

Name ____________________ Style B C D

Class ____________________ Task Sheet # __________

Date ____________________ Music: Note heads

To the student: A note head may have a stem.

Stems go <u>up</u> on the <u>right</u> side of the head.

Ex: 

Make note heads with stems going up in the boxes below.

Stems go <u>down</u> on the <u>left</u> side of the head.

Ex: 

Make note heads with stems going <u>down</u> in the boxes below.

If a note is on or below the third line the stem will go up.

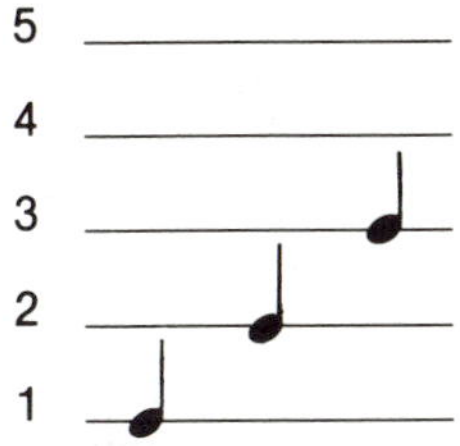

If a note is above the third line the stem will go down.

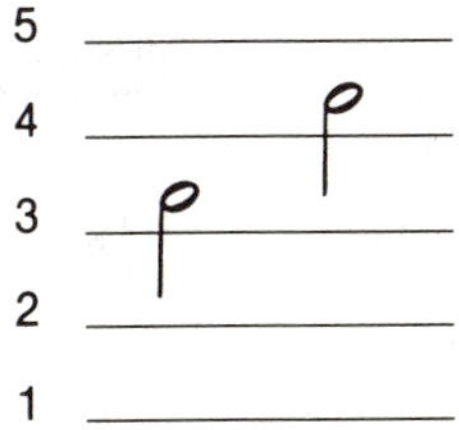

Place a stem on each note head, following these two rules.

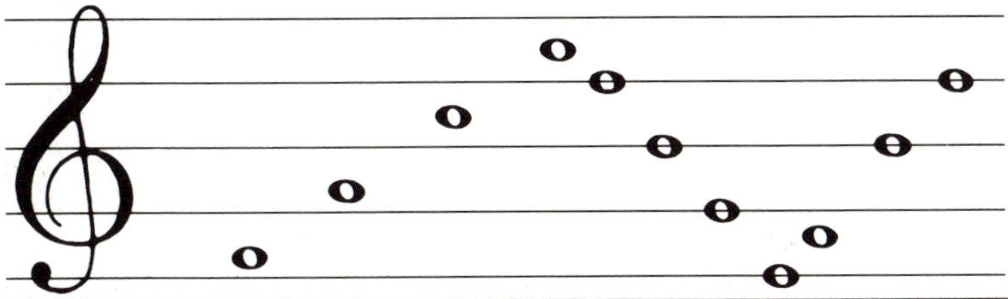

Figure 5.4. A Task Sheet for an Episode in Music

Name _____ Style Ⓑ C D

Class _____ Task Sheet # _____

Date _____ English Literature _____

<u>Macbeth</u>

To the student: Follow the directions for each of the three sections below.

1. Identify the speaker of the quote:

_____ a. "To beguile the time, look like the time; bear welcome in your eye, your hand, your tongue; look like the innocent flower, but be the serpent under it."

_____ b. "There's no art to find the mind's construction in the face."

_____ c. "What's done cannot be undone."

_____ d. "Come what come may, time and the hour runs through the roughest day."

_____ e. "But cruel are the times when we are traitors and do not know ourselves."

_____ f. "When our actions do not, our fears do make us traitors."

_____ g. "More needs she the divine than the physician."

_____ h. "Things without all remedy should be without regard; what's done is done."

_____ i. "Life's but a walking shadow, a poor player that struts and frets his hour upon the stage and then is heard no more. It is a tale told by an idiot, full of sound and fury, signifying nothing."

_____ j. "Let every man be master of his time."

2. For the following two questions, identify by quotes the passages that supply the answer. These two questions are not an exercise in interpreting, but one in the identification of factual information as presented in the text.

   a. List five quotes that indicate the strong and weak points in Lady Macbeth's and Macbeth's characters. Follow this form:

Lady Macbeth

Weaknesses	Strengths
a. pg. ___, line ___	a. pg. ___, line ___
b. pg. ___, line ___	b. pg. ___, line ___
c. pg. ___, line ___	c. pg. ___, line ___
d. pg. ___, line ___	d. pg. ___, line ___
e. pg. ___, line ___	e. pg. ___, line ___

Figure 5.5. A Task Sheet for an Episode in English Literature

b. Select one minor character in the play that impressed you, and identify seven quotes that describe the character.

a. pg. ____, line ____

b. pg. ____, line ____

c. pg. ____, line ____

d. pg. ____, line ____

e. pg. ____, line ____

f. pg. ____, line ____

g. pg. ____, line ____

3. Contrast the following characters to Macbeth. Contrast Macbeth's motives and patterns of deterioration to each of the following characters (supply only the page and line; do not write the quote).

	Motives		Pattern of Deterioration	
Macbeth	pg.___, line___ pg.___, line___		pg.___, line___ pg.___, line___	
	pg.___, line___ pg.___, line___		pg.___, line___ pg.___, line___	
Duncan	pg.___, line___ pg.___, line___		pg.___, line___ pg.___, line___	
	pg.___, line___ pg.___, line___		pg.___, line___ pg.___, line___	
Guards	pg.___, line___ pg.___, line___		pg.___, line___ pg.___, line___	
	pg.___, line___ pg.___, line___		pg.___, line___ pg.___, line___	
Banquo	pg.___, line___ pg.___, line___		pg.___, line___ pg.___, line___	
	pg.___, line___ pg.___, line___		pg.___, line___ pg.___, line___	
Lady Macduff	pg.___, line___ pg.___, line___		pg.___, line___ pg.___, line___	
	pg.___, line___ pg.___, line___		pg.___, line___ pg.___, line___	
Young Siward	pg.___, line___ pg.___, line___		pg.___, line___ pg.___, line___	
	pg.___, line___ pg.___, line___		pg.___, line___ pg.___, line___	

Figure 5.5. (*continued*)

Biology (Anatomy) – The Skeletal System

Subject Matter: _____   Lesson# _____   Date _____

The overall objective of the lesson: To identify the bones of the shoulder girdle and their relationships to each other.

	OBJECTIVES	SUBJECT MATTER		LOGISTICS		
Episode No.	Subject Matter and/or Role	Specific Tasks	Style	Organization of Learners, Equipment, Task Sheets, etc.	Time	Comments
1.	To arouse curiosity	Show a short tape of arm movements in dance, daily tasks, throwing a stone, shooting a basketball. OR: shoot the tape in the classroom, select appropriate movements, and show it.	B[a]	Video equipment Tape	5 min.	
2.	To identify the parts of the humerus	1. Learners examine the bone & identify the parts of the humerus using the anatomy manual p. 2. Learners fill in the names of these parts on task sheet 1, containing a sketch of the bone.	B	Collection of bones Task sheet 1	10 min.	
3.	To identify the parts of the clavicle	1. Learners examine and identify the parts of the clavicle, using the manual p. 2. Learners fill in the names of the parts on task sheet 2. 3. Learners identify the position of the clavicle in relation to the humerus using the skeleton as a model.	B	Bones Skeleton Task sheet 2	10 min.	
4.	To identify the parts of the scapula	1. As in episode 3 with the scapula. Manual p. 2. As in episode 3 with task sheet 3. 3. Learners identify the relationships of the scapula to the humerus and to the scapula.	B	Bones Skeleton Task sheet 3	10 min.	
5.	Closure: To review the parts from memory	1. Learners call the name of the parts of each bone as the teacher points to the parts (individually and in a group). 2. Same. Teacher points randomly to various parts.	B		5 min.	

[a]A canopy style; see Chapter 9.

Figure 5.6. Plan for a Biology Lesson

   The starting point is deciding which aspect of the subject matter will be taught in the lesson: What is the overall objective of the lesson? To reach this objective, learners must participate in a series of episodes, each with its specific tasks. Success in each task and reaching the objective of each episode directly contribute to the attainment of the *overall objective* of the lesson.

   Next is the decision about the selected style, in this case Style B. This will determine the behaviors of the teacher and the learner in order to reach the objectives (T-L-O). This is followed by logistical considerations that involve decisions about organization of learners, equipment, materials, task sheets, and so on, all of which are aspects of class management.

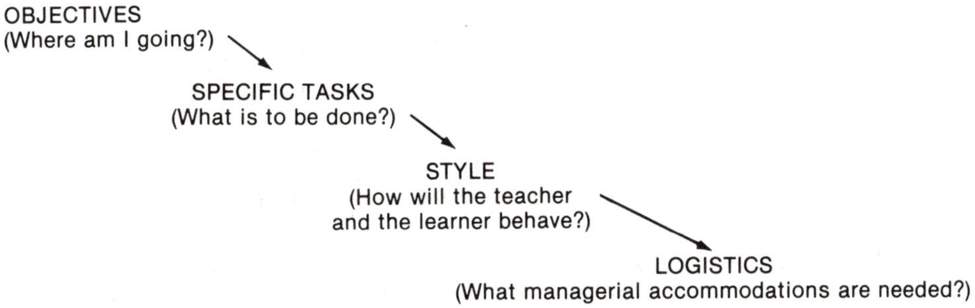

OBJECTIVES
(Where am I going?)

SPECIFIC TASKS
(What is to be done?)

STYLE
(How will the teacher
and the learner behave?)

LOGISTICS
(What managerial accommodations are needed?)

Figure 5.7. Flow of Planning

The next step in the planning involves setting time parameters for each episode. This provides the teacher with guidelines for time distribution during the lesson. At this point the planning is completed and the lesson is ready. The comments column is used by the teacher for his/her assessment of the lesson and suggestions for the next lesson. Subsequent lessons can be planned in the same manner and, if needed, several lessons can be strung in a sequence that constitutes a unit, a topic, or a theme.

The lesson plan shown in Figure 5.6 illustrates the planning loop that connects the various elements of the lesson and ensures its flow. In summary, this loop goes from objectives to logistics, as diagrammed in Figure 5.7.

Note that when logistical decisions are made, the teacher must take into consideration factors such as the number of learners and the amount of available equipment and organize the class for maximum participation in the tasks. (See the section on "Organizational Formats" in Chapter 9).

IMPLICATIONS OF STYLE B

As the Spectrum unfolds and more decisions are shifted to the learner, more things happen to the learner. The teacher must know and understand the ever-expanding network of implications because then, and only then, will the teacher be able to orchestrate the multiple dimensions—philosophical, psychological, social, and cognitive—that often affect the class simultaneously. Each event, each decision made in the classroom has consequences. So once again let's examine the implications of this new relationship that develops in the practice style. The reality of episodes in this style implies that:

1. The teacher values the development of deliberate decision making.
2. The teacher trusts the learners to make the nine decisions.
3. The teacher accepts the notion that both the teacher and the learner can expand beyond the values of one style.

4. Learners can make the nine decisions while practicing the tasks.

5. Learners can be held accountable for the consequences of their decisions as they participate in the process of individualization.

Verbal Behavior

In order to produce the new reality of Style B and inculcate a sense of mutual *trust,* the teacher must make several adjustments in his/her verbal behavior. The first and perhaps the most difficult adjustment is to shift the pronoun "I" to "you." This requires awareness and deliberateness. Refrain from saying: "I want you to. . . ." Instead say: "Your task is to . . ."; "Your role is. . . ." Just as Style A is an "I" style, Style B is the beginning of the "you" style. Learners, in a rather short time, pick up this linguistic difference with all its connotations.

The second adjustment needed is in the way the teacher talks about the transfer of the nine decisions from teacher to learner. The appropriate verbal behavior is: "In this style nine decisions are shifted to you. The nine decisions are posture, location. . . ." The key word is *shift.* Shift is a neutral word that conveys to the learner the intent of Style B. During the introduction of Style B the teacher should avoid saying: "I will allow you . . ."; "I will give you . . ."; or "I will bestow upon you. . . ." These phrases focus on the position and power of the teacher and connote that the decisions may be taken away.

Reward and Reprimand

One of the differences between the practice style and the command style is in the conception and use of the reward and reprimand systems. In the command style the learner is rewarded for obeying and following; in the practice style the learner is rewarded for initiating—for making the specific nine decisions. Behaviors that would be reprimanded if demonstrated in the command style are now invited and rewarded—seemingly a paradox.

How then can the teacher ascertain that there will be no confusion and discontent about the rewards and reprimands? The concept of *episodes* mitigates this potential conflict and paradox. For each new episode, the teacher announces the style and makes sure that learners are clear about the expectations of the style, the roles of the teacher and the learner, and the change in the *basis* for rewards and reprimands—that is, that the shift is not only in the decisions made, but also in the consequences of these decisions. When this is done, the systems of reward and reprimand that accompany each style are anticipated with clarity, openness, and honesty.

Style B and Feelings

When the nine decisions are shifted to the learner, a whole new dimension in the relationship between the teacher and the learner begins to evolve—the dimension of *trust*. In this style, trust develops in two directions: (1) the teacher learns to trust the student to make the decisions appropriately, and (2) the student learns to trust the teacher to be consistent in shifting the decisions and in providing private feedback. This style is, indeed, the beginning of the "weaning process" for both teacher and learner.

As Style B is introduced in the classroom, the teacher should be aware of several possible behaviors by learners. Some learners are overwhelmed by the sudden presence of options. The shift of these decisions may be too demanding. This feeling can produce one of two types of behaviors. At one extreme, the learner "freezes"—learners who are not able to make any of the decisions may become immobilized and simply freeze in one spot. They need to be told what to do. They need more time to learn to deal with one decision at a time. At the other extreme, the learner exhibits random behavior, roaming around, and inability to start a task and stay with it.

Patience and acceptance of the learner's limitation at this initial stage will enhance the trust and will help the learner overcome the sense of frustration and inability.

STYLE-SPECIFIC COMMENTS

Experiences in the operation of the practice style have produced a variety of style-specific findings and insights. The following comments refer to the use of this style and its impact. Consider and think about these comments; examine them as you proceed in developing this style in your class.

Style B is the teaching style most commonly used in schools. About 80 percent of episodes in all subject areas use one form or another of this style. The sequence of presenting materials, assigning students to related factual tasks, providing performance time, and offering feedback about the performance of the tasks represents a four-step model that is universally used in schools. This model is the essence of Style B. It is pervasive and it is effective. Studies in Spectrum classes have verified the efficiency of this style, in which time-on-task is as high as 70 percent (Shirey et al. 1978).

In the initial introduction of the practice style to a class, it is imperative to explain to the learners the new roles of the learner and the teacher, the concept of shifting decisions, and to specify the nine decisions. This explanation sets the expectations for everyone's behavior and makes it possible to hold the teacher and the learner accountable for behaviors that are consonant with their respective roles. These behaviors do not develop automatically; they need to be understood and practiced.

When Style B is used, some learners may test the parameters set by the teacher. It is quite natural to do so. This testing can take place in any one of the nine decision areas. It will be manifested by pushing the boundaries of that decision—for example, selecting odd places for location or assuming an unusual posture while performing the task. As long as these behaviors do not interfere with other learners and do not constitute safety hazards, perhaps the best response by the teacher is to simply wait. The testers will find out soon enough that some of their decisions are interfering with their own learning and participation. At times the teacher might need to remind the learners about the parameters, either publicly to the entire class or privately to certain individuals.

Style B provides the teacher with time to offer individual feedback. In a class of 25–30 students, it is possible during the impact set to come in contact with almost every learner during episodes that last about 20 minutes.

In many classes one observes the temptation and the practice to respond mostly (or only) to those who raise their hands. These students usually draw the teacher's attention to difficulty in doing the task. Teachers often invite this behavior by saying: "Raise your hand when you have a problem and I'll come to you." This procedure has a number of liabilities:

1. Only those who want contact will raise their hands.
2. Only those who identify themselves get the attention.
3. All the learners will know that the teacher is available only to those who have difficulties.
4. All the learners will know who has difficulty—hence, there is a reduction of privacy.
5. Learners know that they can manipulate the teacher and keep him/her away by *not* raising their hands.
6. Those who *do not* raise their hands may not know whether their performances are correct or not.
7. Some learners may produce errors deliberately in order to have contact with the teacher.
8. The teacher does not know how each individual is performing.

In Style B learners should ask questions for clarification only. Questions for clarification refer to what the teacher has explained and to unclear parts of the subject matter. Answers are given and learners move on with the task. This procedure is necessary to keep everyone on the way to the objective. It does not connote rigidity or interference with the learner's thirst for knowledge. Teachers must learn to distinguish between relevant questions, which represent the student's genuine quest, and those used for manipulation. Some students learn to ask questions that take the class on a tangent. In some classes learners have been reinforced to do so. This has been rationalized by the notion of encouraging "free expression." In reality it gives license to learners to go in any direction (many of which are irrelevant to the situation at hand) and thus manipulate the teacher and the rest of the class.

As learners begin to take responsibility for time decisions in Style B, the teacher must be alert to the issue of wasting time. One technique used by students to stretch the time parameters is to engage in a variety of activities unrelated to the task. When the teacher announces, "Time is up," one often hears a grumble and statements from various spots: "I have not finished . . ."; "We did not have enough time." "Okay," says the teacher, "take 10 minutes more." If this occurs once in a while there is no problem. But when it becomes the way time is handled in the class, then the learners are in control of the time. As a result:

1. They learn to procrastinate.
2. They learn not to produce.
3. They learn that they control the time.
4. They learn to manipulate the teacher.
5. They do not learn to concentrate and accomplish the task.

Perhaps the best way to handle this is by maintaining the original time parameters, stopping the activity on time, and collecting the assigned tasks. With consistency and appropriate reward and reprimand systems, students learn the reason for and the value of time parameters.

Although Style B provides for learners to make decisions about attire and appearance, this is not always possible. In some situations this decision is made by the institution and therefore cannot be made by the individual learner. For example, some schools require uniforms for all the students, many provide uniforms for teams, and so on. Such restrictions should be clarified when Style B is explained to the learner.

When Style B is used, it sometimes happens that a considerable number of learners makes the same error when performing the task and/or making the decisions (role error). This requires an adjustment decision by the teacher, who should stop the action of the class, repeat the explanation and/or demonstration, and ask the students to continue. This technique of recalling the learners for group feedback has several advantages:

1. It is time-efficient. The same feedback is given to all those who made the same error. To do it individually is a waste of time.
2. During this time learners can ask questions and the teacher can ascertain that most or all learners understood the correction.
3. It may reinforce those who have performed correctly.

Since Style B is designed for individual and private practice, communication among or between students must be kept to a minimum. When a student talks to a peer, he/she interferes with the other person's decisions. Style B must not be perceived as a "no talking" style, but as a style that provides for private practice time.

At the elementary school level two phenomena may occur in the initial stages of Style B. First, individual learners often follow the teacher around to show what they have learned and to seek feedback. Second, learners often stop after one performance and wait for the teacher to get to them for feedback. In both situations the quickest and most neutral way to handle the learner's behavior is to review with the learner the teacher's role in Style B. Reassure your learner that you *will* get to him/her, just as you get to all other learners in the class.

Sometimes, because of the different performance levels of the learners, the teacher will assign different groups a different level of the task, or different tasks. In Style B the teacher makes this decision to accommodate differences in performance. In another situation, the learner may be asked to select, for example, three out of five available tasks. In this case the teacher has made the subject matter decisions about the task design, but the learner makes the decisions about which tasks to select for the present episode.

Learners occasionally finish a task before the time allotted for it is up. This may occur in all styles except the command style. The resulting *interval time* (also referred to as *transition time*) must be considered when planning the lesson because this interval invites learners to engage in decisions that may not be appropriate for the episode. The teacher should plan an interval activity available for learners who finish their task early. A choice of two or three interval activities could always be available during a certain number of lessons, weeks, or the entire semester.

When Style B is used, the teacher should take care to use verbal behavior that is appropriate to this style. The following behaviors should be avoided: "Your role is simply to. . . ." "Your role is very impor- tant. . . ." "My role is just to. . . ." These modifiers are not helpful. They project a value that is not an accurate description of the roles. During the postimpact phase, the teacher who comes to a learner for individual and private contact should not ask: "How are you doing?" This will shift the postimpact decision of evaluation to the learner. In Style B it is the teacher's role to make the postimpact decisions. Style B teaches the learner to receive private feedback from the teacher.

The following statements may project "value" about the speed of performance: "Oh, you are the first to finish." "You have not finished yet?" "You finished already?" All these comments, when said with a particular intonation, may project the cultural value of speed. You may want to reconsider how you use them.

A useful aid in Style B (and other styles) is the wall chart, which identifies the purpose, the roles and the decisions (see Figure 5.8).

By identifying the specific roles of the teacher and the learner, and by doing a decision analysis of various programs, strategies, models, and educational games, it becomes possible to place them in the Spectrum; they always represent a given style. "Mastery Learning," for instance, is an excellent example of Style B, operating over a long period of time; the teacher makes the preimpact decisions, particularly about the appropriate tasks for the learner. The learner is engaged in doing the tasks (impact), and the teacher assesses the performance in order to decide about the next step

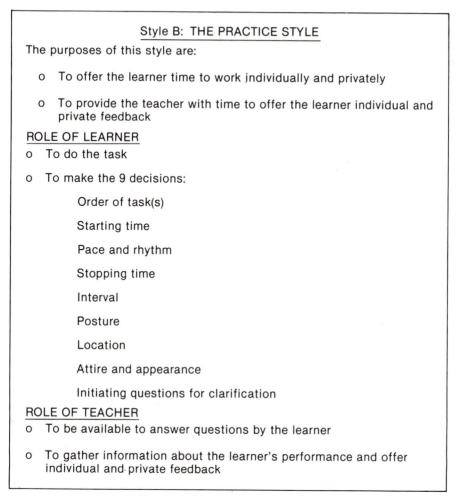

Style B: THE PRACTICE STYLE

The purposes of this style are:

o   To offer the learner time to work individually and privately

o   To provide the teacher with time to offer the learner individual and private feedback

ROLE OF LEARNER

o   To do the task

o   To make the 9 decisions:

Order of task(s)

Starting time

Pace and rhythm

Stopping time

Interval

Posture

Location

Attire and appearance

Initiating questions for clarification

ROLE OF TEACHER

o   To be available to answer questions by the learner

o   To gather information about the learner's performance and offer individual and private feedback

Figure 5.8. Style B Classroom Chart

(postimpact). The tasks are factual, concrete, with correct answers (responses).

Strategies for question-and-answer activities that involve recall of particular facts in a given subject area represent a form of Style B (see the section on "The Canopy" in Chapter 9). Some coaching procedures (or coaching behaviors) are excellent examples of Style B done with high intensity and precision.

The purpose of this analysis is to identify what a model is and what it is not. Knowing a model's boundaries helps us know which objectives it can reach. We shall return to this theme later in this book.

The charts shown in Figure 5.8 and Table 5.1 can be used as aid materials or wall charts.

TABLE 5.1. THE ANATOMY OF STYLE B: THE PRACTICE STYLE

Decision Sets	Teacher's Decision Categories	Learner's Decision Categories
Preimpact	All decisions, minus the *specifics* of the decisions that are shifted to the learner in the impact set	Not involved
Impact	Implementing the preimpact decisions *minus these* ⟶ Delivering all subject matter Observing the performance of the learner Adjustment decisions (May make parameter decisions)	⎡ Order of tasks Starting time (per task) Pace and rhythm Stopping time (per task) Interval Location Posture Attire & appearance Initiating questions for ⎣ clarification Performing the task
Postimpact	All postimpact decisions Assessing the teaching style itself	Not involved

STYLE B AND THE DEVELOPMENTAL CHANNELS

As we conclude Style B, let's once again hypothesize about the relative placement of the learner on each of the developmental channels. As we did in Style A, we'll use as an illustration the criterion of *independence* (see Figure 5.9). The question that arises is: How independent is a learner in making decisions about . . . ?

The Physical Developmental Channel. Since nine decisions are shifted to the learner, the learner is more independent in making decisions about his/her physical reality. This is primarily due to the shift in decisions about posture and pace and rhythm. The placement on the physical developmental channel is therefore slightly away from "minimum."

The Social Developmental Channel. Since the location decision is shifted to the learner, he/she can select a location that is close to a friend, where some communication can occur. In this style each learner is expected to perform the task privately; nonetheless, some verbal (and nonverbal) communication and social interaction does take place. The learner, therefore, is placed slightly away from "minimum" on the social developmental channel.

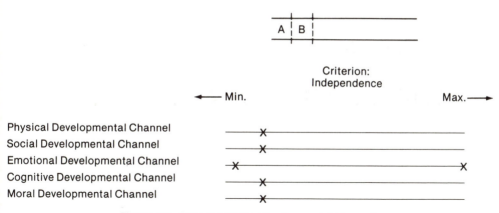

Figure 5.9. Style B and the Developmental Channels

The Emotional Developmental Channel. The placement is dual on the emotional developmental channel. Some students feel quite independent in making the nine decisions and are independent about their feelings. These are placed toward "maximum." Others may feel stress in making the nine decisions; they are not sure of themselves, they may not be accustomed to making these decisions and, therefore, they do not feel independent about their emotional positions. These learners are placed toward "minimum" in this channel.

The Cognitive Developmental Channel. Since Style B calls for memory and recall as the main operation in reproducing a model, the analysis of the cognitive developmental channel is similar to that of the command style. The placement of the learner is toward "maximum" in memory and toward "minimum" in other cognitive operations.

The Moral Developmental Channel. The shift of the nine decisions begins to develop trust. Development of trust hinges upon honesty. In Style B the learner has the opportunity to demonstrate a degree of honesty in independently making the nine decisions. The placement on the moral developmental channel is therefore slightly away from "minimum."

When criteria other than independence are selected, the placement on the channels will change and a different developmental picture will emerge.

In summary, the practice style is efficient and widely used, and helps us meet important education goals.

CHAPTER 6

Style C: The Reciprocal Style

Style C, the reciprocal style, is about partnership; it is about a relationship between learners. In this style, which is conducted in pairs, students learn to perform the task and receive feedback from their partners. A new dimension—social interaction—becomes the focus of episodes in this style. Students learn to work with each other, talk to each other, and listen to each other. Patience and tolerance develop while tasks are being done and immediate feedback is being exchanged. Indeed, with the reciprocal style a new reality evolves in the classroom with new roles for the learners and for the teacher.

In order to facilitate this process, a different social arrangement must occur in the classroom. This arrangement is called the *triad*. The triad (Figure 6.1) involves three people: the teacher and two learners. One learner is the doer (L_d), the other is an observer (L_o). All three have specific roles to play and specific decisions to make.

$$L_d \qquad L_o$$

$$T$$

Figure 6.1. The Triad

Before we examine the multiple relationships that develop in Style C, let's identify the structure of this style and the roles of each participant in the decision-making process.

THE ANATOMY OF STYLE C

The anatomy of Style C calls for more decisions to shift from the teacher to the learner. The shift occurs in the postimpact set as shown in Figure 6.2. The role of the teacher is to make decisions in the preimpact set; the role of the doer (L_d) is to make the nine decisions in the impact set as in Style B and to perform the task. The role of the observer (L_o) is to make the decisions in the postimpact set and offer feedback to the doer based on criteria prepared by the teacher. When the task is completed, the doer and the observer switch roles.

	A	B	C
	A	B	C
Preimpact	(T)	(T)	(T)
Impact	(T) $\longrightarrow$ (L)		(L_d)
Postimpact	(T)	(T) $\longrightarrow$ (L_o)	

Figure 6.2. The Shift from Style B to Style C

Directions of Communication

In order to facilitate the new relationships among the doer, observer, and teacher, specific directions of communication must exist. The possible directions of communication are illustrated by the doubleheaded arrows in Figure 6.3.

Figure 6.3. Possible Directions of Communication in Style C

Since the two major purposes of style C are (1) to develop and enhance the new role of "the observer," and (2) to develop a productive social relationship between the partners, the desirable directions of communication are those shown in Figure 6.4. The two arrows highlight the two major purposes of the style. They show the reciprocal communication between the observer and the doer, and the reciprocal communication

Figure 6.4. Desirable Directions of Communication in Style C

between the teacher and the observer. If the teacher does communicate with the doer, he/she will violate the shift of decisions in this style and will usurp the role of the observer. There is, however, one exception to this rule. When danger is imminent, either physical or emotional, the teacher must intervene, talk to the learners, and prevent the mishap (Figure 6.5). Throughout the episode, however, the teacher observes the behaviors of both the observer and the doer in order to be aware of the events that take place in the class.

Figure 6.5. Style C Communication with Teacher Intervention

OBJECTIVES OF STYLE C

The specific subject matter objectives and behavior objectives of Style C are as follows:

Subject Matter Objectives	*Behavior Objectives*
To learn the specifics of the subject matter	To learn to observe, to compare, and to contrast
To learn the steps involved in a given task	To learn to give and receive feedback from peers
To learn to correct errors immediately	To learn to respect, tolerate, and accept others' differences in performance
To learn to give and receive immediate feedback concerning the performance of the task	To expand socialization as a result of these new behaviors

IMPLEMENTATION OF STYLE C

Description of an Episode

Style C episodes are fundamentally different from those in the previous two styles. You can actually "see" a different social interaction and a different process of decision making. After the teacher introduces the style to the class and explains the shift of decisions, the learners select their partners and make the decision about who will be the first doer and observer. The doer picks up the task sheet and/or other materials and begins doing the task. The observer picks up the criteria sheet and assumes his/her role as an observer and a provider of feedback. Shortly after the doer begins performing the task, the observer compares the performance against the criteria (prepared by the teacher). The observer is engaged in assessing the performance and deciding whether or not there are any errors. When the observer is ready, he/she offers feedback to the doer. After a few episodes in this style, students learn to offer the corrective, value, and neutral forms of feedback. The doer receives the feedback, acts upon it if necessary, and continues with the performance of the task. The partner continues with the observer's role until the doer completes the task. The learners then switch roles and continue with the episode. The new doer proceeds with the task and the new observer offers feedback. While this process of reciprocation evolves, the teacher moves about from pair to pair, observes the interaction, and offers feedback to the observer. And thus flows an episode in a different style that accomplishes the learning of the task and the learning of new social behavior.

How to Do It

The Preimpact Set. In the planning phase, the teacher makes all the decisions in the preimpact set with a focus on:

1. Selecting and designing the subject matter.
2. Designing the criteria sheet.
3. Determining the logistics appropriate for the episode.

The Impact Set.

1. The teacher addresses the entire class and states the objectives of Style C:
   a. To work with a partner.
   b. To offer feedback to the partner.
2. The teacher explains the social arrangement of Style C by:
   a. Identifying the triad (see Figure 6.1).
   b. Explaining that each person in the triad has a specific role and that each learner will take turns in the roles of doer and observer.
3. The teacher explains the role of the doer:
   a. To do the task.
   b. To make the nine decisions as in Style B.
   c. To initiate questions and communicate only with the observer.

4. The teacher describes the role of the observer:
   a. To have the performance criteria (prepared by the teacher).
   b. To observe and/or listen to the performance of the doer.
   c. To compare and to contrast the doer's performance against the criteria.
   d. To draw conclusions about the accuracy of the performance.
   e. To offer feedback to the doer.
   f.`To initiate, if necessary, communication with the teacher.
5. The teacher introduces the role of the teacher:
   a. To offer feedback to the observer.
   b. To answer questions by the observer.

Steps 1–5 set the *behavior expectations* for the episode. Since the reciprocal style is quite new to most learners, it is desirable to review these steps with the class for the first two or three episodes in this style. After that, stating the designation of the style by name or letter is sufficient to establish the expectations for the episode.

6. The teacher delivers the task by explanation, demonstration, use of media, or a combination of these.
7. The teacher delivers the criteria. This involves:
   a. Explaining the criteria to the class and showing a sample of them. The teacher does not explain the specific answers, only the *use* of criteria (see the section on "The Criteria Sheet" below). If the students have not had the experience of using specific criteria as a source of feedback, it is important during the first two or three episodes in this style to take the time for detailed explanation of how to use the criteria for observing task performance in a given subject matter.
   b. Explaining how to offer feedback. The teacher acquaints the students with the four feedback forms, explains the purpose of each, and conducts short exercises to provide the students experience in using the appropriate verbal behavior. In this context the teacher can also design short exercises in error detection, a necessary skill for the role of observer.
8. The teacher identifies the logistics necessary for the operation of the episode—that is, the place to pick up task sheets, criteria sheets, needed materials, and equipment; the place to drop off completed task sheets; and so on.
9. The teacher identifies the interval task in case the pair has completed their task before the time parameters expire.
10. The teacher establishes the parameters appropriate for the episode (time, interval, etc.).
11. Once the parameters and the logistics have been stated, the teacher proceeds: "Select a partner and decide who will be the doer and who will be the observer first. Then begin."

12. The students begin by selecting partners, picking up the task and criteria sheets, and settling down to the performance of their roles. The doers start making the decisions appropriate to their roles in performing the task, and the observers follow through with the decisions appropriate to their role in offering feedback. Initially, this process may take a few minutes, but after two or three episodes in this style, students go through the logistical aspects rather rapidly and start with the task performance in a minimum amount of time.

The Postimpact Set. The teacher, meanwhile, waits for a few minutes and observes the partners settling into their roles. Then, systematically and swiftly, the teacher moves from one observer to another. The teacher stays with each observer just enough time to hear some of the specific verbal behavior in the interaction, then offers the appropriate feedback to the observer (*not* to the doer) and moves on to the next observer. It is imperative, during the first few episodes, to visit all observers. The role of the observers and the expected behaviors require strong reinforcements. These short and frequent contacts are essential for establishing the observer as the source of feedback.

At the end of the episode the teacher offers feedback to the entire class, addressing the role of the observers. The specific verbal behavior may take the following forms (either positive-value or corrective statements):

- "You have performed your roles as observers very well today."
- "The feedback offered by the observers was specific and was well done."
- "I see you know how to observe and use the criteria."
- "The observers need more time to learn how to offer feedback privately."

Note that the feedback offered by the teacher at the end of the episode does not include comments about the performance of the task. This was done by the observers during the episode. The purpose of the feedback to the entire class at the end of the episode is to enhance the new role of the observers and the doers.

SELECTING AND DESIGNING
THE SUBJECT MATTER

Tasks designed for Style C should accommodate the decisions that the learners have to make in this style. Primarily we are concerned with the decisions that the observer is invited to make.

There are two categories of tasks available for Style C: product tasks and process tasks.[1]

Product tasks are those where a short final result is sought. They require the doer to respond either by choosing between yes/no or true/false or by supplying the answer. The following examples require yes/no or true/false responses:

- The capital of Colorado is Denver.   Yes ____   No ____
- The tibia and fibula are calf bones.   True ____   False ____
- Israel gained independence in 1948.   True ____   False ____

As you can see, this kind of product task requires the learner to remember and recall a single correct response. The observer, by using the criteria, can verify the correctness or incorrectness of the response. Now, if the response is *incorrect,* the observer, by saying so, actually tells the answer to the doer.

Examples of product tasks that ask the learner to supply the answer include:

- $5 \times 7 =$ _____ .
- The capital of Nevada is _____ .
- The Thirty Years War began in _____ .
- The Olympic Games of 1968 took place in _____ .
- Beethoven wrote (#) _____ symphonies.

In these kinds of product tasks the learner is also required to remember and recall in order to provide the correct answer. But there is a difference in relation to the feedback. The observer, by noting an incorrect response, does not supply the answer.

Let us examine the first example. If the learner states that $5 \times 7 = 36$, the observer, by saying "Incorrect," only alerts the doer to the need to do the task again, but does not supply, by inference, the correct answer. The doer has to do the multiplication once more.

Process tasks involve several steps, each of which is crucial to the end result—for example, long division, use of instruments, a series of gymnastics movements, use of a map to follow the routes of explorers, experiments in chemistry, following a recipe in baking.

In this kind of task design, the observer has to follow the process continuously in order to offer feedback to the doer. In process tasks continuous feedback is needed because errors may occur any place along the process. Process tasks invite the observer to concentrate and remain involved throughout the process.

Since there are many new aspects to be learned in Style C, product tasks should probably be used in the initial episodes. To keep Style C going

---

[1] These two categories also apply to Styles B, D, and E. They are introduced here because this distinction is vital to the understanding of the observer's behavior in Style C.

TABLE 6.1. ASSETS AND LIABILITIES OF PRODUCT TASKS AND PROCESS TASKS

	Assets	Liabilities
Product Tasks	1. Materials are easy to prepare. 2. Tasks are available in textbooks. 3. They are more comfortable for nonreaders. 4. It is possible for the very young to engage in the task.	1. The observer may wander while the doer does the task. 2. When there is an error, it is obvious what the correct answer is. 3. The socializing process is at minimum.
Process Tasks	1. The observer learns to follow a process. 2. The observer is engaged more often. 3. The observer is intensively comparing and contrasting. 4. The socializing process is at maximum. 5. The observer receives more information about the subject matter. 6. The observer can see the relationships among parts of the subject matter because of the clue questions (see the next section on "The Criteria Sheet"). 7. The observer is engaged in mental practice before he/she does the task.	1. Materials take a longer time to prepare. 2. Some doers may need a longer time to do the task; hence after switching roles the second doer may run short of time. 3. Nonreaders may find such tasks frustrating.

in your class, however, process tasks must be used with increasing frequency. Process tasks keep the observer engaged in the subject matter and the performance of the doer; they invite interaction, and thus they reach the objectives of the reciprocal style.

Table 6.1 summarizes the assets and liabilities of the two kinds of task designs for Style C.

THE CRITERIA SHEET

Since one of the major purposes of Style C is to develop and enhance the new decision making shifted to the observer, it is necessary to supply the observer with the tools needed for the new role. The crux of a successful operation in this style is the preparation of the *criteria sheet*. The availability of criteria in the hands of the observer establishes the emotionally safe conditions that evolve in the reciprocal relationships between the doer and the observer. The behavior of the observer is guided by the criteria, and the source of feedback to the doer is the criteria, not the idiosyncratic notions of

Name _____   Style   B Ⓒ D

Date _____   Task Sheet # _____

Class _____   Syllabication — vowels heard

Doer 1

To the doer: This task has two parts:
1. Divide the words into syllables.
2. Underline the vowels <u>heard</u> in each word.

travel	suffer	unsold	softness	airplane
boat	melted	ribbon	locate	goodness
label	replant	mislead	below	painting
marble	notice	cowgirl	promise	lonely
propeller	helpful	open	refill	basement

Figure 6.6. Task Sheet for Doer 1

the observer. This condition establishes *equality* in roles when the partners reciprocate. Both learn to offer feedback based on observation and adherence to criteria. Both learn the use of information regarding the subject matter and the appropriate behavior in their respective roles of doer and observer.

The criteria sheet includes the following components:

1. The description of the task(s) as given to the doer.
2. The answers to each exercise and/or the process of arriving at the answer (in process tasks).
3. Clues (questions or statements) to help the doer focus on corrections.
4. Samples of feedback offered to the doer when the performance is correct and when it is incorrect.

Figures 6.6 and 6.7 show a typical task sheet used by the doer and the related criteria sheet that illustrates the four components listed above. The designations "Doer 1" and "Observer 1" serve as organizers. When the

Do not write on this sheet.

Style Ⓒ D

Criteria Sheet # _____

Syllabication — Vowels heard

Observer 1

To the observer: Offer feedback to the doer while he/she is doing the task.

If the task is done correctly, say:

- That is correct.
- That word is correctly divided into syllables.
- You underlined all the vowels heard in the word.
- You are doing well on this task.

If there is an error, let the doer know where the error is without giving the answer. Say:

- That is incorrect.
- The word is not correctly divided into syllables.
- Say the word aloud.
- Another vowel needs to be underlined.
- An incorrect letter was underlined.
- Too many letters were underlined.

(If the doer cannot at this point do the task, ask the doer to go to the next one.)

The answers:

trav/el	suf/fer	un/sold	soft/ness	air/plane
boat	melt/ed	rib/bon	lo/cate	good/ness
la/bel	re/plant	mis/lead	be/low	paint/ing
mar/ble	no/tice	cow/girl	prom/ise	lone/ly
pro/pel/ler	help/ful	o/pen	re/fill	base/ment

Figure 6.7. Criteria Sheet for Observer 1

learners switch roles, the sheets containing different exercises will be marked "Doer 2" (Figure 6.8) and "Observer 2" (Figure 6.9). Note the information part on both sheets (name, class, the topic at hand). The letters at the top right corner indicate that the task sheet and the criteria sheet can be used in other styles (specifically the task sheet in B and D; the criteria sheet in D). Since in this case they are used for Style C, the letter "C" is circled.

Name _____   Style B Ⓒ D

Date _____   Task Sheet # _____

Class _____   Syllabication — vowels heard

Doer 2

To the doer: This task has two parts:
1. Divide the words into syllables.
2. Underline the vowels <u>heard</u> in each word.

thunder	shadow	Friday	darkness	thankful
pancake	express	music	displease	wagon
pepper	cottage	useless	stove	sunshine
dishpan	depart	please	motel	pencil
tablet	princess	tulip	nine	expect

Figure 6.8. Task Sheet for Doer 2

Figures 6.10 and 6.11 are the task sheet and criteria sheet for a typical process task. In this example, the observer gets involved with the doer's process of doing the task. The criteria sheet provides the observer with the specific steps that are necessary for doing this task. In each step the observer knows whether the performance of the doer is correct or not. The observer, then, can offer the appropriate feedback.

A General Guide for the Design of a Criteria Sheet

When you design the criteria sheet, delve into your experiences and anticipate the mistakes that learners might make in the tasks. Identify possible trouble spots by recalling where mistakes were made in the past. Now, if you were to give the feedback, what would you say? Write down these details on the criteria sheet so that the observer can be as precise as possible in giving feedback. It is wonderful to watch the faces of the observers when their doers succeed in performing the task.

Any of the following suggestions for observers can be incorporated

Do not write on this sheet.

Style   B Ⓒ D

Criteria Sheet # _____

Syllabication — Vowels heard

Observer 2

To the observer: Offer feedback to the doer while he/she is doing the task.

If the task is done correctly, say:

- That is correct.
- That word is correctly divided into syllables.
- You underlined all the vowels heard in the word.
- You are doing well on this task.

If there is an error, let the doer know where the error is without giving the answer. Say:

- That is incorrect.
- The word is not correctly divided into syllables.
- Say the word aloud.
- Another vowel needs to be underlined.
- An incorrect letter was underlined.
- Too many letters were underlined.

(If the doer cannot at this point do the task, ask the doer to go to the next one.)

The answers:

th<u>u</u>n/d<u>e</u>r	sh<u>a</u>d/<u>ow</u>	Fr<u>i</u>/d<u>ay</u>	d<u>a</u>rk/n<u>e</u>ss	th<u>a</u>nk/f<u>u</u>l
p<u>a</u>n/c<u>a</u>ke	<u>e</u>x/pr<u>e</u>ss	m<u>u</u>/s<u>i</u>c	d<u>i</u>s/pl<u>ea</u>se	w<u>a</u>g/<u>o</u>n
p<u>e</u>p/p<u>e</u>r	c<u>o</u>t/t<u>a</u>ge	<u>u</u>se/l<u>e</u>ss	st<u>o</u>ve	s<u>u</u>n/sh<u>i</u>ne
d<u>i</u>sh/p<u>a</u>n	d<u>e</u>/p<u>a</u>rt	pl<u>ea</u>se	m<u>o</u>/t<u>e</u>l	p<u>e</u>n/c<u>i</u>l
t<u>a</u>b/l<u>e</u>t	pr<u>i</u>n/c<u>e</u>ss	t<u>u</u>/l<u>i</u>p	n<u>i</u>ne	<u>e</u>x/p<u>e</u>ct

Figure 6.9. Criteria Sheet for Observer 2

when you are preparing the criteria sheet. Some of the proposed verbal behavior is applicable to any subject matter.

Suggestions for Instructions to the Observer

1. When offering feedback to the doer, you may, if necessary, ask any of these general questions: "Are the directions clear to you?" "Are you clear about the task?" "What is the task asking you to do?"

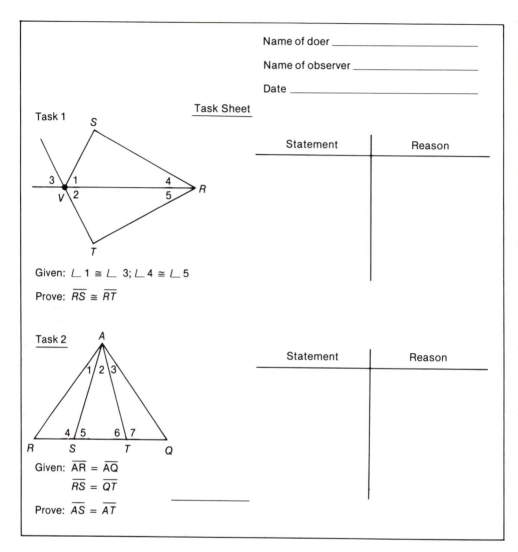

Figure 6.10. Task Sheet for a Process Task

2. If the doer performs the task correctly, you may offer a general comment or a specific comment.
    a. To make a general comment, say: "That is correct"; "You know this subject matter very well"; or "Your answer is correct."
    b. To make a specific comment, identify the specific items that were correct. See Figure 6.12 for examples of what to say.

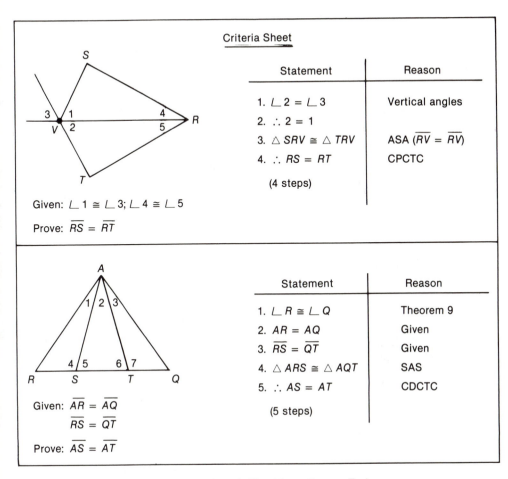

Figure 6.11. Criteria Sheet for a Process Task

3. If the doer has errors, you may offer a general comment or a specific comment.
   a. To make a general comment, say: "That is incorrect"; "Check this section again"; "Please read this question again. There is an error here"; "This is incorrect. Try it again"; or "Reread this paragraph and you will find the answer."
   b. To make a specific comment, cite the specific item that was incorrect. See Figure 6.13 for examples of what to say.
4. Remember that your role as the observer is:
   a. To have the criteria.
   b. To observe and/or listen.

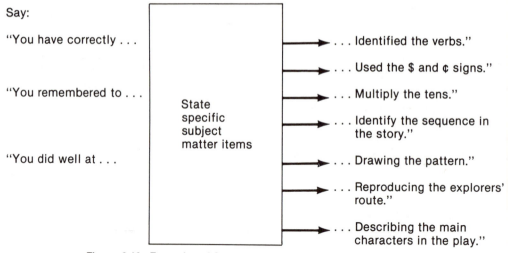

Figure 6.12. Examples of Specific Comments for Correct Responses

c. To compare and contrast (against criteria).
d. To draw conclusions about the performance.
e. To communicate results to the doer, during and after the performance.
f. To initiate, if necessary, communication with the teacher.

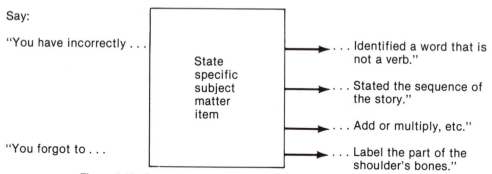

Figure 6.13. Examples of Specific Comments for Incorrect Responses

STYLE-SPECIFIC COMMENTS

Pairing Techniques

In implementing the reciprocal style, one of the practical questions that has to be answered is: How can students be paired up? Obviously there are a number of available techniques and procedures; each has its assets and liabilities. Some of these possible pairing techniques are:

1. The teacher selects and assigns partners.
2. Random selection (drawing a number, etc.).
3. Students select each other.
4. By alphabetical order of names.
5. By height.
6. By weight.
7. By seating arrangement.
8. By sex.
9. By assigning one student to do the selection.
10. By achievement scores.

Which of these possibilities will facilitate the essence of Style C, the evolvement and development of a *relationship* between two students? Since the role of the observer revolves around assessing the performance of a peer (a power position!), it is fraught with sensitive possibilities. Lots of things can happen between the doer and the observer. It is imperative, therefore, that initially students select partners with whom they like to be and work.

Therefore, the third technique—students select each other—is desirable. This option seems to accommodate the giving and receiving of feedback. It is more reassuring to engage in the new behavior with a selected person whom one can trust.

This pairing technique is the most effective one during the initial episodes in Style C. As time goes on, however, and your students become adept at the decisions and processes of this style, you may be ready to change the pairing procedures by rotating partners. Of course you may try any of the other techniques, but rotation allows student selections to remain the most effective focal point of the selection process. You may say to your students: "For the last several episodes in Style C you worked with a partner. Today select someone you have not worked with." You may hear a grumble from your students, but they will follow through. It may take a couple of extra minutes, but they will settle down to their roles and tasks. After all, you have just upset an established social balance. Have patience and give them time. Most of your students will learn to do the job with a new partner. Let them stay with the new partner for a few episodes and then change again. The verbal behavior here could be: "Select a partner with whom you have not worked before."

At every rotation stand back and observe. Watch how your students make the selections, see how they approach new partners, listen to what they say. Take note and see if new bonds are cemented or if they invite peril. You will learn a great deal about your students. You will verify old notions about some and you'll form new notions about others. Watch and see how the objectives of Style C are realized. Watch and see how well each learner learns to exhibit patience, tolerance, sensitivity, and appropriate verbal behavior during the communication with a new peer.

Several teachers have contributed stories about some fundamental changes in attitude that occurred in their classes as a result of frequent use of this style. One change occurred in the relationship between black and white students. The teacher reported that the particular design of Style C (which was used every day throughout the year) served as an equalizer in her class. The reciprocation in offering feedback and frequent rotation of partners created opportunities for everybody to work with and help each of the other students. The use of the criteria established safety and equality of roles and objectivity of feedback. Thus it drastically reduced the reliance on idiosyncracies and the potential of volatile conflicts. Instead, a climate of mutual appreciation and trust *eventually* evolved in that class.

Another change was reported by several early-grade teachers concerning the relationships between the sexes. The reluctance of boys and girls to work together was significantly reduced.

It must be emphasized that these changes occurred after a relatively long period of time during which Style C became a part of those students' reality. It was a result of the teachers' trust in their students and the teachers' tenacity in reaching for the objectives intrinsic to this style.

A third and a rather fascinating story was about a third-grade class that had one learner who was extremely advanced in mathematics. Gary was doing algebra and calculus while the rest of the class was struggling with three-digit additions. Since this learner was different, he was isolated by most of the students in and out of class. The teacher, however, decided that Gary needed the experience and benefit of Style C. He needed to experience different relationships with the members of the class. His peers needed to develop different attitudes toward him.

The teacher decided that Gary would participate in Style C doing the arithmetic along with the rest of the class. Initially it was tough. No one wanted to work with him. But slowly the learners who were Gary's partners (on a rotation basis) realized that he had human qualities besides his mathematical gift. The observers who worked with him learned that the criteria sheet provided them with knowledge to offer feedback to Gary. Again the availability of criteria served as the role equalizer. Gary, in turn, learned to receive feedback from his peers and learned to give feedback. He learned *to be with* his classmates. He did not walk home alone anymore.

These anecdotes highlight a major characteristic of Style C—its ability to reduce stigmatization. Style C teaches people to communicate, to socialize, and to tolerate (which is not the same as accept) individuals who are stigmatized.[2]

Once more we see the inextricable bond of the O–T–L–O; moreover, we see the two sets of outcomes of each style—subject matter outcomes and behavior outcomes. The combination of both are the forces that constantly affect the development of the person.

---

[2] For a captivating treatise on stigmatizing behavior, see Erving Goffman, *Stigma*.

Hazards of Style C

Despite the seemingly smooth-sailing description in the previous sections, all kinds of hazards can appear when a Style C episode is in progress. The following are some potential hazards cited by teachers:

1. The "troublemakers" will get together and raise hell.
2. Some students will dominate when they are in the observer's role.
3. Observers will not know how to correct the doers, despite the explanation of roles and the criteria sheet.
4. Partners will fight; there will be personality clashes.
5. One partner will goof-off.
6. One of the partners will do all the work.
7. They will cheat.
8. Some students will experience rejection ("I don't want you as a partner").
9. The observer will not perform his/her role.
10. The doer will not do the task.
11. Choosing partners will consume too much time.
12. It will take time before they will begin the task.
13. Learners will disagree and use abusive language.
14. Some doers will take a lot of time; there will be no time to switch roles.
15. Noise level in the class will increase.
16. Some doers will not be able to do the task.
17. The teacher will overlook some pairs.
18. Some doers will go to the teacher for feedback.
19. One or more learners will not be selected.
20. The doer will go to the teacher to complain about the observer.
21. The criteria sheet is incomplete or confusing.
22. Organization of the class and the materials is confusing.
23. The teacher will communicate with the doer.

When discipline problems occur in the classroom, they always emanate from someone's behavior. The hazards that have been just identified must, then, emanate from the doer, the observer, or the teacher. Let us, therefore, categorize these hazards according to their source, and then we'll suggest ways of treating them.

Hazards Emanating from the Doer

10. The doer will not do the task.
14. Some doers will take a lot of time; there will be no time to switch roles.
16. Some doers will not be able to do the task.
18. Some doers will go to the teacher for feedback.
20. The doer will go to the teacher to complain about the observer.

Hazards Emanating from the Observer
2. Some students will dominate when they are in the observer's role.
3. Observers will not know how to correct the doers, despite the explanation of roles and the criteria sheet.
9. The observer will not perform his/her role.
21. The criteria sheet is incomplete or confusing.

Hazards Emanating from Either or Both Doer and Observer
4. Partners will fight; there will be personality clashes.
5. One partner will goof-off.
6. One of the partners will do all the work.
7. They will cheat.
8. Some students will experience rejection.
11. Choosing partners will consume too much time.
12. It will take time before they will begin the task.
13. Learners will disagree and use abusive language.
15. Noise level in the class will increase.
19. One or more learners will not be selected.

Hazards Emanating from the Teacher
17. The teacher will overlook some pairs.
21. The criteria sheet is incomplete or confusing.
22. Organization of the class and the materials is confusing.
23. The teacher will communicate with the doer.

In this chapter we'll focus on hazards that emanate from the teacher. Removing the hazards that are caused by the teacher's oversight will improve the conditions for successful episodes in this style. It will also eliminate some of the hazards emanating from the doer or the observer, which will be discussed in more detail in Chapter 16.

The major responsibility of the teacher in this style is the preparation of an accurate and detailed criteria sheet. This always helps the observers maintain their roles. There are three indicators that will convey to the teacher that something is not appropriate with the criteria sheet:

1. Several observers demonstrate confusion.
2. Observers ask too many questions for clarification.
3. Observers often ask the same question.

When these indicators are evident, the teacher needs to correct the situation by doing any of the following:

1. Resolve it on the spot, by an immediate correction of the criteria. If, for example, there is an error in a word or computation in the criteria, the teacher stops the work momentarily and announces the

correction to the entire class. The same can be done if the criteria sheet is missing a small part. The teacher can say: "Class, stop for a minute. Observers for task 2, please correct item 78. The '4' should be a '3.' Please continue." Or: "Observers, I have made an adjustment decision. The section that was omitted from the criteria sheet is written on the board."

2. Clean up the criteria for the next episode.
3. Stop the episode and move on to a different task in order to avoid any further confusion or inaccuracies. At times this is the best solution. The preimpact decision making was obviously not complete and caused the problem. The teacher should tell the class that he/she needs more time to prepare a more appropriate criteria sheet. Most students can readily understand and accept this adjustment.

Many potential hazards stem from overlooking some pairs. If this occurs with some frequency, the excluded pair(s) may respond by demonstrating inappropriate behavior. It is imperative in Style C to get around to all observers. If it is impossible to do it in one episode, the teacher must note the ones not visited and follow through during the very next episode in this style.

The third potential hazard is evident with teachers who are disorganized in handling materials and equipment and thus often encourage inappropriate behavior. The inappropriate behavior will manifest itself by excessive traffic in the classroom, which in turn invites tangential talking. This kind of social activity delays the beginning of task performance, and procrastination may permeate the entire episode. At times disorganized teachers blame the students for all the mishaps and do not see that these responses are the result of inappropriate logistical and organizational decisions. Clear organization, placement of materials in fixed places, and clear procedures for mobility in the class will reduce such potential deviation and ensure successful episodes in Style C.

One of the most potent hazards is teacher communication with the doer. By talking directly to the doer the teacher steps outside the announced roles. If this behavior occurs two or three times in a row, the trust that evolved will be tarnished and the episode will be aborted. Style C will cease to operate in that class.

The "Odd" Learner. A hazard that often occurs is the situation of the extra student, which results from there being an odd number of students in the class. This problem is exacerbated when the same student is repeatedly not selected. In classes with an odd number of students, the teacher can take one of three approaches. First, the teacher can ask that "odd" student to join one of the extant pairs as either (1) a second doer or (2) a second observer. Neither arrangement is totally satisfactory because it may be difficult for one observer to see two doers, and it is certainly more difficult for one doer to receive feedback from two observers. In instances where the task involves a series of rapid steps (such as in gymnastics or diving), the second arrangement may be desirable. One observer then observes a specified number of steps and the second observer observes the rest of the steps.

The second approach is more functional. The "odd" student is asked to do the task in today's episode in Style B and the teacher gives him/her the feedback. When this approach is chosen, the teacher should not say to the student: "I'll be your partner." There are three reasons for this:

1. There can be no reciprocation because it does not make sense for the teacher to be the doer.
2. It ties up the teacher and interferes with the role of offering feedback to the observers.
3. Some learners may deliberately choose to be the "odd" learner in order to have the teacher all to themselves.

The third approach is to move the learner to Style D (see Chapter 7).

Cases in which the same student is repeatedly not selected are more serious. When a student is not selected by classmates there must be a reason. Often the reason reflects some sort of *stigma* attached to the excluded student. Perhaps the best way to deal with this issue is to conduct an episode in group discussion dealing with issues of stigma, sensitivity to other people, and so on. This kind of an episode (conducted in Style H) provides an opportunity for exchange of ideas, feelings, and solutions focusing on the issues and not the particular person involved.

Miscellaneous Comments

The teacher may conduct a special episode to introduce the learner to the feedback forms. Although some learners may have picked up the verbal behavior by listening to the teacher during episodes in Style B, everyone participating in a Style C episode needs to be thoroughly acquainted with the forms and the verbal behavior and purposes of each. These feedback forms are not professional secrets known only to the teacher. Expanding the learners' understanding of human communication is one of the teacher's roles.

Sometimes learners may benefit from practice in using the criteria before a Style C episode is conducted. The teacher can design short episodes specially designed for the purpose of error detection.

Most students appreciate the equality of roles in Style C and usually follow through with appropriate behavior and enjoyment. At times, however, a superior performer (labeled as "bright," "talented," or "gifted") who has always been singled out, reinforced, and perhaps unduly praised demonstrates impatience in this style. When this happens, the teacher should help the learner reexamine his/her individual preference (or habit) and should explain the need for a "non-versus" conception of classroom experiences. Since one of the objectives of education is the development of social interaction, the gifted need to experience episodes in Style C. With patience and dialogue with the learner, a teacher can help expand the self-perception of the learner who has been accustomed to the special position.

At times learners who see themselves as "slower" like to be the observers first. The possession of the criteria sheet first seems to provide a degree of security.

With respect to time-on-task, or ALT, seemingly in Style C each learner participates in doing the task only half of the time. However, engaging in the role of the observer provides that learner with a different kind of learning that does not hinder the performance of the task itself (see Goldberger et al. 1982).

With respect to time parameters, switching the roles of doer and observer is the learners' decision in Style C. The teacher may remind the class that half of the episode's time has elapsed, but the learners decide when to switch roles. If the time is unequally distributed and one of the partners cannot finish the tasks, the learner will have to deal with this in the subsequent episode.

Style C knows no age boundaries. Many people, regardless of age, enjoy working with others, observing and being observed, giving and receiving feedback. This style has been used with learners of all ages, from preschoolers to adults. The success of such episodes depends on the knowledge, insights, and creativity of the teacher. Appropriate selection of tasks, precise criteria, and verbal behavior relevant to the age levels are the ingredients necessary for success.

Several misconceptions about Style C occasionally emerge in the minds of teachers.

1. "In this style the smart one works with the 'dummy.' " Style C is not designed to differentiate levels of "smartness." On the contrary, the major contribution of this style is creating a condition where both partners are equal in their roles. Both partners have the opportunity to use their capacities within the social context of this style and to adjust their emotions to accommodate the interaction process.

2. "In Style C the teacher is not working." On the contrary, the teacher is teaching the learners the new behaviors of being an observer of and a receiver of feedback from a peer. Nor is the notion that "the observer is doing my job" appropriate. The teacher is constantly engaged in giving feedback, but about a different aspect of the educational process. The teacher is still accountable for the events and the processes in the lesson.

3. "This style is not for the learner who has difficulties in comparing and contrasting performance with criteria." On the contrary, this

---

Style C: THE RECIPROCAL STYLE

The purposes of this style are:

o To work with a partner

o To offer feedback to the partner, based on criteria prepared by the teacher

ROLE OF LEARNER

o To select the roles of doer and observer

o The *doer* does the task (as in Style B)

o The *observer* compares the work of the doer with the criteria, draws conclusions, and offers feedback to the doer

o At the completion of the task by the doer, doer and observer switch roles

ROLE OF TEACHER

o To monitor the observers

o To give feedback to the observers

o To answer the observer's questions

Figure 6.14. Style C Classroom Chart

style is excellent for learners who need more time in these cognitive operations. They need practice, and what better opportunity than with a partner who is equal in role and supportive in behavior? The cooperative nature of Style C invites most learners, sooner or later, to participate.

4. "The observer cannot evaluate the doer." Style C is not an evaluating style. The roles are confined to offering feedback by criteria to improve the performance of the task.

5. In style C learners work in partnership. The observer offers feedback to the doer based on criteria prepared by the teacher. See Figure 6.14.

TABLE 6.2. THE ANATOMY OF STYLE C: THE RECIPROCAL STYLE

Decision Sets	Teacher's Decision Categories	Learner's Decision Categories
Preimpact	All decisions minus the *specifics* of the decisions that are shifted to the learner	Not involved
Impact	Implementing the preimpact decisions Delivering all subject matter and the criteria Observing the performance of the doer and the observer Adjustment decisions	Doer: Decisions as in Style B Communicating with the observer Performing the task
Postimpact	Decisions about the performance of the observer Assessing the performance of doer and observer in their respective roles Assessing the teaching style itself	Observer: Assessing the doer's performance based on criteria established by teacher Decisions about: Observing Comparing and contrasting Drawing conclusions Communicating results to doer

The chart shown as Table 6.2, which lists the decisions made by the teacher and by the learner, can be used as a wall chart or classroom aid.

Logistical Aids

Two logistical aids that expedite the clarity of introducing and maintaining the operation of Style C are style charts and signs.

The Style Charts. Three types of style charts can be used. The first type delineates the roles of the doer, the observer, and the teacher (see Table 6.2). This chart will serve you well when you introduce the style, and can be used when reminders are needed during the episodes. The visual representation of the roles makes them clear and permanent. The second type of style chart is a list of options in verbal behavior that can be used by the observer for feedback purposes. The third chart can display the triad and the desirable directions of communication (see Figure 6.4).

Signs. Signs can be used to organize the reams of task sheets and criteria sheets for both "innings" of a Style C episode. You can prepare two signs for the first inning with the designations d_1 and o_1 and two signs for the second inning, d_2 and o_2. These can be placed on tables or attached to walls. Next to them you can place the appropriate pack of papers. It is best to keep these four signs in a fixed place. It will teach your students routines and order. It will avoid confusion, frustration, and waste of time.

IMPLICATIONS OF STYLE C

Many of the implications of Style C are self-evident. The comments in the previous section alluded to implications for verbal behavior, choice of subject matter, social interaction, and communication. In addition, when this style is in operation it implies that:

1. The teacher accepts the socializing process between observer and doer as a desirable goal in education.
2. The teacher recognizes the importance of teaching learners to give accurate and objective feedback to each other.
3. The teacher is able to shift the power of giving feedback to the learner for the duration of Style C episodes.
4. The teacher learns a new behavior that requires refraining from direct communication with the performer of the task (the doer).
5. The teacher is *willing* to expand his/her behavior beyond Styles A and B and takes the needed time for learners to learn these new roles in making additional decisions.
6. The teacher *trusts* the students to make the additional decisions shifted to them.
7. The teacher accepts a new reality where he/she is not the only source of information, assessment, and feedback.
8. The learners can engage in reciprocal roles and make additional decisions.
9. The learners can expand their active role in the learning process.
10. The learners can see and accept the teacher in a role other than those intrinsic to Styles A and B.
11. Learners can spend time learning (by use of the criteria sheet) in a reciprocal relationship without the constant presence of the teacher.

Style C is a charming style that brings people safely together. But its most contributing asset for you, as a teacher, is that you will learn about qualities your students possess that you cannot learn in Styles A and B. It is, indeed, impossible to learn from those styles—beautiful and efficient as they are—how your students emerge and function in the attributes that are intrinsic to the reciprocal style.

STYLE C AND
THE DEVELOPMENTAL CHANNELS

With the differences between Style C and the previous styles, it is most interesting to hypothesize about changes in the relative position of the learner on the developmental channels.

Placement Using the Criterion *Independence*

Independence remains the primary criterion by which we observe the relationships between this style and the developmental channels (see Figure 6.15).

The Physical Developmental Channel. Since the nine decisions that were shifted to learners in Style B are still made by the doer and the observer, the placement on the physical developmental channel is the same as in Style B—slightly away from "minimum."

The Social Developmental Channel. Since the very essence of Style C is social interaction and interpersonal communication, the degree of social independence is high, and therefore the placement of the learner on the social developmental channel is closer to "maximum" than it was in previous styles. The placement is not *at* "maximum" due to the existence of parameters on the social interaction in the form of the criteria sheet. The learners, therefore, are not maximally independent in the possible options and forms of communication.

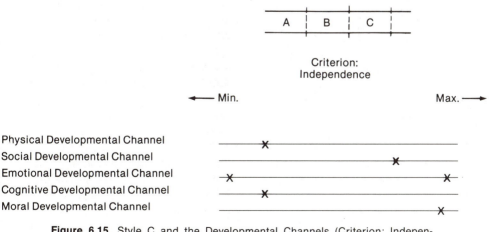

Figure 6.15. Style C and the Developmental Channels (Criterion: Independence)

The Emotional Developmental Channel. In Style C, as in the previous styles, there is dual placement on the emotional developmental channel. Since the state of emotions is so closely intertwined with the social possibilities in this style, some learners who leap into the social interaction are quite independent in their emotions during such episodes. These students are placed toward "maximum" in this channel. Others, more shy and reluctant, demonstrate less independence in their emotional state; hence they are placed toward "minimum."

The Cognitive Developmental Channel. In Style C, the learners are engaged in memory, recall, and in the additional operations of comparing, contrasting, and concluding. Thus there is greater independence in cognitive engagement. The placement on the cognitive developmental channel, therefore, is further away from "minimum."

The Moral Developmental Channel. The placement on the moral developmental channel is closely related to the conditions evolved by the nature of the social interaction. Engaging in a relationship that requires honesty and trust demands that learners be more independent in accepting these values and demonstrating them in their behavior. The placement, therefore, is toward "maximum."

Placement Using the Criterion *Peer Communication*

For comparison, let us use another criterion—that of *peer communication*—and hypothesize about the new relationships that emerge between Style C and the developmental channels. For each channel we will identify the component (variable) of peer communication that affects the placement on that channel. Since the success of Style C hinges primarily on the behavior of the observer, the analysis and the placements on the channels will pertain mainly to the observer. Figure 6.16 shows the new picture that emerges when the criterion of peer communication is used.

The Physical Developmental Channel. When peer communication is used as the criterion, it has no impact on the physical developmental channel; hence the designation of NA (not applicable).

The Social Developmental Channel. One of the main components (variables) of peer communication is acceptance—acceptance of another person regardless of performance level. The very structure of Style C provides learners with the opportunity to see another person's successes and failures and to learn to accept the person just the way he/she is at that time. This level of acceptance places the observer (who learns to demonstrate acceptance of the doer) toward "maximum" on the social developmental channel.

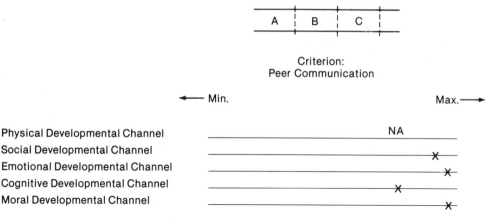

Figure 6.16. Style C and the Developmental Channels (Criterion: Peer Communication)

You may select another component of peer communication and see what happens to the placement on this channel.

The Emotional Developmental Channel. In order for the observer to be accepting, he/she must develop and exhibit patience and tolerance. Therefore an observer who is exhibiting patience and tolerance in the communication with a peer is placed toward "maximum" on the emotional developmental channel. It is interesting to note that the doer may not show patience and tolerance, but the observer *must*.

The Cognitive Developmental Channel. Since the observer uses the criteria sheet for assessing the performance of the doer, the observer must therefore exhibit cognitive precision. This places the observer toward "maximum" on the cognitive developmental channel.

The Moral Developmental Channel. Honesty is the main component in peer communication when feedback (by criteria) is offered to the partner. The demand for honesty in the behavior of the observer is quite apparent. When an observer has learned to exhibit this honesty in giving feedback to the doer, he/she is placed toward "maximum" on the moral developmental channel.

The Purpose of Developmental Channel Analysis

These analyses of relationships between a given style and the position of the learner on the developmental channels are not a mere academic exercise in hypothesizing. The intent is to understand the intrinsic relationship between specific behaviors (the specific decisions that learners make in each style) and the consequences of these behaviors. Here we seek to understand the consequences in terms of growth and development in particular aspects (developmental channels) of human existence. This is an attempt to understand the organic relationship between what people do and what they become. In educational terms it is a way of looking at the relationships between means and goals.

You are familiar now with three landmark styles. Each represents a different reality initiated by the teacher and carried out by the teacher and the students. Episodes in Style C continue the weaning process begun in Style B and enable teachers and students to engage in sharing decisions in new ways. Those who have used all three styles successfully have demonstrated mobility across a significant portion of the Spectrum.

CHAPTER 7

Style D: The Self-Check Style

As an introduction to Style D, you are invited to do the puzzles in Figure 7.1 and check your solutions against the answers given on p. 116.

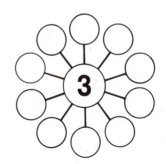

1. Which exit, A or B, will get you out of this maze?

2. Use numbers from 1 to 14 in the circles so that the sum of any 3 numbers in a straight line is 18.

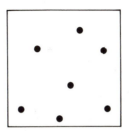

3. Divide the square so that each dot is in a separate section.

Figure 7.1. Three Puzzles

Have you ever observed or participated in any of the following episodes?

- Shooting baskets
- Playing darts
- Bowling
- Embroidering a printed pattern on a pillow
- Multiplying numbers using a computer that flashes a smiling face on the screen
- Answering questions in a textbook and verifying the answers by reading them at the end of the book
- Assembling a toy following the manufacturer's instruction sheet
- Turning on and off any instrument
- Solving a maze
- Following directions when driving somewhere
- Using a hand calculator

All these episodes have in common an essence that is fundamental to Style D, the self-check style. The essence of these episodes is the availability of immediate and precise feedback that the participant can get by him/herself. The feedback is intrinsic to the task. The structure of the task instantly provides information about:

1. Yes/no ("I am successful"; "I am not successful.")
2. Correct/incorrect ("I know the correctness of my performance.")
3. The score ("I know the measured value of my performance.")

The purpose of Style D is to learn to engage in self-check (self-feedback) without relying on the teacher or the partner, and to learn to use performance criteria provided by the task itself or by media (answer sheets, calculators, computer, etc.). This new decision—the decision about assessing oneself against specific criteria—presents the learner with new skills, new responsibilities, and new demands. This additional step toward self-reliance serves many people as a motivating force for continued participation in tasks at hand.

OBJECTIVES OF STYLE D

Style D offers the learner a new set of subject matter objectives and behavior objectives:

Subject Matter Objectives

To do the task
To continue to learn how to use the criteria
To learn how to correct errors in the task performance
To increase time-on-task

Behavior Objectives

To wean oneself from dependency on the teacher or on a partner, and to begin relying on oneself for feedback
To use criteria for verification of one's performance
To maintain honesty about one's performance
To accept discrepancies and one's limitations
To continue the individualizing process by making the decisions shifted to the learner in the impact and postimpact sets

THE ANATOMY OF STYLE D

In Style C the students learned to engage in the postimpact decisions. The observer's role was to assess the performance of a peer and offer feedback to a peer. In Style D there is an additional shift of decisions; each learner is engaged in *self-check*—each learner makes the postimpact decisions for him/herself.

The shift of decisions is shown schematically in Figure 7.2.

The teacher's role is to make all the preimpact decisions (as in the previous styles), and to ascertain that the learner learns the behaviors involved in the postimpact phase. The role of the learner is to do the task while making the nine decisions in the impact set, and then engage in self-check by using the provided criteria. The learner is making decisions in the postimpact set that correspond with his/her own performance of the tasks.

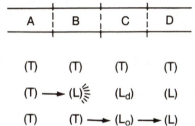

Figure 7.2. The Shift from Style C to Style D

IMPLEMENTATION OF STYLE D

The Nature of Style D Episodes

Perhaps the most striking aspect of a Style D episode is the carryover from the two previous styles. In Style B learners learn to do the task. In Style C they learn to use criteria and give feedback to a peer. In Style D the learners use the same skills for self-assessment. This does not necessarily mean that the learner must move sequentially from B to C to D, but it certainly helps in accumulating skills. It is quite fascinating to observe a class that has experienced all three styles and knows both the roles and the appropriate decisions to make.

Episodes in Style D actually provide learners with the opportunity to become more self-reliant in knowing what they have or have not done in the performance of the task. When the learners disperse in the classroom, gymnasium, or playing field, they begin performing the task, stop frequently to look at the criteria sheet, compare their own performance with the criteria, and then move on. They either repeat the task to correct or maintain the performance, or go on to a new task. Style D is the first style that allows time for self-assessment decisions. For learners to experience these decisions they must engage in several subsidiary behaviors: They pause to read and internalize the criteria, and they pause after the performance of a task to think about their performance. At times they may engage in "self-negotiation," expressing concern or joy. These behaviors are overt and observable. Taken together they present a different picture of what goes on in the classroom. A great deal more than just performing tasks occurs in Style D episodes.

Self-checking behavior is possible because the teacher's role has changed. The verbal behavior that is specific to this style develops and maintains the operation and the spirit of such episodes. The teacher's role in this style is to move about from one learner to another observing how the learners are doing in their new role of self-checking. The teacher initiates communication with each learner and addresses the learner's participation in the *process* of self-feedback. Initially most learners need guidance and reinforcement in this process; it is the first time (on the Spectrum) that they're involved in making *this* decision for themselves. So the teacher's presence is vital to every learner. In order to maintain the decisions shifted to the learner and enhance the role of the learner, the appropriate verbal behavior after a learner checks his/her work is: "How are you doing on the task?" This question invites the learner to focus on his/her role in judging the performance. The learner responds by telling the teacher about his/her perception of the performance. If there is an error in the performance, undetected by the learner, the teacher could say: "Before continuing, check the criteria again." This redirects the learner to the step where the error occurred. The teacher stays with the learner until the error is corrected. This kind of dialogue is *crucial* for shaping the behavior of the learner in Style D. The teacher must not look over the learner's shoulder and walk away. The one-to-one contact with feedback about the learner's new role is the essence of the teaching behavior in this style. When the dialogue with one learner is over, the teacher moves on to the next learner. This process of one-to-one contact began in Style B; it continues in Style D. When the episode is over the teacher, in a closure, offers general feedback to the whole class about the participation in self-check.

It should be noted that there are times in Style D when the learner, after engaging in self-check, still has difficulties with the task. The teacher's role is to stay within the behavior of this style by asking questions concerning the learner's understanding of the task and the criteria. The teacher can furnish additional explanation of the task, but the learner must learn to do the assessment. The teacher should have patience and stay with the learner within the boundaries of this style. Only when this process is exhausted is it appropriate to shift momentarily to Style B, which is efficient, swift, and helpful. When a learner gets stuck on a given task, there is no need to press the process of self-check, which may increase the frustration and decrease the skill. Removing the obstacle by explaining the task (or the missing part) takes a moment, and then the learner can continue both with the subject matter and the process of self-check.

How to Do It

The following steps describe the role of the teacher and the role of the learner as they make decisions in the preimpact, impact, and postimpact sets of a Style D episode.

The Preimpact Set. The teacher makes all the decisions in the preimpact set with the focus on:

1. Selecting and designing the subject matter (tasks).
2. Identifying and/or designing the criteria sheet.
3. Determining the logistics appropriate for the episode.

The Impact Set. As in Styles A, B, and C, the teacher sets the scene by explaining the style and delivering the tasks. The teacher's role in the impact phase is as follows:

1. To explain the purpose of this style.
2. To explain the role of the learner, describing the decisions involved in self-check and the difference from Style C.

3. To offer feedback about how well the learner is participating in the *process* of self-check. The teacher explains to the learners that he/she will not address feedback to the performance of the task because it is the role of the learner to do so. However, the teacher will be available for questions about the task.
4. To present the task(s).
5. To explain the logistics.
6. To establish the appropriate parameters (mainly time and location).
7. To invite the learners to begin.

The Postimpact Set. The role of the learner in the postimpact phase is:

1. To assess one's performance against the criteria.
2. To give feedback to oneself.
3. To correct the errors and to repeat the performance.

The role of the teacher is:

1. To ascertain that each learner is engaged in self-check.
2. To observe the decision making of each learner.
3. To answer questions initiated by the learner.
4. To offer feedback to each learner about his/her participation in the role of self-check.

SELECTING AND DESIGNING THE SUBJECT MATTER

Tasks designed for Style D should accommodate the decisions that the learners make in this style. Primarily we are concerned with the process of giving feedback to oneself. There are two kinds of tasks that are conducive to this behavior: (1) tasks with intrinsic feedback and (2) tasks that require an outside source of verification.

The first kind of task supplies the learner with immediate information needed for knowing *yes* or *no*: "Yes, I am successful"; or "No, I am not successful." Getting out of a maze, shooting a basket, lighting a match, and most target games in sports are examples of such tasks. The performance of the task is either correct or incorrect, and the information about its correctness is built into the very structure of the task. The end result instantly provides the feedback. In order to correct a failed performance, the learner needs to *repeat* the task; and if the task is within the learner's range of cognitive and neuromuscular ability, additional few attempts will provide success.

The second kind of task does not supply immediate information about the correctness of its performance; the learner needs to rely on an available outside source of verification such as a criteria sheet, an answer sheet, a calculator, a computer, or a videotape. All these are sources that the learner can use without the intervention of the teacher; they serve, in effect, as surrogate teachers. A learner who is engaged in doing a series of long-division exercises, for example, may not know whether each step of the process is correct nor whether the end result is correct. The use of an answer sheet can supply this information. The use of a calculator *after* the task is completed can serve as a source of verification. In a gymnastics routine there could be errors in the performance that are unnoticed by the learner; the use of a videotape can offer the learner the information needed for corrections. This information is available for the learner to use in the process of self-check.

Probably all subject matter areas contain tasks that fall into the second category—that is, they require an outside source of verification. The skill of the teacher is recruited in Style D in selecting and designing tasks that develop the self-check process. The creative capacity of the teacher is manifested by the design of the criteria and the use of various techniques and technologies—all used for accommodating and enhancing the self-check process. Indeed, there are times when tasks that provide intrinsic feedback also require the use of criteria. A learner who repeatedly fails in the performance needs information not only about the end product, but also about the process of getting there. Correcting continuous failure in shooting a basket may require information about correcting the form of the throw and this information must come from an outside source. The same is true for the maze exercise or any other similar tasks.

The criteria that are used for both kinds of tasks supply the answers to the following questions:

1. Where is the error?
2. Why did the error occur?
3. How do I correct the error?

In Style D there is a very particular relationship between the design of the task, the availability of criteria, and the decisions that the learner has to make in order to accomplish the objectives of episodes in this style. Teachers who are using this style for the first time should be aware that a student who has very little background in a given subject matter may not be able to perform successfully in the initial step of learning certain tasks. Frustration takes over and the use of criteria for self-assessment may not even be attempted. Obviously the teacher needs to be alert to such possibilities and assess the learner's readiness for episodes in this style. This does not mean, however, that the learner should be excluded from such experiences. Different tasks must be selected as the initiation to the self-check process.

IMPLICATIONS OF STYLE D

The implications of Style D are powerful. It is the first time on the Spectrum that the learner has the opportunity to assess and judge him/herself. This is quite a step toward self-reliance. Many tasks in life require the ability and the skill to do this; moreover, they require honesty in participating in this process. Experiences in school can develop and enhance this responsibility. Episodes in this style further develop reciprocal trust. The teacher learns to trust the student in evaluating performance, and the student learns to trust the teacher in the shift of this decision. The sharing of power via the evaluation decisions—a sharing that began in the reciprocal style—continues and expands in the self-check style.

If part of schooling is, indeed, providing opportunities for the development of human qualities, then episodes in Style D must appear in high frequency; these qualities do not sprout without actual experiences that nourish them.

Specifically, Style D implies that:

1. The teacher values the learner's independence.
2. The teacher values the learner's ability to develop a self-monitoring system.
3. The teacher trusts the learner to be honest during this process.
4. The teacher has the patience to ask questions focusing on the process of self-check as well as the performance of the task.
5. The learner can work privately and engage in the self-checking process.
6. The learner can identify his/her own limits, successes, and failures.
7. The learner can use self-check as feedback for improvement.
8. The new classroom reality that evolves in Style D episodes creates conditions for examining one's self-concept. The condition for honesty in self-assessment indeed demands a look at oneself and a need to decide about one's conduct and one's responsibility for its consequences. Learning to be honest with oneself, learning to recognize and accept one's errors, is a moral demand that did not impinge on the learner's self in the previous styles.

STYLE-SPECIFIC COMMENTS

Verbal Behavior

The teacher's verbal behavior must reflect the intent of this style and must support the roles of the teacher and the learner. The purposes for communication between the teacher and the learner are:

1. To ascertain that the learner can compare and contrast his/her own performance against criteria.
2. To listen to what the learner is saying.
3. To lead the learner to see discrepancies (when they exist) by asking questions.
4. To tell the learner about the discrepancies if the learner cannot see them.

With regard to items 3 and 4, the teacher should be careful not to increase the learner's frustration by asking questions that the learner cannot answer or by withdrawing feedback. This may require an adjustment decision. The learner's feelings are more important than the structure of the style. The teacher can momentarily switch to Style B and offer feedback to the learner about the performance of the task.

To initiate communication with the learner in Style D, the teacher asks a general question: "How are you doing?" The learner has several options in answering it:

1. "Fine!"
2. "I can't do the task, and I'm not sure why."
3. "I can't do the task, but I know how to correct it."
4. "I can do the task and I understand each part of the criteria."

In each case, the first response by the teacher is to acknowledge the learner's behavior in the process of self-check ("I see that you know how to use these criteria."). The next step is to deal specifically with the situation. If the learner has answered "Fine," the teacher might ask: "What was fine?" This invites the learner to focus on his/her specific performance and communicate the information to the teacher. The teacher can then assess the learner's ability to compare the performance with the criteria.

If the learner is not sure why he/she can't do the task, the role of the teacher is to ask: "What part of the task is not clear?" If clarification is needed the teacher offers it. This is followed by ascertaining that the learner understands the criteria. When leaving the learner the teacher can say: "I'll be back in a while to see how you progress."

When the learner believes he/she knows how to correct the error, the teacher may stay with the learner for a moment and ask: "Have you identified the error?" The teacher then observes the correcting effort and is available for feedback.

Situations where the learner states he/she can do the task and understands the criteria call for observation of the results and offering feedback to the learner. The point is that the teacher's verbal behavior is not an arbitrary habitual statement to the learner, but rather a careful, targeted question that invites the learner to focus on the task and the criteria. It takes time and awareness on the part of the teacher to *shift* the verbal behavior from

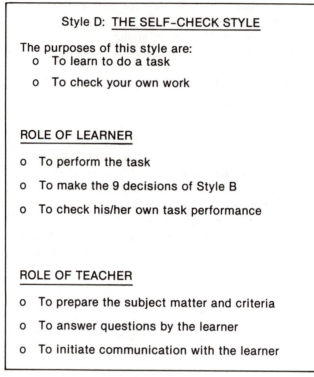

Figure 7.3. Style D Classroom Chart

statements that put the teacher in focus to questions that put the learner in focus.

Logistical Suggestions

In order to facilitate each learner's role in the postimpact phase, the criteria can be supplied by:

1. Distributing individual (photocopied) criteria sheets.
2. Using transparencies.
3. Writing the answers on the chalkboard.
4. Posting the criteria sheet in several places in the room.

The charts shown in Figure 7.3 and Table 7.1 should be posted in order to remind the learner of the purposes of Style D and the respective roles.

TABLE 7.1. THE ANATOMY OF STYLE D: THE SELF-CHECK STYLE

Decision Sets	Teacher's Decision Categories	Learner's Decision Categories
Preimpact	All decisions as in Style C, with a focus on the design of tasks and assessment criteria	Not involved
Impact	Implementing the preimpact decisions Delivering the tasks and the criteria Observing the performance of the learner Adjustment decisions	The nine decisions in Style B Performing the task
Postimpact	Acknowledging the learner's performance Initiating communication with the learner concerning the process of self-checking Assessing the teaching style itself	Self-assessment decisions about the performance of the task

STYLE D AND THE DEVELOPMENTAL CHANNELS

Once again we will use the criterion of *independence* to examine the placement of the learner on the developmental channels while engaging in Style D (see Figure 7.4).

The Physical Developmental Channel. In Style D, as in Styles A, B, and C, the learner is not independent in making decisions about his/her physical development; hence the placement is toward "minimum" on the physical developmental channel.

The Social Developmental Channel. Style D is a very solitary style. The work is done individually and with considerable privacy. The structure of this style does not call for interaction and communication among learners. Therefore social development during such episodes, in terms of contact, is very minimal; however, the development of respect for another person's right to privacy is high. The placement on the social developmental channel is therefore slightly further from "minimum," perhaps similar to that of Style B.

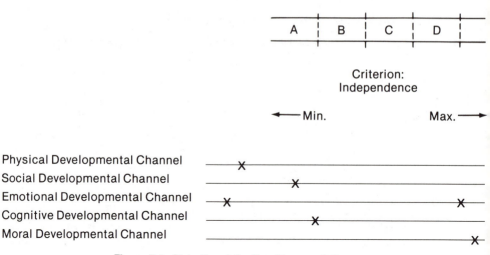

Figure 7.4. Style D and the Developmental Channels

The Emotional Developmental Channel. There are learners who are emotionally independent and can accept and sustain the condition of assessing themselves without the need for frequent external verification. There are others who find difficulties in adjusting to the solitude conditions of the style. Therefore the placement on the emotional developmental channel is dual.

The Cognitive Developmental Channel. The role of self-assessment in the postimpact phase requires the learner to engage in the operations of comparing, contrasting against criteria, and then drawing conclusions about his/her performance. The placement on the cognitive developmental channel is therefore further away from "minimum" than with the previous styles.

The Moral Developmental Channel. The requirements for honesty and integrity in this style invite independence in weighing these values. Assessing him/herself with honesty places the learner further toward "maximum" on the moral developmental channel.

Style D allows learners to continue the weaning process that began in Style B by taking responsibility for checking their own answers and assessing their own task performance. As they become more proficient in using criteria and engaging in honest self-assessment, they will develop the skills and increased maturity that will prepare them to assume the new decision-making responsibilities of Style E.

CHAPTER 8

Style E: The Inclusion Style

THE CONCEPT OF INCLUSION

We shall begin this chapter with a story. Holding a rope level about one foot above the ground, we asked a group of students to jump over this obstacle one by one (Figure 8.1). When all had cleared the rope we asked them: "What shall we do with the rope now?" Instantly the answer came forth: "Raise it!" We raised the rope by a few inches and asked the students to jump over it again. All the students cleared the rope once more. "And now?" we asked. "Raise it again!" was the answer. We continued raising the rope a few inches each time and the students continued to jump over it.

At a given height the inevitable happened. Some students were unable to clear the rope; they walked a few feet away and sat down. As we continued raising the rope, more students failed to clear the rope until there was only one student left—and then none. "This experience," we said, "expresses the concept of *exclusion*."

We then asked: "What can be done with the rope to create a *condition for inclusion*?" There was a moment of silence. All the participants were immersed in thoughts. "I know," announced one student, "I know what we

Figure 8.1. Horizontal Rope

Figure 8.2. Slanted Rope

can do—let's *slant* the rope.'' We raised one end of the rope to chest level and placed the other end on the ground (Figure 8.2). "Jump over the rope again," we said. Within seconds the students dispersed opposite various heights and began jumping. All the students cleared the rope. "Do it once more," we urged them. Again all students cleared the rope. "This experience," we said, "expresses the concept of *inclusion*."

Over the years we have had many auspicious opportunities, here and abroad, to repeat this experience. The results have been identical and the behavior universal: The condition represented by raising the "horizontal rope" *always* excludes people, and the condition represented by the "slanting rope" *always* includes.

What does all this mean? Can you remember one significant moment in your schooling when you were excluded? Do you remember how you felt? Should we always strive toward conditions where everyone is included? Or only sometimes? If the latter, when and for what purpose do we provide for inclusion? How does the concept of inclusion fit into a competitive society?

Let's follow *one* student who is engaged in this experience and do an analysis of the decisions that the student is making. When a student is facing the slanted rope, his/her initial decision is about where to begin. The student must ask the question: "At what height do I begin?" In order to answer this question, the student momentarily engages in self-assessment, gauging his/her capabilities in reference to the options in the task. When a conclusion is reached, the student is ready to enter the experience. At this point the student performs the first jump successfully. Without exception the first attempt is always successful. Students always select a "safe" height for the first attempt. After evaluating the first attempt the student is ready for the subsequent decisions: "What do I do next?"

Let's assume that the entry point was at X (Figure 8.3).

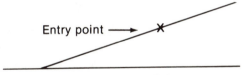

Entry point ⟶ ✗

Figure 8.3. Entry Point

The student now has three options (Figure 8.4):

1. To jump over the same height (X)
2. To jump over a lower point (A)
3. To jump over a higher point (B)

Taking the first option could mean: "I did it well here; I want to do it again"; or "I want to verify my success." The second option could mean: "I think I would feel more comfortable at a lower point"; or "It is easier here." The third option could mean: "I think I can do it at a higher point"; or "I am ready to be challenged by more." Regardless of the height and the number of jumps, the student must make a choice among these three options after every jump.

Style E is the first style on the Spectrum that invites the learner to make such decisions. In all previous styles the task was designed to a single standard and the teacher made these decisions for the learner. Now the learner makes the decisions, choosing among the available *options* with the *same* task.

What are the specific objectives of this style? What is the new role of the teacher? How do we apply the slanted rope concept to various subject matter areas?

OBJECTIVES OF STYLE E

As in the previous styles, Style E has both subject matter objectives and behavior objectives.

Subject Matter Objectives
To accommodate individual
   differences
To design options within the same
   task
To offer a range of options that
   provide entry points for all
   learners

Behavior Objectives
To learn to make a decision about
   the entry point by choosing the
   initial performance level
To learn to evaluate one's
   performance and then decide
   about the next step
To learn to accept the reality of
   individual differences in the
   ability to perform tasks
To learn to deal with congruity or
   discrepancy between one's
   aspiration and the reality of one's
   performance
To learn about honesty in selecting
   the appropriate level and honesty
   in self-evaluation

INCLUSION ENSURES CONTINUED PARTICIPATION

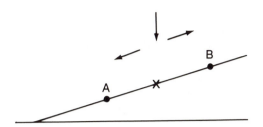

Figure 8.4. Options after Entry

THE ANATOMY OF STYLE E

In Style E the shift of decision occurs in two sets: Decisions are shifted to the learner in the impact set *and* in the postimpact set (Figure 8.5). In the preimpact set the teacher continues to make all the decisions, but now with the focus on designing the options within the tasks.

In the impact set the role of the teacher is to introduce the style and explain the shift of the new decisions, and to introduce the subject matter and the criteria. The role of the learner is to assess him/herself in relation to the available options, to decide on the entry point, and to do the task at the selected level.

In the postimpact set the role of the learner is to evaluate his/her performance of the task and to decide about further placement in the range of options. The role of the teacher is to gather information about the learner's performance by asking questions, to answer questions for clarification, and to offer feedback about the role.

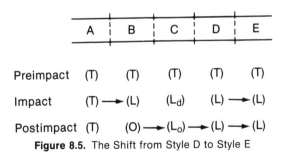

Figure 8.5. The Shift from Style D to Style E

IMPLEMENTATION OF STYLE E

Description of an Episode

One of the ways to introduce the concept of Style E to students is to present them with the actual experience of the slanted rope. It is real and vivid. Most, if not all, learners can identify with it. It creates an immediate reality of inclusion. The teacher, then, explains that among episodes in the other styles there will be times for participating in this style. This is followed by the description of the roles and the shift of decisions. After the teacher delivers the tasks and the criteria, each learner picks up the materials that are designed for inclusion and ponders the question: "Where do I begin?" Since the task and the materials are arranged to accommodate various levels of performance, each learner takes a moment to examine the available options.

Once a decision is made about the entry point, each learner—materials in hand—makes the rest of the now-familiar decisions about location, order, starting time, pace and rhythm, and so on. Each learner proceeds and privately engages in performing the task at the level of his/her choice. As the task performance continues, learners begin making the decision about self-evaluation. The self-evaluation decision can take place after the completion of *each* individual task, after several tasks, or after all the tasks have been completed. The inclusion of all learners is quite visible.

While all this is in process the teacher moves about, makes private contact with each individual learner, and gathers information about the performance. The appropriate verbal behavior during this initial contact with the student is: "How are you doing on your task?"; or "How is it going?" This question focuses on the learner's self-evaluation decision. The learner will respond by offering the necessary information, which lets the teacher know the standing of the learner in the given task and/or his/her feelings. If any questions for clarification are asked, the teacher answers them. At this point the teacher gives the learner feedback about the *role* and then moves on to the next learner. Learners who finish their task on the level they selected may then either go on to a *different* task that is available during the interval, or they may select another *level* of the first task and continue the performance. At the end of the episode the teacher addresses the entire class and offers feedback about the learners' ability to make the decisions in Style E. This kind of closure is necessary during the first few episodes in this style. Learners must be strongly reinforced in their new roles. Later on, only periodic feedback about their role in this style is needed.

How to Do It

The Preimpact Set. The teacher makes all the decisions in the preimpact set with the focus on:

1. Selecting and designing the tasks by the "slanted rope" principle (see the section below on "The Individual Program").
2. Identifying and/or designing the criteria.
3. Determining the logistics appropriate for the episode.

The Impact Set. In the impact set, the sequence of events is as follows:

1. The teacher sets the scene by introducing the concept of inclusion. One episode of the actual experience with the "slanted rope" will suffice for understanding and internalizing the concept.
2. The teacher states the major objective of this style: to include all learners by providing options within the same task.
3. The teacher describes the role of the learner, which is as follows:
   a. To survey the choices.
   b. To select an initial level as an entry point to the task.
   c. To perform the task.
   d. To assess his/her performance against criteria.
   e. To decide whether or not another level is desired or appropriate.
4. The teacher describes the role of the teacher, which is as follows:
   a. To observe the learners in making the decision about the level and the performance of the task.
   b. To answer questions by the learner.
   c. To initiate communication with the learner.
5. The teacher presents the subject matter, describing the "Individual Program" and identifying the factor that determines the "degree of difficulty" (see the sections on these concepts below).
6. The teacher explains the logistics and establishes the necessary parameters.
7. At this point the students begin to engage in their individual roles and tasks.

The Postimpact Set. The sequence of events in the postimpact phase is as follows:

1. Learners use the criteria sheet to assess their performance and decide about engagement in tne next task.
2. The teacher observes the class for a while, then moves about and offers individual and private feedback to each learner. The verbal behavior is the same as in Style D with the added dimension of verifying (not approving) the appropriateness of the learner's selection of the level.
3. At the end of the episode, the teacher offers feedback to the entire class about their role in decision making.

SELECTING AND DESIGNING THE SUBJECT MATTER

The crux of episodes in Style E is the design of tasks that offer options to the learner. The teacher is always faced with the need to select and/or design materials that accommodate the decision shift in the inclusion style. These

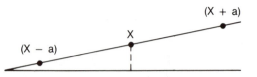

Figure 8.6. Optional Degrees of Difficulty

materials cannot be a random nor a casual collection of tasks. The design must adhere to particular principles and the tasks must be organized in particular ways. These principles and designs are discussed in the following sections.

The Principle of Degree of Difficulty

The condition represented by the slanted rope offers the learner options within the *same* task. These options differ from one another due to their *degree of difficulty*. Let's go back to the slanted rope. Any point along the rope, say X (Figure 8.6), represents a particular degree of difficulty in performing the task of jumping over the rope. Another point on the rope, for example X + *a*, represents a different degree of difficulty. Due to increased *height* the degree of difficulty is greater than it was at the previous point. In the same manner another point on the rope, X − *a*, represents a different degree of difficulty. In this case, due to reduced height, the degree of difficulty is smaller than that at point X.

   Now, regardless of where the initial point X is located, and regardless of the magnitude of the step *a*, any choice of height to the right of X will be an increase in degree of difficulty and any choice to the left of X will represent a decrease in the degree of difficulty. All the points, together, along the slanted rope comprise the *range* of degree of difficulty in this task: jumping over the rope. The degree of difficulty is intrinsic to the design of the task itself, and is not dependent on the participating person. Point X + *a* on the rope is of greater difficulty than point X for *any* person.

Identifying the Factor That Determines the Degree of Difficulty

In the case of the rope, what *factor* makes the difference in the degree of difficulty? Indeed, it is the *height* of the rope at any given point. Height, then, is an *intrinsic factor* that is specific to this task. Manipulating this factor—that is, changing the height—creates the options that result in inclusion. How, then, can we use this principle in *any* task in any subject matter area? How do we design options within tasks in arithmetic, spelling, identifying places on a map, shooting basketballs, learning another language,

Figure 8.7. Hammering a Nail

or doing exercises in grammar or in language arts? Before we answer these questions let us first use another example that is vivid—a task using tangible things. Then we'll transfer the principles of this task design to other areas.

The task is to hammer a nail (up to its head) into a piece of wood with minimal number of hits. The equipment for this task is a flat piece of wood, a nail, and a hammer (Figure 8.7).

Some students, due to lack of experience or limitations in neuromuscular skill, may not be able to perform this task adequately; yet we want to create for them conditions for success. How do we rearrange the task so that it provides options for inclusion?

The first step is to identify the factor or factors that are *intrinsic* to this particular situation and task. For example:

1. Type of wood: hardness of wood
2. Size of the nailhead
3. Size of the hammer
4. Angle of the nail
5. Distance between the hammer and the nail

The crux of the matter here is that each of these factors is always present when hammering a nail and each affects the performance of the task. Let us examine each factor separately. Suppose we want to create a condition for *inclusion* by manipulating only the first factor. In order to create a range of degree of difficulty around this factor, we need to have an assortment of pieces of wood with varying degrees of softness or hardness. It is always less difficult to hammer a nail into soft wood and harder to do so with hard wood.

When options of different types of wood are presented to a learner, he/she can select the type most conducive to success in driving in the nail. It is possible to visualize these options with various types of wood by placing them on a "slanted rope" diagram (Figure 8.8). In this case the options do not represent minute or continuous increments as with the rope. The

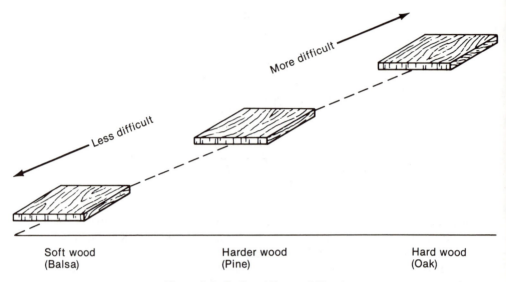

| Soft wood
(Balsa) | Harder wood
(Pine) | Hard wood
(Oak) |

Figure 8.8. Optional Types of Wood

principle, however, is the same. The soft piece of wood is equivalent to the lower point of the slanted rope and the other pieces of wood, with gradually increasing hardness, are equivalent to the gradual increase of the rope's height; hence, the range in degree of difficulty. When this assortment of types of wood is arranged by degree of difficulty, opportunities are increased for including more people in the successful performance of this task, and, at the same time, offering more challenging levels of performance to more proficient students. The use of a single type of wood may exclude some participants and not offer sufficient challenge to others.

Let us now examine the second factor: the size of the nailhead. It is more difficult to hit a long nail with a tiny head, and it is less difficult to hit a long nail with a large head. This factor is represented in Figure 8.9. When options in the size of the nailhead are available, students can decide which nail fits their *present* ability in this task. Using only medium-sized nail-heads will inevitably exclude some students from even entering the task and they will not learn how to hammer a nail. At the same time, with larger nailheads, more proficient students will be denied options that provide more challenge.

The third factor, the size of the hammer, offers us a rather rich range of options. There are many different sizes of hammers available (i.e., various head sizes, weights, and handle sizes) that will certainly offer any learner ample choice and an opportunity to find his/her entry point into this activity.

The same procedure can be followed with any other identified factor. Sometimes two factors can be combined to vary the conditions for the

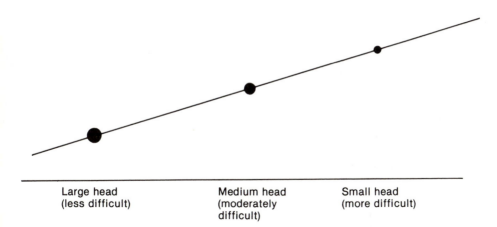

| Large head
(less difficult) | Medium head
(moderately
difficult) | Small head
(more difficult) |

Figure 8.9. Optional Nailhead Sizes

options in degree of difficulty. In the present example using different nailhead sizes *and* different hammer sizes certainly multiplies the number of options and increases the possibilities for inclusion.

All this is quite clear and operational in such concrete tasks as jumping over a rope or hammering a nail. The factors can readily be identified and manipulated by the principle of degree of difficulty. It is a bit more difficult and more subtle when this principle is applied to other areas. Nevertheless the principle remains the same and the technique of factor analysis is used in the same way: First, identify the factor that is an intrinsic part of the task—an internal ingredient of the activity—and then identify the range. Ask: Using the given factor, what would make this task more difficult or less difficult?

The Issue of Quantity and Quality

All human activities can be perceived as having both *quantitative* and *qualitative* dimensions. The quantitative dimension represents the "how muchness" of things, events, people, and performances. Our language provides us with words and phrases that reflect and define the quantitative dimension. We can say:

- "He ran 5 miles."
- "She read 30 pages."
- "He pole-vaulted 18 feet."
- "I swam 2 miles."
- "I ate a lot."

- "He is very tall."
- "I lost 15 pounds in two months."
- "Dinner will be ready in 20 minutes."
- "I finished 50 math exercises."
- "It took three hours to find all the details for making the map of population shift."
- "That car cost $8,000."
- "The concert lasted for two hours."
- "Fifty dancers participated in the performance."
- "On our vacation we visited eight countries."

The common denominator of all these statements is the *quantitative* dimension. Each answers the questions: "How much?" "How many?" Each represents our quantitative perception of reality, a perception that is a part of our daily life and without which we probably could not survive.

Every subject matter area consists of a great deal of information that is intrinsically quantitative. Many tasks, in every area, represent this quantitative dimension. Moreover the very essence of *mastery* of task performance is quantitative because it is rooted in and manifested by repetition. Rarely, if ever, does one master anything in a single attempt. Doing the task more than once, repeating the performance in order to master the particular skill or the particular behavior, is the cornerstone of learning and development. The characteristics of the quantitative dimension are that it is concrete, measurable, finite, and intrinsic to any task.

The *qualitative* dimension represents the perceived "goodness" or "wellness" of things, events, people, and performances. Here, too, our language provides us with words and phrases that express the human capacity to attribute qualities to the perception of reality. We can say:

- "He ran beautifully."
- "She read those pages with passion."
- "He pole-vaults so gracefully."
- "The food was so tasty."
- "Since he lost weight, he looks so well."
- "That is a pretty car."
- "The concert was magnificent; the tones of the violinist were superb."
- "She is a very elegant woman."
- "The dancers performed in perfect harmony."
- "Some of the countries we visited were more beautiful and interesting than others."

The common denominator of all these statements is the *qualitative* dimension. Each one *attributes* a particular quality to the thing, the event, the people, or the performance. They all include value words that project the subjective feelings, opinions, and reactions of the observing individual.

This extraordinary human capacity to perceive, sense, and attribute qualities to reality is a capacity without which we probably could not survive. The characteristics of the qualitative dimension are that it is not concrete, not measurable, not finite, and not intrinsic to the task. The qualitative dimension is external to the task; it represents an attribution.

It is fascinating to realize how these quantitative and qualitative dimensions get intertwined. Consider, for example, how we judge "good" reading or the quality of a student's reading performance. Is it not judged by roughly calculating the *relationship* (or ratio) of number of pages read to speed of reading to comprehension of *what* was read? And is it not true that the student's comprehension (not interpretation) of what was read is judged by the amount of accurate information gleaned from reading? All these aspects of reading are quantitative and not qualitative. Number of pages, speed, and amount of comprehended information are all quantitative. When these quantitative aspects of reading are viewed through their interrelationship (the ratio of one to the other), we then *attribute* a quality to the act of reading. A student who can read *more* pages in *less* time and can accurately answer *more* factual questions is deemed a "good" reader. So we assign qualitative attributions to performance judged by quantitative measures.

Despite the importance of the qualitive dimension, however, it is quite difficult to design a task with a range of options that focus specifically on this dimension. This problem will become clearer once we have examined some typical task designs that incorporate degree-of-difficulty options.

Task Designs That Incorporate Degree-of-Difficulty Options

Let us apply the principle of degree of difficulty to arithmetic when the task is adding whole numbers. The question is: How do we take this one task of adding and design options that are more difficult and less difficult? If we use the *number of digits* as the factor, then logically the least difficult exercise is adding two single digits, starting with the lowest values. On the "slanted rope" diagram it will appear as shown in Figure 8.10. In this design, level 1 consists of tasks that start with the smallest whole number to which numbers with graduated values are added and the sum does not exceed 9. At level 2, larger single-digit numbers are added and their sum is now a double-digit number but no larger than 11. (Figure 8.11). In level 3, one double-digit number and one single-digit number are added, the sum of which will not exceed 19 (Figure 8.12). And thus a series of exercises in *each* level is designed with larger and larger values. These designs (Figures 8.10, 8.11, 8.12) are examples used to illustrate the principle of degree of difficulty. The

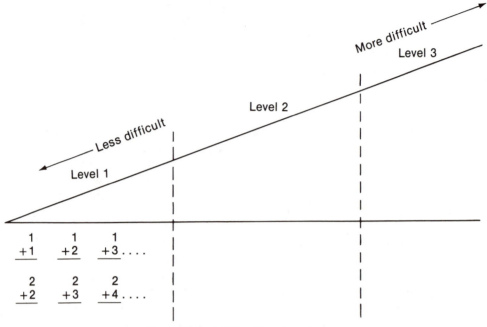

Figure 8.10. Addition Exercises: Level 1

lines of demarcation between the levels, here, are arbitrary. The teacher can design/select different exercises within each level, based on factors other than the number of digits.

In summary, this design:

1. Represents the concept of degree of difficulty within the same task (addition).
2. Provides the learner with options where the learner can select the entry point.
3. Provides several exercises in each level for practicing purposes.
4. Provides access to verification of results and self-evaluation after the performance. This evaluation and self-feedback can be in the form of an answer sheet, use of a calculator, or use of a computer that presents the tasks and the feedback.
5. Represents the quantitative dimension. The increments that determine the degree of difficulty are manifested by the number of digits to be added and by the complexity of the mental operation required with the increased difficulty. In each level the learner has to do more than in the previous one.

Three Types of Design. There are three basic types of design: (1) classical design, (2) semiclassical design, and (3) cumulative design.

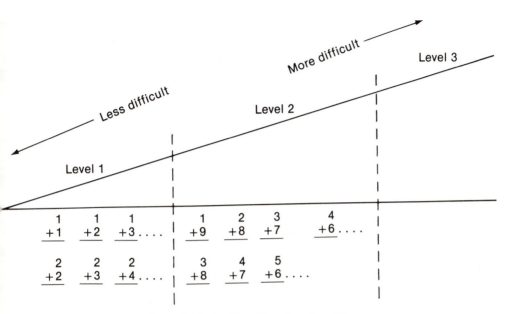

Figure 8.11. Addition Exercises: Level 2

The *classical design* reflects the following:

1. The available increments are very small and constitute a continuous range of degree of difficulty. (The slanted rope is an example.)
2. The range of options emanates from the *intrinsic* factor inherent in the activity. (In the case of the slanted rope it is height.)
3. Anyone who can successfully perform the task at a given level can also perform the task on levels with a lesser degree of difficulty.

The *semiclassical design* reflects the following:

1. The increments are not continuous; at times they are steps with gaps in between.
2. The factor represented as intrinsic (e.g., the number of digits in the addition exercises) does not always offer a clean range of degree of difficulty. The verification of the relative difficulty is not always possible.
3. Performance at a given level does not necessarily ensure success in levels with a logically lesser degree of difficulty. We generally assume, for example, that a learner who can add single digits to 8 can do it to 4. But this may not always be so. In the reality of doing the

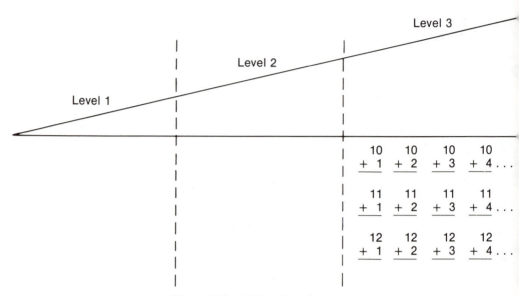

Figure 8.12. Addition Exercises: Level 3

exercises it is possible that *some* learners might be able to perform accurately a task with a greater degree of difficulty and yet make errors with tasks of lesser difficulty.

The *cumulative design* reflects the following:

1. The increments are arbitrary.
2. The factor is *external.*
3. In order to participate in a given level, the learner has to do all the previous levels in succession. Suppose, for example, the task is to cite the names of presidents of the United States in sequence. Clearly, citing the names of all the presidents has the highest degree of difficulty. It is less difficult to cite only 20 names, 10 names, and so on. Each level, then, is arbitrarily determined by the number (quantity) of names that the learner chooses to cite at that moment. This factor of "number of names" is an external factor that is superimposed on the design. Indeed, it affects the degree of difficulty in memorizing; it is harder to remember 41 names than to remember 5 names of presidents. To do the most difficult level, the learner has to remember all the names of the presidents by citing, in sequence, the names in level 1, level 2, and so on—indeed, a cumulative task.

Let us examine two further examples that illustrate the principles of cumulative design and classical design. Another vivid example of cumulative design is the activity of doing push-ups. Let us say that the range represented to the learner is 1 to 30 repetitions, and let us assume that the learner assesses him/herself as capable of doing 20 push-ups. However, it is *impossible* to enter the range at 20. The learner must always start at 1, then do 2, 3, and so on until 20 is reached. It is also possible that a failure to perform the task will occur at any place before 20 push-ups are completed. The feedback is built in; the learner knows the results of the performance and can make the decisions about what to do next.

An excellent example of the classical design is the Universal weight machine for the development of strength. In many gymnasiums and health clubs one can see participants in Style E experiences as they use this machine. The various tasks (pushing, pulling, lifting, etc.) are presented on charts and by the design of the machine itself. Each task is designed to activate and develop a particular group of muscles. Increasing degrees of difficulty are built into the design of the machine via its graduated weight system. Each participant selects his/her entry point, decides the number of repetitions, speed of the movement, when to start, when to stop, how long to rest between exercises, and so on. At any point the participant knows his/her rate of success; the feedback is intrinsic. In this classical design for the inclusion style, the task is to push, pull, or lift; the factors are the amount of weight (intrinsic) and the number of repetitions (external). The range of options is presented by the available graduated weights.

Task Design and the Qualitative Dimension. All of the examples given thus far reflect the *quantitative dimension* of the task design. Let us return for a moment to the issue of the *qualitative dimension* of task design. Since the qualitative dimension is external to the task, and since it represents quality attributed to the task by an outside source, we are confronted with a series of questions: What is the definition of "quality" in a given subject matter area? Can quality be attributed to all tasks in all subject areas? We can say: "He danced beautifully!" But can we also say: "She did the multiplication beautifully"? We can say "You performed Beethoven's Third Piano Concerto with utmost sensitivity and passion." But can we also say: "You produced this series of maps in social studies with sensitivity and passion"? Certainly we can say: "These maps were beautifully done!" These questions trigger thoughts and discussions that are within the realms of philosophy, cultural standards, and personal preferences, but they are also relevant to the practical issue of designing tasks for the inclusion style. How do we design options within the same task that will represent a range of degree of difficulty in quality? Shall we ask the learner to select among levels of aesthetics? Is it possible to ask the student to select the point of entry in a range of "wellness"?

While we continue to contemplate the answers to these questions, it seems quite difficult at this point to propose a practical guide for the design of a task on the slanted rope representing the qualitative dimension. Do you have any thought about this matter?

Name of the task:

o   Identify the rank order for the key and the supporting factor(s)
o   Indicate the range

	External Factors	Range
_____	Number of repetitions	
_____	Time	

Intrinsic Factors

_____	Distance
_____	Height
_____	Weight of implements
_____	Size of implements
_____	Size of target
_____	Speed
_____	Posture
_____	Other

Figure 8.13. A Factor Grid

The Factor Grid

As a technique for identifying and selecting the factors that affect the degree of difficulty, one can use a *factor grid*. This grid is a tool that offers a way of thinking about both the intrinsic and external factors affecting the design of tasks. The factor grid shown in Figure 8.13 is from the discipline of physical education, which is rich in concrete tasks and concrete factors.[1]

The grid suggests two kinds of factors: intrinsic and external. The intrinsic factors are a part of the given task's structure. Some tasks may have all of the factors shown in Figure 8.13 and others may have only some. The external factors are superimposed on the performance of the task. Both kinds of factors affect the degree of difficulty of the given task; any one of the factors can be changed (or manipulated) to vary the degree of difficulty.

Once the teacher has selected the task, the next step in using the grid is to decide which intrinsic factors can be manipulated to provide for inclusion in the ensuing episode. Sometimes tasks are affected by two or more factors. For example, throwing a ball at a target with an overhead throw readily suggests size of target and distance from the target as possible key factors. The teacher must decide which one will serve as the key factor in planning

---

[1] Adapted from Muska Mosston and Sara Ashworth, *Teaching Physical Education*, 3rd ed. (Columbus, Ohio: Charles E. Merrill Publishing Co., 1986).

Name of the task: Chip Shot

	External Factors	Range
_____	Number of Repetitions: 10	
_____	Time:	

Intrinsic Factors

__2__	Distance	Lines A, B, C (3 yd., 5 yd., 7 yd.)
_____	Height	
_____	Weight of Implements	
_____	Size of Implements	
__1__	Size of Target	Small target 10 ft.; large target 30 ft.
_____	Speed	
_____	Posture	
_____	Other	

Figure 8.14. Factor Grid for Chip Shot Practice

and which one will be the supporting factor for the given episode. This choice is related to the task's objective. The rank order is indicated by writing the numbers (1, 2, . . .) on the line to the left of the factor.)

Next, the teacher identifies the range of possibilities in the key factor from which the learner will select his/her entry level. For example, in the case of the size of the target, the range may include targets with varying diameters: small, medium, large; or 10 in., 20 in., 30 in.; or 15 cm, 30 cm, 45 cm. The range for the supporting factors is also identified.

If the teacher selects one of the external factors as the key factor (e.g., the choices in the number of repetitions of a given task will be 5, 10, 15, 20, etc.), this is indicated under "Range." If not, a specific quantity is indicated on the line next to the external factor.

The speed factor can be placed on a range from slow to fast, controlled by a metronome, the music, or the pitching machine as in tennis or baseball.

The posture factor involves the position(s) of the body required to perform a static and/or a dynamic task. (It is also referred to as the *form, basic skill,* or *technique* of a given sport or dance.) If a learner cannot do the task, then manipulating the factors of distance, time, or size of target will not help. The entry point here is created by a modifying the posture—changing the angle between body parts, adding further extension, and so forth. For example, if a learner cannot do the T-scale, the teacher can introduce (on a range) modifications in the angle of the lifted leg or the position of the upper body. This will be the entry point that includes all learners. Later on, factors such as repetition and time can be added. Knowing what is less difficult or more difficult in the posture factor is derived from biomechanical analyses of the task.

Figure 8.14 shows how the factor grid can be used for the golf chip shot. Note that the two intrinsic factors selected for inclusion are the size of target and distance. The external factor involves the number of repetitions. With this identification the teacher can offer the learner a program of activities.

The factor grid is equally suited to other disciplines in other subject matter areas. In a reading exercise, for example, the intrinsic factors are identified as the speed of reading, the number of errors, and comprehension of the content (Figure 8.15). When these three operate in appropriate juxtaposition, the objective of reading is accomplished. It is possible that for some learners slower reading may produce fewer errors and greater comprehension, but the availability of these various levels in each factor provides legitimate entry points for more learners. Obviously the best reader is the fastest one with minimal errors and maximum correct answers.

The flaw in this design is in a portion of the self-feedback. A learner can assess the speed and the number of correct answers (by use of an answer sheet), but he/she may not be able to identify the errors that occur during the reading.

An external factor of repetition may be assigned to the reader. The teacher and/or the learner will have to decide whether or not it is worthwhile to repeat the reading of the same page.

The factor grid for a social studies exercise (Figure 8.16) provides the teacher with a reasonable idea about the structure of this task and how to accommodate different levels of performance. In this case the degree of difficulty is directly related to memory of the information previously learned by Style B or D. This episode, then, is done for review purposes.

The task: Reading one page	
External Factors	**Range**
_____ Number of Repetitions _____ Time	
Intrinsic Factors	
_____ Speed _____ Number of errors permitted _____ Number of correct answers _____ Other	3 min. 2½ 2 1½ 8–10 5–7 2–4 1 3 4 5 6

Figure 8.15. Factor Grid for a Reading Exercise

Identifying the factor grid in any given subject matter is quite a challenge for the teacher. It requires insight into the structure of the task, analyzing its inherent elements, separating them from the external factors, and seeing how each factor is the source for options arranged by the "slanted rope" principle.

The Individual Program and the Criteria Sheet

The central purpose of the inclusion style is to provide an opportunity for each learner to enter the activity on his/her level, *maintain* the participation in the activity, and engage in self-feedback. The individual program offers the learner a task or a cluster of tasks, each arranged by the "slanted rope" principle. This program engages the learner in doing the task(s) over an extended period of time. One technique that accommodates these conditions is the *individual program*.

One form of the individual program is a task sheet that presents the learner with a variety of options within the same task. Let us examine such a task sheet for the chip shot in golf (Figure 8.17). This individual program has the following features:

1. Space for general information (name, date, program number, etc.)
2. General instructions to the student.
3. Instructions on how to do the task, which in this case also serve as the performance criteria for the details of the chip shot.
4. Presentation of the task.

The task: Identifying locations on a blank map of your state.

External Factors	Range		
___ ?			
___ ?			
Intrinsic Factors			
✓ Amount of information			
a. Cities	a. The Capitol	Capitol + 2 others	Capitol + 5 others
b. Towns	b. 2 towns	5 towns	8 towns
c. Rivers	c. Largest river	Largest + 2 others	Largest + 5 others
d. Lakes	d. 1 lake	3 lakes	5 lakes
e. Mountains	e. Tallest	Tallest + 1 other	Tallest + 2 others
f. Other			

Figure 8.16. Factor Grid for a Social Studies Exercise

Name _____   Style   B   C   D   E

Class _____   Individual Program # _____

Date _____

Golf — Chip Shot

To the student:

1. Select an initial level and circle the number you expect to do.
2. Do the task and blacken out the number of the actual performance.
3. Compare your execution of the task with the performance criteria.
4. Decide whether to repeat the test at the same level or at a different level.

Chip shot

Criteria:

1. Stand with your feet close together.
2. Bend your knees slightly, as though starting to sit.
3. Contact the ball off your left heel.
4. Follow through along the path of the ball, keeping the left wrist firm at contact.
5. Refrain from letting the club head pass the left hand.
6. Keep the flight of the ball low.
7. Hit to a predetermined spot and have the ball roll to the cup.

The Task: Choose a distance (line A, B, or C) and a target area (either the large or the small). Take 10 chip shots and record the number of times you hit the target area.

Line   A _____   _____

Line   B _____   _____

Line   C _____   _____

Distance	LARGE TARGET										
A	0	1	2	3	4	5	6	7	8	9	10
B	0	1	2	3	4	5	6	7	8	9	10
C	0	1	2	3	4	5	6	7	8	9	10

Distance	SMALL TARGET										
A	0	1	2	3	4	5	6	7	8	9	10
B	0	1	2	3	4	5	6	7	8	9	10
C	0	1	2	3	4	5	6	7	8	9	10

Figure 8.17. An Individual Program for the Golf Chip Shot

5. Delineation of options in the target sizes and the distances from the targets.
6. A recording chart for the anticipated and actual performance.
7. Semiclassical design.

This program can be used for several episodes to serve as a guide for learning the chip shot and monitoring its progress. It was designed by using a factor grid for this task. Clearly the structure of this task suggests the size of the target and the distance from it as intrinsic factors. The number of repetitions and the number of successful shots are external factors.

This kind of an individual program in the field of sport entertains a special dimension that programs in other fields in the curriculum may not possess. Repeating the same task (and the same program) over and over again enhances the performance of the particular skill, which is a part of a larger involvement—in this case, the game of golf itself. Proficiency in the neuromuscular activities related to the chip shot requires repetition and continuous practice and is necessary for success in the overall game. This dimension may or may not apply to other fields. Once one has learned the multiplication table, for example, it is probably not necessary to practice it over and over again as a part of engaging in other mathematical activities. An individual program is very useful in the initial teaching of a given task, but once the learner has learned the task, he/she can move on to other tasks and other programs.

The next example is an individual program task sheet for a "telling time" exercise for young children (Figure 8.18). The intrinsic factor that determines the degree of difficulty here is the position of the hand(s). In this case the learner needs a criteria sheet in order to verify his/her telling of time. The criteria sheet may be designed as shown in Figure 8.19. As you can see, not all tasks represent an instantly recognizable progression in degree of difficulty. As an exercise in design, you might try to devise a more precise progression for this exercise.

IMPLICATIONS OF STYLE E

In this section we will consider Style E in the areas of subject matter design, feelings, verbal behavior, and logistics.

Subject Matter Design

Differentiating the design of subject matter in order to accommodate different students has been quite prevalent in schools. Usually it takes the form of selecting particular units or courses. These have been designated by different names such as *advanced, remedial, compensatory,* and so on. The attempt is made to identify chunks of information, acts, and concepts that

Name _____	Style B C D E
Date _____	Task Sheet # _____
Class _____	

To the Learner: 1. Select the level.
2. Read the time of the three exercises on that level and write it in numbers.
3. Decide whether or not to do another level.

Task	Level			
Telling Time Factor: Position of the hand	1. Position of the hand to the hour	12 ↑ ___:00	→3 ___:___	9← ___ ___
	2. Position of the hand to the half-hour	→3 6 3:___	7 6 ___:___	8 6 ___ ___
	3. Position of the quarter- hand to the quarter-hour	9←→3 9:___	9← 1 ___:___	10 ___ ___
	4. Position of the minute hand at 5– minute intervals	2 7 6 2:___	12 6 5 ___:___	↗ ___ ___
	5. Position of the minute hand at 1–minute intervals	2 4 5 2:___	10 2 ___:___	↕ ___ ___

Figure 8.18. An Individual Program for Telling Time

150

Level			
1	12:00	3:00	9:00
2	3:30	7:30	8:30
3	9:15	12:45	10:15
4	2:35	12:25	2:05
5	2:22	10:11	12:28

Figure 8.19. Criteria for Telling Time Exercise

the student will be able to handle on his/her own level of ability. This level is usually identified via various testing procedures conducted by the teacher or outside experts. The learner is then placed in the class, group, or course that deals with a commensurate level of subject matter. This arrangement represents the single-standard principle for *that* part of the subject matter and for *that* group of students. It is a design representing Style B, since the learner does not choose the level nor is the learner engaged in self-feedback.

The implications of the inclusion style to the design of subject matter are rather serious and demanding. The reality created by this style is so different that it takes time to accept the concept that *each* single task can be analyzed and rearranged to accommodate *multiple* entry points into the subject matter. The concept of inclusion, philosophically accepted in books and speeches, requires considerable thinking and effort when it reaches the level of actually doing it in the classroom. Implementing this concept via task design requires a more profound understanding of the structure of the subject matter in general and of the purposes of each specific task. The implications for the teacher who is ready to accept this style involve changing one's conception of task design. This means that the teacher is willing to see that *each* single task can have options that are *legitimately* less difficult or more difficult for a given period of time. It means that the teacher is able to accept *where* the learner *is* at the given time and start from there. It means that offering options within the task is more important for the teacher than protecting arbitrary standards that have nothing to do with the present ability of the student.

Feelings

In one workshop we asked the participants to reminisce about *one* instance in their lives where they were *excluded,* either in school or outside. It was astonishing to realize that it took only a few seconds and most participants were ready with their stories. Apparently the past experiences of having been excluded made a considerable impact on them. They did not have to strain in order to conjure up memories. Some of the stories were amusing but most were serious and painful. All reflected a sense of rejection, embarrassment, and stigma. Most of the stories were from childhood. When the stories were over there was silence in the room. We were all immersed in thoughts about the various forms of exclusion and the powerful feelings they evoked in us.

Episodes designed for inclusion evoke the opposite feelings—they evoke a sense of belonging, a sense of being involved, a sense of achievement, a sense of being wanted. It is uncanny to watch students in these episodes. It is like seeing an invisible banner waving above each head proclaiming: "I am in, not out!"

We also recall a presentation to a PTA that included a demonstration of the slanted rope in action. The demonstrators were children of the attending parents. The concept and the demonstration were generally received with warmth and appreciation. That night there were no "stars" and no one sat out on the bench. The parents saw their children, regardless of ability, engaged in making decisions about themselves and participating with zest and joy. When the applause subsided one father stood up and said: "Thank you very much for the presentation and demonstration. The children were very lovely but *you* don't understand life. What you showed us tonight is not the real world. In life you compete, you exclude and get excluded!" and he sat down. There was utter silence in the auditorium.

What was going on here? Was it a conflict of values? Was it a conflict of perception of reality? Or was it a lack of understanding of the "non-versus" feature of the Spectrum—the idea that Style E is one among several options?

Ability and Aspiration. There are several aspects of the emotional domain that Style E evokes in most people because it reveals the potential gap between ability and aspiration. For example, a learner's reality may be that he/she can perform only at a moderate level of difficulty while his/her aspiration reaches to a much higher level. A gap exists and an inner conflict may develop. The reverse is true, too. In reality a learner may be able to perform tasks with a high degree of difficulty, yet he/she aspires to perform only on a level of lesser difficulty. Again a gap exists and a conflict may develop.

Let us examine some of the reasons for such gaps and consider ways in which the resulting conflict can be resolved.

When the student's aspirations are below his/her real ability, one or more of the following factors may be involved:

1. The student is not be interested in the task.
2. The student is not motivated.

3. The reward for effort is too small.
4. The student is lazy.
5. The student has learned that this behavior draws attention from the teacher.
6. The subject matter is not relevant to the student.
7. The student fears failure.

The last item, fear of failure, can be a potent inhibitor of aspiration. It manifests itself in the following behaviors:

1. Staying on the same level relatively too long.
2. Using rationalizations such as "I don't like. . . ."
3. Resisting risk taking; avoiding trying a level of greater degree of difficulty.
4. Pretending to be lazy.
5. Showing an "I don't care" attitude.
6. Becoming ill.
7. Stating "I'm pleased with where I am."

When the student's aspirations are above his/her real ability, any of these factors could be the cause:

1. The student is ambitious.
2. The student is competitive.
3. The student wants to do what is "best."
4. The student seems to enjoy failure.
5. The student wants to please the teacher.
6. The student does not know how to assess his/her ability.
7. The student is a risk taker.

With reference to risk taking, it should be noted that this ingredient of the emotional structure was in hibernation in Styles A–D. When the teacher makes the decision about where the learner *should* be, there is no need to take risks. One can take risks only when there are choices. In Style E, particularly when the learner's reality is considerably lower than the level of aspiration, he/she must exhibit the capacity for risk taking if the gap is to be reduced.

Because it is often difficult to discern the exact reason for an observed gap between aspiration and ability, we sometimes make inaccurate assumptions about learners. It is imperative to be constantly aware that the very structure of Style E creates conditions for these behaviors to surface. Therefore patience and appropriate verbal behavior are mandatory during the interaction that takes place privately with the particular learner. The following steps are helpful in resolving some of these situations.

1. **Observe the behavior.** Observe the learner's decision and verify if, indeed, there is a gap between reality and aspiration. Do not rush to conclusions. An inaccurate assessment by the teacher followed by an inappropriate statement may infringe on the learner's integrity.
2. **Ask questions.** Ask the learner about his/her self-assessment and reasons for the decisions. Weigh the information given to you.
3. **Provide evidence.** You may have knowledge of the learner's performance ability from prior experiences; talk about it and listen to the learner's response. Just offer the information, do not moralize.
4. **Decide how to use the interplay of Styles B and E.** You may, momentarily, switch to Style B by telling the learner to enter on a different level and observing the performance and the reaction of the learner. Then switch back to Style E. Ask the learner to proceed with making that decision.

This private, one-to-one interaction sends a clear message to the learner: You care not only about the task, but also about the learner's sense of self. You are available to deal with one of the most crucial and difficult aspects of human development—the relationship between reality and aspiration—which in turn affects the self-concept of the individual.

Verbal Behavior

As in Styles A–D, the pivot around which the Style E relationship revolves is the verbal behavior of the teacher. This style, too, has its own language rules. There are words and phrases that will *initiate* and *maintain* the spirit and process of the style, and there are words and phrases that will *abort* it almost from the beginning. The awareness of the verbal behavior appropriate to Style E begins with the introduction of the ''slanted rope'' idea. If a teacher who is presenting the actual rope situation to a class uses the words ''do your best'' while explaining the idea of inclusion, the results are often *not* congruent with the objectives of this style.

The instruction ''do your best'' is seemingly an innocent one but its consequences are not quite so. This phrasing is rooted in the tradition of a competitive principle that inculcates in the young that ''doing your best'' is always the best thing to do. This may be true for some people some of the time, but for many it creates unbearable pressure to perform all the time at levels beyond their reach. This, in turn, results in exclusion with all its emotional and psychological trimmings.

Lest this sound like a treatise against competition, let us remind you of the ''non-versus'' notion and the idea of episodes in a variety of styles. If we value the concept of inclusion and consider it as one of the goals of education, then it is mandatory to provide frequent opportunities for inclusion style episodes in the reality of the school. During the day there are episodes that call for competition and there are episodes that invite the learners to do what *they can* without challenging them to do what they *cannot.*

Moreover, Style E does not eliminate the essence of competition; it only presents it in a different form. Instead of competing with others against a single standard, the learner has the opportunity to find out where he/she stands in face of multiple standards.

We have arrived at these insights by examining failures. When teachers told us that the slanted rope did not work quite the way we had described it, or that it did not work for them, we were puzzled. After repeated analyses of the episodes and reexamination of the concept, it became clear that the so-called failures of this idea often were a direct reflection of the teacher's verbal behavior.

The appropriate *initial* verbal behavior, therefore, is: "In this style you make the decisions where to enter the activity. You decide which option is for you." The focus is on the *learner's decision,* about his/her choice of challenge, not the teacher's. The focus of Style E is to nourish the delicate process of evolving a reasonable and realistic self-concept.

In the postimpact set, when the teacher makes individual, private contact with the learner, it is imperative to maintain the role of the learner in accordance with the shift of decisions. Since the learner is the one who makes the evaluation decisions about the performance, the *first* verbal contact is the question: "How are you doing on the task?" This question instantly focuses on the *learner's* role in the postimpact phase. If the learner responds by telling the teacher about the performance and the information is accurate, the teacher's feedback is: "I see that you know how to do self-evaluation"; or "You made your postimpact decisions properly." This kind of verbal behavior reinforces the learner's ability to perform the role. The reinforcement for doing the task comes from the performance itself and from the criteria card.

If the learner is not performing the task accurately, the teacher says: "Before you continue, check your work against the criteria." Again, this statement invites the learner to focus on his/her role without being judgmental or corrective. If necessary the teacher reviews the role of the learner by asking: "What is your role in this style?" If the learner knows it, the teacher responds: "Yes, you know your role; let me see you do it." If the learner fumbles at recalling the role, the teacher privately reviews the steps and the decisions that are part of the learner's Style E role.

The following are examples of other verbal behaviors that distract from the potential success of Style E and should therefore be avoided:

1. "You can do better than that."
2. "*You* can do that?"
3. "You *can* do that?"

4. "You can do *that*?"
5. "You can do that, too?"
6. "Good for you!" (surprise)
7. "Will you ever be able to . . . ?"
8. "How many times are you going to do this level?"
9. "You did that level yesterday."

These are all familiar sentences and it is very tempting to use them. Clearly they can be viewed as encouraging and motivating. They are comfortable for us, they maintain *our* position as the decision makers and the source of feedback. But they are not compatible with the purposes of this style. They do not strengthen the learner's role in the decisions that were shifted to him/her for the duration of *this* episode. In Style E the students learn to make these evaluations by themselves, for themselves.

STYLE-SPECIFIC COMMENTS

Although Style E is conducive to the needs of every learner at certain times, it is most applicable to special education and remedial programs. Students with limitations have experienced many moments of exclusion and rejection. One of the ways to reverse this reality is to conduct frequent episodes in the inclusion style. It is not sufficient to offer a variety of general activities in a given subject matter; rather, inclusion should be built into each task. The design of options within a given task invites the learner to participate and feel included.

At times this style is useful with a learner who is stuck and cannot perform tasks with the rest of the class that may be in a Style B episode. A short episode in Style E for this learner can be very helpful in moving him/her on.

Style E produces an interesting phenomenon that did not surface in styles A–D. There are good performers who have difficulty with Style E episodes. They seem to function well in conditions where they are told what to do and where they know the "pecking order." Their goal is to be the best and their arena must facilitate those needs. Because their emotional structure requires the kind of feedback that frequently singles them out as being the best, shifting to Style E sometimes disturbs them. Now each learner is "okay" in his/her level, and accepting that all learners are equal in such episodes is sometimes quite difficult. Learning to be oneself and make all the decisions of this style is demanding, as is breaking the emotional dependency on the teacher. This can often be a painful and delicate process.

Students who have frequently been excluded often react quite positively to Style E episodes. They love this style. For many it is the first time they have been included over a longer period of time. These students identify with Style E because they have an entry point that allows them to participate and succeed in the task, and they see a chance for continuous progress and development.

Although Style E is inviting to most learners, for students in special education it is perhaps mandatory. It is an excellent style to start with before introducing the others. Perhaps all students need to experience the "non-versus" realities.

Style E must not encourage the learner to remain on one level of performance (rationalized by the learner's decision). When it is apparent the learner is stuck (e.g., because of laziness or poor self-concept), it is the role of the teacher to discuss the matter with the learner and move the learner on without violating the integrity of the learner or the style. One approach for breaking this stagnation is to use episodes that combine Styles B and E. The teacher assigns tasks (Style B) on various levels; when the learner can, in fact, perform them, he/she evolves a clearer sense of self-assessment and renewed motivation. These Style B episodes are immediately followed by Style E, where the learner resumes the role of making decisions about the level.

At times the issue of cheating will surface in Style E episodes. Having the answer sheets (criteria) available creates conditions conducive to cheating. Here again it is the role of the teacher, as pedagogue, to intervene and deal with this moral aspect of behavior without admonishing or penalizing. Helping the learner to accept his/her present level of accomplishment will reduce the need to cheat.

Every so often a learner will brag about his/her level of performance. This is a wonderful opportunity for the teacher and the learner to deal with the issue of accepting all learners, regardless of their choice of level, which reduces the need to single oneself out. Generally students who experience Style E with reasonable frequency learn to accept each other and appreciate the individual differences that exist in the class.

Style E is highly private in terms of the decision itself, although not necessarily in terms of the engagement in the activity. This privacy must be respected. The teacher cannot be invisible in a classroom; but the decisions about the level must remain within the private domain of each learner.

Operationally Style E offers the teacher and the learners longer periods for independent practice. The individual program, therefore, should be designed for a series of episodes containing a number of tasks and levels. Infrequent, single episodes in this style do not create the opportunity to reap the full benefits of the style. Learning to be more independent takes time, and the design of the individual program can accommodate this objective.

Perhaps the single, most important feature of Style E is its power of inclusion. It enables the stigma caused by exclusion in various classes to be reduced. The invitation to participate offered by the slanted rope is so powerful that sooner or later all learners who have previously been excluded (regardless of reason) join in. It is as if the learner says: "I have a place, too. I belong!" (See Figure 8.20 and Table 8.1.)

Style E: THE INCLUSION STYLE

The purposes of this style are:

   o   To learn to select a level of a task you can perform

   o   To check your own work

ROLE OF LEARNER

o   To make the 9 decisions of Style B

o   To examine the different levels of the task

o   To select the level appropriate for you

o   To perform the task

o   To check your own work against criteria prepared by the teacher

o   To ask the teacher questions for clarification

ROLE OF TEACHER

o   To prepare the task and the levels within the task

o   To prepare the criteria for the levels in the task

o   To answer questions by the learner

o   To initiate communication with the learner

Figure 8.20. Style D Classroom Chart

STYLE E AND THE DEVELOPMENTAL CHANNELS

Again we will use the criterion of *independence* to examine the position of the learner on the developmental channels when Style E is used (see Figure 8.21). The question is: How independent is a learner in making decisions about . . . ?

The Physical Developmental Channel. In physical education episodes involving physical tasks, the learner is highly independent about his/her

TABLE 8.1 THE ANATOMY OF STYLE E: THE INCLUSION STYLE

Decision Sets	Teacher's Decision Categories	Learner's Decision Categories

Preimpact	All decisions as in Style D
	Designing the levels of
	  performance in each task
	Preparing the criteria for the
	  different levels
		Not involved

Impact	Implementing the preimpact
	  decisions
	Delivering the tasks, the levels,
	  and the criteria
	Observing the performance by
	  the learner
	Adjustment decisions
		The nine decisions of Style B
		Selecting the appropriate level
		  within the task
		Performing the task on his/her
		  level

Postimpact	Acknowledging the learner's
	  performance
	Initiating communication with
	  the learner concerning the
	  process of self assessment
		Self assessment decisions about
		  the selection of his/her level,
		  and the performance of the
		  task

physical development. In other tasks the learner is still independent about the physical domain even though the focus of the tasks is not physical. Therefore the placement on the physical developmental channel is toward "maximum."

The Social Developmental Channel. The condition for social interaction in Style E is the same as in Styles B and D, but since Style E is a private and individual style, it does not call for socialization. In this style, however, one learns to respect other people's privacy. One learns to respect other learners' private choices of levels in the range of difficulty. The placement

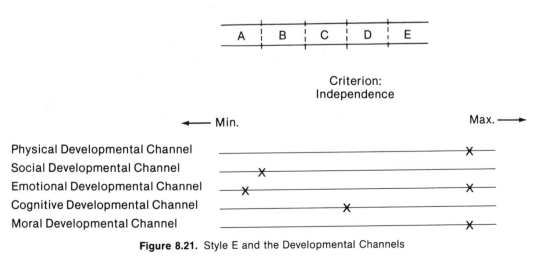

Figure 8.21. Style E and the Developmental Channels

on the social developmental channel is therefore somewhat further away from "minimum."

The Emotional Developmental Channel. As in previous styles there is dual placement on the emotional developmental channel. Some students need to make and take comfort in making the decision of where to enter the "slanted rope" exercises. This places them toward "maximum" on this channel. These students are more independent in accepting where they are on the range of options. On the other hand, there are students who cannot deal with the available choices; they are anxious, unsure and, at times, afraid. These students need more time to learn to cope with choices and to feel comfortable with their own entry decisions. For the time being, these students are placed toward "minimum" on this channel.

The Cognitive Developmental Channel. In Style E the learner is engaged not only in memory and recall but also in the cognitive operations of comparing and contrasting, assessing, and evaluating. Therefore the placement on the cognitive developmental channel is further away from "minimum."

The Moral Developmental Channel. Perhaps one of the major contributions of Style E to the student's development is that it forces a confrontation with honesty. Assessing and evaluating oneself against options and against criteria require a particular state of emotions that permits one to be honest in doing the evaluation and in accepting the verdict. Being honest with oneself is one dimension of moral development. Being independent in demonstrating the ability to be honest places the student further toward "maximum" on the moral developmental channel.

It may seem like quite a burden to remember and integrate all the specifics of Style E. In order for this style to make its intended contribution, the teacher needs to have a clear understanding of the concept of inclusion and specific knowledge of how to design tasks that reflect the "slanted rope" principle. Without the intricate and subtle adaptations in the teacher's verbal behavior, for example, learners cannot reap the full benefits of Style E. So think about the power of this style. Think about its capacity to invite and embrace every student in your classes. The efforts you invest in studying Style E will pay off when you see all your students enjoy a new reality in your class—the reality of inclusion.

CHAPTER 9

About Styles A–E

We have traveled a long way since the command style and we have experienced the uniqueness of each of five different styles. As a cluster, however, Styles A–E share several characteristics in common. In this chapter we will examine a variety of concepts and issues that apply to all the styles in this cluster and that should be considered in conjunction with the specificity of each style.

THE GOAL OF REPRODUCTION

As a cluster, Styles A–E represent the human capacity for *reproduction*— reproduction of ideas, skills, and models. We have seen that a portion of life experiences and a portion of school knowledge are the results of this basic human capacity. The goal of this cluster, therefore, is to teach and to learn about the past and to reproduce the known—that is to reproduce those parts of the past that are relevant to our understanding of ourselves and our world. Each of the styles in this cluster engages the learner in a different way of moving toward this goal.

All the styles in this cluster share in common the characteristics shown in Figure 9.1. Each style in this cluster, due to its particular structure (O–T–L–O), contributes to the accomplishment of a portion of the reproduction goal. The decision structure of each style defines what the style *can* and *cannot* do; it defines the *boundaries* of the style. This notion of boundaries is helpful in understanding that each style can accomplish only a portion of the objectives and goals of education. Together Styles A–E can reach the full ramifications of *reproduction*.

161

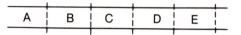

REPRODUCTION OF

o Past Knowledge

o Facts

o Specific Skills

o Rules

o Particular models

o Traditions and rituals

o Cultural events

MAINLY VIA

o Memory and recall

o Repetition

Figure 9.1. Characteristics of Styles A–E

EPISODES AND LESSONS

Any face-to-face relationship between teacher and learner constitutes an episode. An *episode* is a period of time within which the teacher and the learner are in the same style, heading toward the same objective. This is shown schematically in Figure 9.2. Each episode has its specific objectives, its particular tasks (subject matter), and is conducted in a particular style. Thus each episode represents a particular reality in which the teacher and the learner participate in a particular relationship defined by the style used during that time.

A *lesson* can be conceived, planned and executed as a series of consecutive or concurrent episodes. The use of *consecutive episodes* represents the decision to conduct the lesson in a manner that moves the entire class from style to style and from task to task.

In a four-episode lesson, like that shown in Figure 9.3, the content of the first episode could be a review of the previous lesson's work; the second episode could involve doing familiar tasks; the third episode could focus on

←– – – – – Time – – – – –→

O – T – L – O

Figure 9.2. An Episode

Episode 1	Episode 2	Episode 3	Episode 4
Style B	Style D	Style A	Style B
(5 min.)	(20 min.)	(10 min.)	(15 min.)

Figure 9.3. A Lesson Composed of Consecutive Episodes

precision work; and the fourth episode could be used for presenting and practicing new materials.

The use of *concurrent episodes* (Figure 9.4) represents the decision to conduct the class in a manner that provides the opportunity for different groups (or individuals) to engage in different styles and different tasks at the same time.

Concurrent episodes provide some flexibility in terms of the mobility of the learners and the teacher. The groups (or individuals) can rotate and switch styles and tasks at the completion of each episode, time decisions can be more flexible, and the teacher can make the decision about his/her presence and role with a particular group. It is important to realize that in the example shown in Figure 9.4 not only are four different tasks being performed concurrently (these tasks may be in the same subject matter or in different ones), but also four different behaviors are being practiced— different teaching behaviors and different learning behaviors. In the language of the Spectrum, four different O–T–L–O are in process concurrently.

DELIBERATENESS AND SPONTANEITY

One of the most fascinating and sensitive issues in educational debate is the issue of *deliberate* teaching versus *spontaneous* teaching. These two descriptors of teaching have a multiplicity of meanings and connotations to

Style B Task 1 10 learners	Style C Task 2 10 learners
Style D Task 4 4 learners	Style E Task 3 7 learners

Figure 9.4. A Lesson Composed of Concurrent Episodes

teachers. In courses or workshops on teaching, have you ever heard the participants make any of the following comments?

- "This idea is okay, but I teach my way."
- "It sounds logical, but it is too restrictive."
- "It's not me."
- "It is artificial."
- "I don't want to lose my spontaneity."
- "I am a creative teacher."

These statements express a deep concern for the maintenance of one's integrity, and at the same time project resistance to any proposal that invites introspection and possible change of behavior—teaching behavior in this case. Spontaneity is viewed, at times, as a reflection of one's inner qualities, abilities, personal choices, and integrity. Deliberateness is perceived, at times, as succumbing to external models, procedures, and rules. Some people have elevated spontaneity to a virtue, while others accept deliberateness as a necessity. So once again we are facing a dichotomy, a tug-of-war, a "versus."

Rather than perpetuate the combat between opposing positions, let us try to understand the meanings of each term and the possible interplay between the two. First, let's define each term and describe its characteristics. According to the *Random House Dictionary* (1973), *deliberate* means "carefully weighed or considered; studied; intentional." *Spontaneous* means "coming or resulting from a natural impulse or tendency; without effort or premeditation; natural and unconstrained; unplanned."

It is quite obvious that both deliberate and spontaneous dimensions exist in our personal and professional behaviors. The issue is not which one must predominate, but rather when is each behavior most appropriate and what are the criteria for such a choice.

In teaching, deliberateness means conducting an episode in a manner that maximizes the congruity between the intent and the action. In such an episode, both teacher and learners know in advance the objectives of the episode and both adhere to the expected teaching behavior and learning behavior. At the end of the episode, both teacher and learners know the outcomes and can assess them in relationship to the intended objectives. (In the language of the Spectrum the O-T-L-O in a given episode was expected in advance, was adhered to during the flow of the episode, and was used as the criterion to assess the congruity between the intent and the action.)

In teaching, *spontaneity* can be viewed in two ways. First, it is a response to the unexpected in the flow of an episode. Something unusual has happened; something has interrupted the sequence of events and this interruption calls for an instant response from the teacher—perhaps humor, anger, puzzlement, redirection, or silence. Each of these responses is drawn from the teacher's personal repertoire, experience, and wit.

What happens next may be unpredictable. Often some or all of the students may respond spontaneously. In any case, the next step in this first scenario is to reenter the flow of the episode. This view suggests that spontaneity is an intermittent behavior, a behavior used when called upon *within* the flow of an episode. When the interruption has been dealt with (resolved), the episode continues in the intended deliberate manner.

Second, spontaneity may be viewed as a behavior that governs the *entire* episode. The scenario, here, is different. In a totally spontaneous episode the objectives are not predetermined, the expected teaching and learning behaviors are not known, and the outcomes cannot be assessed in relationship to the intended objectives. Spontaneous episodes are triggered by a stimulus unknown in advance, the flow can take any direction, and the end results (outcomes) cannot be anticipated.

Indeed, both deliberate and spontaneous episodes exist in schools. The fundamental question that arises is: What is the most desirable ratio between these two types of episodes? The cluster of Styles A–E represents a schema for alternatives in teaching behaviors wherein each style serves as a guide for the deliberate behaviors and provides for spontaneity *within* the style. This *interplay* between the deliberateness of each style and the spontaneity that occurs within it creates a reality that is flexible and purposeful. It seems imperative here *not* to equate the deliberateness/spontaneity issue with the historical dichotomies of teacher-centered/student-centered, structured classroom/open classroom, direct teaching/indirect teaching, authoritarian education/permissive education, and so on. These dichotomies always reflected a "versus" position, a philosophical position that represents only a portion of human reality.

From the psychological point of view, a call for deliberate teaching behavior can trigger *fear*—fear of the unknown, fear of errors, fear of accountability. In our professional behavior we have all evolved habits, patterns and beliefs that seem natural and spontaneous to us. They cushion our feelings with comfort and equilibrium. Any attempt to expand or change our present behavior may cause discomfort, disequilibrium, anxiety, and fear. These emotions become particularly strong when specific new models serve as criteria for the new behavior. Yet there are many activities where concrete models are perfectly well accepted as learning guides—for example, in learning to play the piano, to speak a new language, to play tennis, or to use a new tool. Why then should we fear them in learning teaching behaviors that are new to us?

Learning to be deliberate is fundamental to professional behavior; it provides a framework for our actions, criteria for correcting mishaps, and landmarks for achieving intended goals. Research on teaching and learning behavior notes the importance of deliberateness or intentionality. Contributions from these findings suggest that it is helpful

1. To recognize the importance of deliberateness, the awareness of what we do

2. To recognize and accept the initial "awkward phase" (Joyce 1981) that is a part of learning any new skill/behavior
3. To be willing to practice the new behavior, to accept corrective feedback, and to practice again
4. To be willing to approximate the "idealized model," to accept corrective feedback, and practice again
5. To continue until the new behavior becomes familiar, smooth, and natural

Successful implementation of *all* the styles in the Spectrum calls for deliberate behavior spiced with appropriate spontaneity.

INDIVIDUAL DIFFERENCES

One aspect of the individualizing process is the continuous shift of decisions from teacher to learner. Cluster A–E systematically develops this process of individualization. Learners are called upon to make decisions in the impact and the postimpact sets. Learners are called upon to take responsibility for these decisions—responsibility for both the quantitative and the qualitative aspects of the decisions they make. The assumption underlying this cluster and, indeed, the entire Spectrum, is that *all* learners need to learn to make these decisions and learn to be mobile from style to style. This underlying assumption suggests that many (perhaps all) of the decisions in this cluster are *fundamental* for growth and development as a functioning social being.[1]

THE CANOPY

Throughout cluster A–E we have seen episodes with examples of tasks and activities that represented the styles. In these examples there seemed to be a perfect match between the distribution of decisions delineated in the structure of the style and the distribution actually called for by the tasks used in the episode. Under such conditions the styles are designated as *landmark styles*. There are conditions, however, where a perfect match is not possible or desirable. There are conditions where the objectives of the task call for teaching behavior and learning behavior that fall between the landmark styles. Lecturing, showing a film, and giving a test are common examples of activities that cannot be be carried out in a landmark style. Yet, because each of these episodes involves a particular decision distribution between the teacher and the learner, it *can* be placed on the Spectrum and designated as under the *canopy* of the landmark style its decision structure

---

[1] An illuminating overview of individual differences is found in the ASCD publication, *Marching to a Different Drummer* (1985).

most nearly matches. We can determine its placement by making a decision analysis of the episode to identify the proximity of that episode to one of the styles in the cluster. As with the landmark styles, this analysis emanates from the question: Who makes which decisions, about what, and when?

Examples of Placement Analysis

The following examples illustrate a procedure for analyzing episodes for the purpose of placing them in the appropriate canopy position on the Spectrum.

A Lecture Episode. One of the common teaching behaviors in classrooms is the lecture. The major objective of a lecture is the delivery of new subject matter. The decision analysis of the roles of the teacher and the learner yield two conditions, each of which is described and analyzed below.

Condition 1. A lecture can be delivered with the decisions distributed as follows:

Teacher's Decisions	**Learner's Decisions**
Subject matter	Posture
Location (sometimes by the procedure of assigning seats)	What to include in the notes taken during the lecture
Posture (sometimes by assigning a general posture)	
Order	
Starting time	
Pace and rhythm of the delivery	
Stopping time	
Intervals	
Not to permit questions	

Clearly an episode with this distribution of decisions does not represent the command style. It is not equivalent to the chorus, the orchestra, the crew, or the synchronized repetition of words in another language. In a lecture the teacher does not emit a series of single stimuli (commands) with the expectation of corresponding responses from the learners. In a lecture the role of the learner is to listen (be passive) and, at times, to take notes. This episode does not represent the *essence* of Style A. Nor is it an episode in Style B. The learners are not engaged in doing tasks delivered by the teacher, nor does the teacher offer individual and private feedback about the performance of the tasks (although if notebooks are collected and corrected and checked for contents, there will be delayed feedback about the note taking). This episode does not represent the *essence* of style B. However, by noting the distribution of decisions we can place this episode *between* Style A and Style B. The objectives of a lecture dictate particular teaching behaviors and learning behaviors in which the learner makes more decisions than in Style A, but fewer than the nine decisions in Style B.

Given this situation, it is quite legitimate to ask: When does a style cease to be Style A? At what point does it become Style B? What if it is neither A nor B? Underlying these questions is the realization that there are conditions where the landmark styles cannot be used; moreover they should not be used. From this realization the concept of the *canopy*[2] evolved. Under the canopy fall the myriad activities that cannot or should not be conducted by the landmark styles. The designation of the episode just analyzed is $\widehat{B}$ (i.e., it is under the canopy of Style B).

Condition 2. A lecture can also be conducted in a different manner, with a different distribution of decisions:

Teacher's Decisions	*Learner's Decisions*
Subject matter	Location
Starting time	Posture
Order	What to include in the notes taken
Pace and rhythm	during the lecture
Intervals	Asking questions for clarification
Stopping time	

This condition also places the lecture as a canopy $\widehat{B}$ episode. Note, however, the *extraordinary* process that often develops as a result of shifting to the learner the *one* decision of "asking questions for clarification." When the learner can ask questions for clarification *at will,* the following decisions have also been inadvertently shifted:

1. Stopping time. The learner now has the capacity to stop the lecturer at any time.
2. Interval. The learner determines the length of time it will take to ask the question, thus determining the interval between the ideas delivered by the lecturer.
3. Pace and rhythm. Because the student can make the stopping-time and interval decisions, he/she can now interrupt the pace and rhythm of the lecture.
4. Order. These interruptions, at times, determine the order of events during a lecture episode.
5. Quantity. Often the decisions made by the learner affect the quantity of materials delivered in the lecture.

Although this condition is popular with some teachers, it could *invite* manipulation by the learner. The rationale that teachers give for shifting the

---

[2] The concept of the canopy also applies to Styles F–J.

decisions about questions goes something like this: "I want my students to be involved"; "My students are curious"; "They have good questions."

It is not suggested here that teachers should deny students the opportunity to ask questions; rather, it is intended to alert them to the possible implications of shifting this one decision. It is not uncommon to hear students ask questions that they know will take the teacher on a tangent.

Since the purpose of a lecture is to deliver new information, the teacher must be in control. Try it! See what happens when you deliver information this way.

A suitable alternative is to tell the students that questions for clarification can be asked *only after* the teacher has completed the delivery of an idea. When the *teacher* decides that it is time for asking questions for clarification, the appropriate verbal behavior is: "Are there any questions for clarification about what I have said so far?" This way the teacher makes the decisions that keep the lecture moving and at the same time includes the learners in the process.

The flow of a lecture, then, will be as follows:

		Time Examples
Episode 1	Lecture	5 minutes
Episode 2	Questions for clarification	*
Episode 3	Lecture continues	7 minutes
Episode 4	Questions for clarification	*
Episode 5	Lecture continues	5 minutes
Episode 6	Questions for clarification	*

In this case the teacher needs 17 minutes to deliver the subject matter. The time for asking questions for clarification will depend on the number of learners who ask questions and will be regulated by the teacher.

If you identify a different condition for delivering a lecture, apply the decision analysis and identify the place of the episode and its proximity to a landmark style.

An Episode with Flash Cards. The use of flash cards in teaching the identification of words, numbers, shapes, colors, and so on is quite common in elementary school classes. If this episode is conducted in a manner where the teacher makes *all* the decisions, then it is a Style A episode. However, if a teacher calls the learners to sit in a semicircle around him/her in order to establish a more cozy climate for the exercise, the learners will make location and posture decisions (which in this case do not interfere with the accomplishment of the objectives). This episode, therefore, does not represent the landmark Style A, but it certainly reflects the essence of the style. Hence this episode is designated as canopy $\widehat{A}$.

A Film Showing. In an episode of showing a film, there are three decision makers: the teacher, the learner, and—in effect—the film. When we analyze and identify who makes which decisions about what and when, we find one of four distributions of decision making occurs. These are described below as options 1, 2, 3, and 4. Note that in each option the analysis applies only to the *showing* time, not the time before or after the showing.

Option 1. In option 1, the learner makes no decisions. The decision analysis looks like this:

Film's Decisions	*Teacher's Decisions*	*Learner's Decisions*
Subject matter	Selection of subject	None
Order	matter	
Pace and rhythm of	Starting time	
presenting the	Posture of learners	
subject matter	Location for learners	
Interval	Attire and appearance	
Duration	(teacher or	
Stopping time	institutional	
	decision)	
	Starting time	
	Not to permit	
	questions for	
	clarification	
	Not to give individual	
	and private feedback	

When this condition exists, the episode is much closer to Style A than to Style B. This episode is placed, therefore, under the canopy of $\widehat{A}$.

Option 2. There is also another possible distribution of decisions in which the learner makes *some* of the nine decisions. The analysis of decisions in option 2 presents a different picture:

Film's Decisions	*Teacher's Decisions*	*Learner's Decisions*
Subject matter	Choice of subject	Location
Order	matter	Posture
Pace and rhythm of	Starting time	Attire and appearance
presenting the subject	Not to permit	
matter	questions for	
Interval	clarification	
Duration	Not to give individual	
Stopping time	and private feedback	

When a film is shown under this condition, the episode is placed slightly away from Style A and closer to Style B. It is designated as $\widehat{B}$.

Option 3. In the third option the teacher deliberately stops the film after a particular scene in order to ask factual questions and to provide time for the learner to ask questions for clarification. The teacher then continues to roll the film to the next scene, then stops again for questions, and so on. The analysis of decisions will look like this:

Film's Decisions	*Teacher's Decisions*	*Learner's Decisions*
Subject matter	Choice of subject matter	Location
Order	Starting time	Posture
Pace and rhythm	Stopping time	Attire and appearance
Duration	Interval, providing time for learners' questions for clarification	Asking questions for clarification
	Feedback to learner is possible during the pause	

The third option shifts more decisions to the learner, making this episode even closer to Style B. Its style, therefore, is designated $\widehat{B}$.

Option 4. Option 4 is technically the same as option 3. The difference is that the teacher asks questions that produce divergent responses—that is, questions that do not seek one factual correct response (see Chapter 11, "Style H").

Other Episodes. The examples given so far illustrate the analysis procedure that can be used with any episode in order to place it in the Spectrum. The episodes listed below, all representing $\widehat{A}$ and $\widehat{B}$ styles, are very common in classrooms. You are invited to apply the analysis procedure to these episodes, establishing their purposes (objectives), and determining which of the two landmark styles they most nearly resemble.

- Working in groups
- Activities in learning centers
- Assignments asking learners to answer 10 out of 15 questions
- Questions with multiple factual answers
- Writing each of the spelling words in a sentence
- Learners going to the chalkboard
- Preparing flash cards for spelling words
- Seatwork for a part of the class while the teacher is engaged in reading with one group
- Learners presenting oral book reports
- Story time—teacher or learner reading to others
- "Fast and accurate" activities
- Silent reading
- Spelling bee

Each landmark style has its purpose, and the specific objectives of the style define its purpose. The same is true for episodes that are under the canopies of various styles. Regardless of the different labels that are often imposed on such episodes, the analysis of the decisions yields a similar structure for many diverse activities under a particular canopy such as $\widehat{B}$. (By the way, it is interesting to note that about 85 percent of classroom episodes fall under the canopy of Style $\widehat{B}$.) This means that the objectives reached by these episodes are quite similar and not as varied as the superimposed labels might imply. Knowing this helps prevent the confusion that is sometimes caused when different labels are attached to the same activity in order to comply with the day's vogue. The analysis of the episode's decision structure yields a more objective picture of what the episode is or is not.

Assets and Liabilities of Canopy Episodes

In addition to performing the decision analysis it is useful to analyze the assets and liabilities of episodes. When we use the criterion of *degree of individual participation* in the episode, we find that in a landmark style, *each* learner is engaged in each of the decisions delineated by the style. The *structure* of the landmark style provides this intrinsic condition. (Obviously we are not talking right now about some learners, who for one reason or another, are not engaged in the episode.) Because *all* the learners are engaged in the decisions of that style they reap the *assets* of that style. In some episodes under a canopy, however, it is not known if the learners are engaged in the decisions. Therefore, it is important to understand the assets and liabilities of the canopy episodes in order to place parameters on the liabilities of these episodes and thus maximize their assets. To learn how this is done, let us examine the assets and liabilities of two commonly encountered canopy episodes: (1) the lecture and (2) the film showing.

The Lecture. The following are some potential assets and liabilities of any lecture:

Assets	*Liabilities*
1. New materials can be presented.	1. The learner may become overloaded.
2. Time is used efficiently.	
3. Learners get specific facts.	2. The pace and rhythm may not be appropriate for all students.
4. The subject matter is as clear as the ability of the lecturer; there is no "contamination" by inaccurate contributions of the learners.	3. The lecture may be too long.
	4. The lecture may be boring when delivered by a phlegmatic lecturer.

5. Information can be delivered to a large number of students at the same time.
6. The lecture can be very stimulating when delivered by a charismatic lecturer

5. The duration of the lecture may be beyond the attention span of some students.
6. The teacher may repeat a chunk of the lecture because one learner did not understand.
7. If students can ask questions at will, the questions may divert the course of the lecture.

The purpose of any lecture is to deliver new subject matter. The lecture is one of many options for achieving this purpose. Intrinsic to this teaching behavior are the assets and liabilities delineated above. The fact that lecture episodes have liabilities certainly does not invalidate the lecture as a teaching option; rather, it indicates that, to use this option successfully, the teacher should have a thorough understanding of the potential pitfalls. When using the lecture, the teacher should examine the list of liabilities and put parameters on any that apply to his/her situation. The teacher's task is to curb each liability so that students will reap maximum assets of the lecture. Indeed, the teacher's creative capacity can be recruited for designing these parameters. An example of how to handle liability 7 was offered on page 169.

The Film Showing. The assets and liabilities of showing a film are listed below:

Assets
1. Presents subject matter expertly.
2. Motivates.
3. Introduces new subject matter.
4. Entertains.
5. Is sequenced.
6. Is predictable.
7. Focuses the attention of learners.
8. One picture is worth 1000 words.
9. Is authoritative.
10. Uses another mode of communication.
11. Expands on teacher's work.
12. Provides a change of pace.
13. Takes the learner "out of the classroom."

Liabilities
1. Questions can't be asked.
2. Information may be dated.
3. Feedback is limited.
4. Information can be inappropriate.
5. Learner may only appear to be listening.
6. Film may be too long.
7. Equipment may break down.
8. Learners may daydream.
9. Subject matter may be over the heads of some learners.
10. Teacher can't always preview film.
11. Learners sometimes have to endure opinion and propaganda.
12. Teacher does not know how much the learner got out of it.

14. Teaches things other than subject matter.
15. Establishes a model.
16. Provides a vicarious experience.
17. Can repeat the performance exactly the same way.
18. Presents a visual image of aesthetics—e.g., ballet, gymnastics.
19. Presents the totality of a cultural event—e.g., a dramatic play, an ethnic festival, the Olympics.
20. Inflames the imagination in adventure films, love stories, etc.
21. Recreates historical events
22. Affects people's opinions— e.g., propaganda, commercials.

13. Episode is hard to make up if learner was absent.
14. There is opportunity for deviant behavior—e.g., talking, sleeping, eating.
15. Learners cannot retrieve what they have seen.

The teacher who knows these assets and liabilities can do much to reduce the liabilities in order to reach the objectives. For example, preparing questions for the learners so they can focus on specific information will place limits on liabilities 5, 8, 12, and 14. Similarly using a pause during the movie for learners to fill in the information will place limits on liabilities 1, 2, 4, 9, and 11. Can you think of any other solutions to reduce the liabilities?

THE DEMONSTRATION (MODELING)

Since cluster A–E represents the human capacity for *reproduction* of known knowledge, the presentation of tasks in Styles A–E must be done with as much precision as possible. This can be accomplished by the use of the demonstration as a mode of communication. Primarily, a demonstration tells the learner *what* to do and *how* to do it. It presents a concrete model for replication and creates an image—visual and auditory—of the expected performance. A demonstration, therefore, has the following characteristics:

1. It presents a concrete model or an image of the activity—it tells the learner what to do.
2. It establishes, via this model, the performance standard for the learner— it shows the learner how to do it.
3. It can present the entire activity, parts of it, or any combination of the parts.

4. It can be done in a visual mode (e.g., activities in sports, in the use of tools), in an auditory mode (activities in music, in speaking another language), or in a combination of these two (in most subject areas).
5. It is quite rapid.
6. It saves time. A clear demonstration provides for cognitive economy. It takes guessing out of the performance, reduces potential errors, and increases the possibility of accurate replication.
7. It creates two kinds of safe conditions for the learner:
    a. A *safe physical environment* in the chemistry lab, in industrial arts classes, in physical education, in home economics classes, in outdoor education experiences.
    b. A *safe emotional climate* in all subject matter areas. The learner knows quite specifically what is expected of him/her. Demonstrating a model, particularly in the initial stages of learning something new, provides great comfort and security for most people.

All subject matter areas consist of some tasks that require a demonstration of the particular skill, its details, and the correct sequence of behaviors. In preparing the episode, the teacher should examine the tasks to be performed to decide which ones call for a demonstration and which method of presentation is likely to be most effective. Examples of experiences that merit the use of a demonstration are shown in Table 9.1. The demonstration can be presented to the learners by a person or by means of various technologies. Demonstrations are often done by the teacher, the coach, or a student who can perform the task. Or they may be presented via a videotape, an audiotape, a film, photographs (in books, on task sheets, on wall posters, etc.), slides, film loops, or a computer.

Teacher's and Learner's Roles

Since the impact of a demonstration (modeling) is so powerful and effective, the teacher must be rather careful and precise when demonstrating a task in Styles A–E. An erroneously or sloppily demonstrated task unfortunately becomes the model for the learner in that episode. When the demonstration is delegated to other people or technologies, the teacher should exercise the same caution to make certain that the demonstration will depict the desired model.

The role of the learner during a demonstration is to observe, to listen, to ask questions for clarification, and then to participate in practicing the task within the decision structure of the style used in the given episode.

FORMS OF FEEDBACK

Feedback is the information provided to the learner during and/or after the performance of a task. This information usually tells the learner how the job

TABLE 9.1. EXPERIENCES THAT MERIT DEMONSTRATION

Type of Experience	Specific Examples
Learning a language	Pronounciation of words in one's own language; in another language
Learning social manners	Table manners; social interaction
Using some toys	
Using tools	Computer, food processor, electric saw
Using scientific instruments	Microscope, various chemical analyzers
Playing musical instruments	Piano, violin, trumpet
Participating in sports	Initial steps in learning almost any new sport
Participating in cultural activities	Rehearsals for plays, concerts, festivals, parades, graduation ceremonies
Perpetuating tradition	National, regional, ethnic, or family rituals
Participating in religious ceremonies	Weddings, specific services
Learning to perform certain tasks in every job	Sales techniques; setting tables in a restaurant; various plumber's skills; being a receptionist; stacking the shelves in a supermarket; organizing procedures in a law office, a dentist's office

was done—it serves as an assessment of the performance. This information can be delivered to the learner via several modes of communication: symbols, gestures, and verbal behavior.

Symbols are represented by letter grading (A, B, C, etc.), by numbers (1–10), by percentages (0–100%), by awards (for first place, second place, etc.), by ☺ , ☹ . These symbols represent scales on which individual learners are placed. *Gestures* (often called *body language*) are represented by head movements, facial expressions, hand movements, and finger configurations. *Verbal behavior* is represented by various words and phrases, projecting meanings and connotations, which can be changed when spiced with different intonations or cultural interpretations.

Regardless of the mode of communication, there are four *forms* of feedback:

1. Value statements (positive or negative)
2. Corrective statements
3. Neutral statements
4. Ambiguous statements

Each of these forms has its own structure, purpose, and implications. All, however, share the following characteristics:

- They can serve as motivation under varying conditions.
- They can encourage or discourage.

TABLE 9.2. IDENTIFYING VALUE STATEMENTS

Statement	Criterion: Contains a Value Word
"You typed the paragraph **well**, Bobbi."	well
"**Very good**, Mike, you sang it **beautifully**."	very good; beautifully
"I **liked** what you did."	liked
"This is much **better**."	better
"You have a **perfect** paper."	perfect
"I don't **like** your work."	like
"This is incomplete."	—
"You could have done this **better**."	better
"Next time do it this way."	—
"Jason, try it again."	—
"Go back and read the directions, Willis."	—
"Your pronunciation of the French words is **inadequate**."	inadequate
"This was an **excellent** example of the Romantic period."	excellent

- They can change behavior.
- They can affect the improvement of learning.

Identifying the Forms

Value Statements. The single *criterion* for the value statement form of feedback is the presence of a value word like *good* or *bad*. Read the following examples of feedback heard in classrooms and, based on this criterion, try to determine which are value statements:

- "You typed the paragraph well, Bobbi."
- "Very good, Mike, you sang it beautifully."
- "I liked what you did."
- "This is much better."
- "You have a perfect paper."
- "I don't like your work."
- "This is incomplete."
- "You could have done this better."
- "Next time do it this way."
- "Jason, try it again."
- "Go back and read the instructions, Willis."
- "Your pronunciation of the French words is inadequate."
- "This was an excellent example of the Romantic period."

Now look at Table 9.2, which analyzes the statements against the criterion. A boldface value word indicates that the statement belongs in this form of feedback. Statements that do not have a value word belong to a different form of feedback.

It is possible to analyze every feedback statement and determine whether or not it belongs in this form by looking for value words. Sometimes the value word is *positive* and at other times it is *negative; nevertheless,* it projects a value.

Corrective Statements. There are two criteria for identifying corrective statements:

1. The feedback refers to an error. Examples: "You misspelled the last two words." "There is an error here." "This is incorrect."
2. The feedback includes the identification of the error and the correction. Example: "Shaw did not write Othello; Shakespeare did." Sometimes only the correction is offered and the identification of the error is implied. Example: "The answer is 21." This statement offers the correct answer, but it also implies that the answer offered by the learner was incorrect.

Keeping these two criteria in mind, read the following statements and decide which of them are corrective:

- "Risto, 6 times 7 is not 45. It is 42."
- "Jane, this is not the correct definition of CPR."
- "Mike, next time when scuba diving, breathe out continuously as you surface."
- "Incorrect!"
- "Tim, this answer should be: There are 21 counties in New Jersey."
- "You are wrong!"
- "Wally, your answer to question 3 is incorrect. The largest country in the Western Hemisphere is Canada."
- "This is not the way I want it done."
- "Don't do that any more."
- "You could have done it better, Pipsa."
- "You have five shapes in your drawing. The task calls for only three, Zondra."

Now look at Table 9.3, which analyzes each statement against the criteria.

Neutral Statements. Examine the following feedback statements:

- "I see that you finished the math problems."
- "You have done your work."
- "This is a story about dogs."
- "I see that you like the color blue."

TABLE 9.3. INDENTIFYING CORRECTIVE STATEMENTS

	Criteria	
Statement	**Refers to an Error**	**Identifies the Correction**
"Risto, 6 times 7 is not 45. It is 42."	√	√
"Jane, this is not the correct definition of CPR."	√	
"Mike, next time when scuba diving, breath out continuously as you surface."	(implied)	√
"Incorrect!"	√	
"Tim, this answer should be: There are 21 counties in New Jersey."	(implied)	√
"You are **wrong**!"	(Belongs to value statements.)	
"Wally, your answer to question 3 is incorrect. The largest country in the Western Hemisphere is Canada."	√	√
"This is not the way I want it done."	(Belongs to ambiguous statements.)	
"Don't do that any more."	√	
"You could have done it **better**, Pipsa."	(Belongs to value statements.)	
"You have five shapes in your drawing. The task calls for only three, Zondra."	√	

- "You used five different shapes in your design."
- "This is one possible answer."
- "I can see that you are angry."
- Nodding the head.
- A soft grunt "mmm. . . ."
- "Yes."
- "True."
- "You worked half an hour on this."

All these statements share one thing in common: they acknowledge the performance, often by describing some element of it. They do not judge nor do they correct. Note, however, that the tone of voice can affect the perceived meanings of some of these neutral statements, and move them to another form of feedback.

The feedback statement, "That's correct," belongs to the neutral form because it acknowledges, it does not correct anything, and it does not project any value. It states the facts about that answer.

Ambiguous Statements. Examine the following feedback statements (some of which are formulated as questions):

- "You have an error on this page."
- "Are you sure it's correct?"

- "That's one way of putting it."
- "Would you do it again?"
- "Try it again."
- "Did you look at this carefully?"
- "Do it if you want to."
- "We'll get back to it."
- "Tell me about it."
- "I see you did something right."

The common characteristic of these statements is the ambiguity of the information. The learner does not know the real meaning of the statements and is forced to guess the teacher's intent. This is not helpful and often causes frustration.

In daily usage of the language, ambiguous phrases are often safe in social interaction. From the pedagogical point of view, however, ambiguous feedback can hinder efficient learning. It may also suggest to the learner that the teacher lacks knowledge of the task, is not clear about the evaluation criteria, and is not sure about the corrective action.

Perhaps the most prevalent pair of ambiguous feedback phrases are "not bad" and "pretty good." Neither statement reflects a commitment by the teacher; neither offers the learner clear and concrete information about the performance of the task. These linguistic modifiers maintain a safety zone for the teacher but keep the learner in a state of ambiguity.

Assets and Liabilities of Different Forms of Feedback

In analyzing the possible assets and liabilities of each form of feedback, the questions to consider are: What are the purposes of each form of verbal behavior? What does it do *for* the learner? What does it do *against* the learner?

Value Statements.   There are two general types of value statements: positive and negative. The use of *positive value statements* has the following assets and liabilities:

Assets
1. It is pleasing to hear praise about one's performance.
2. It is rewarding and reinforcing for the learner.
3. It usually ensures repeated good performance.
4. It lets the learner know how the teacher feels about him/her at that time.

Liabilities
1. Continuous and lavish positive value feedback tends to lose its effectiveness. The student learns quite quickly that any attempt, any

performance, will be met with rewarding feedback. Some teachers habitually bestow superlatives on their students. Every little poem is wonderful, every statement of opinion is good, every painting is beautiful. These words soon lose their meanings.

2. The learner may become emotionally *dependent* on value feedback for every task. This, in turn, may enhance the need to always be the best, which is quite difficult to accomplish.

3. Frequent and continuous positive value statements create a condition of *reciprocal dependency*. The learner becomes dependent on the teacher, who is the dispenser of the rewards, and the teacher becomes dependent on the student, who is the grateful receiver of what the teacher offers. This situation can be emotionally very soothing; however, it stands as an obstacle for developing some degree of independence and self-satisfaction.

The use of *negative value statements* has the following assets and liabilities:

Assets
1. It informs the learner about the value system that the teacher uses.
2. It may temporarily stop unwanted behavior.
3. It reminds the learner that negative value words are a part of reality.

Liabilities
1. It is not pleasing to hear.
2. It can become rather oppressive to the learner when used continually. One can hear only so many times how "bad" one is, how "poorly" one reads, how "terrible" one's handwriting is, and so on. Eventually one ceases to hear it and no change in the behavior can be expected. (It is important for the teacher to consider the *frequency* and the *magnitude* of value words employed for feedback.)
3. The learner may perceive this feedback in reference to him/herself rather than in reference to the errors made in the subject matter performance.

Corrective Statements. It was pointed out above that there are two types of corrective feedback: (1) statements in which an error is referred to and (2) statements in which the error is identified (if only by implication) and corrected. The principle *asset* of the first type is that it provides the learner with the opportunity to reexamine the area of difficulty. This type has two *liabilities:*

1. If the learner cannot correct the error, frustration may set in.
2. The learner may stay on the problem too long.

Feedback in which the incorrect performance is identified and the correction is offered has the following assets:

1. The correct information is available.
2. The learner can focus on the area where the error is identified.
3. There is no guesswork.
4. Correct performance is more likely to occur.

This type of feedback has only one significant *liability:* The learner does not have the chance to come up with the correction by him/herself.

Neutral Statements. Neutral feedback offers the following assets and liabilities:

Assets
1. It indicates that the teacher acknowledges the performance.
2. It opens the door for more communication between the teacher and some learners. (An initial neutral statement is less threatening to some learners.)
3. It decrease the learner's dependency on the teacher.
4. It can serve as a face-saving technique at a time of tension or conflict.
5. It delays the need for immediate resolution of a situation.
6. It weans learners from expecting value or corrective statements all the time.
7. It can promote the development of self-evaluation.
8. It permits the learner the option of making a value statement about his/her own work, independent of the teacher's view.

Liabilities
1. It may be awkward for both teacher and learner when initially used.
2. Initially it may be confusing to the learner who is accustomed to receiving corrective and/or value feedback.
3. It may cause some learners to prod the teachers for their opinions— for value statements. They will say: "Yes, but how do *you* like it?"
4. It may cause some learners to feel that the teacher does not care.

Ambiguous Statements. Ambiguous feedback has one major asset: It creates a safe climate in some social situations. Its major *liability* is that it interferes with efficient learning and precise performance of tasks.

The Focus of the Feedback Forms

Another difference among the feedback forms emerges when one asks the question: Who or what is *in focus* when each feedback form is in use?

Value Feedback	Corrective Feedback
Projects judgment	Identifies errors or problems
Expresses positive or negative feeling	Identifies the correction
Expresses and, at times, imposes a particular value system	Invites learners to redo the task
Inculcates values	Helps reduce errors
Improves performance	Clarifies subject matter details, standards of performance, and proper behavior
Develops dependency between teacher and learner	Improves skills
Focus: The teacher	Focus: The task

Neutral Feedback	Ambiguous Feedback
Acknowledges the performance and the learner	Creates a safe climate in some social situations
Identifies what happened—is descriptive	Does not offer precise information to the learner
States facts	Hinders efficient learning
Projects a sense of objectivity	
Is nonjudgmental	
Indicates that the teacher is listening	
Saves face; in moments of tension prevents a flare-up	
Focus: The learner	Focus: The teacher

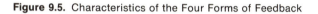

Figure 9.5. Characteristics of the Four Forms of Feedback

When value feedback is in use, the *teacher* is in focus. Although the learner is the receiver of the feedback and is the one who is affected by it, the teacher is in focus because the feedback emanates from the teacher's value system.

When corrective feedback is in use, the focus is on the *task* or subject matter. It is the incorrect performance of the task that invites the use of this form.

When neutral feedback is in use, the focus is on the *learner*. This form of feedback acknowledges the learner and the situation without judgment. It expresses acceptance of the learner for what he/she has done. The learner then, has to deal with this acknowledgment.

When ambiguous feedback is in use, the focus is again on the *teacher*. This form reflects a lack of clarity emanating from the teacher and causes the learner to focus on interpreting or guessing at the teacher's meaning. Figure 9.5 offers a summary of characteristics of the four forms of feedback. Since each of these feedback forms has its particular influence on the learner, no one kind of feedback is exclusively desirable. The subject matter, the situation, the objective, the learner and the teaching style suggest the desirable kind of feedback.

Correct/Incorrect versus *Right/Wrong*

While focusing on the issue of precise *verbal behavior* in feedback, and its impact on the learner, it is useful to examine the use of two pairs of words so commonly used in feedback and so often interchanged: *correct/incorrect* and *right/wrong*. Have you ever listened to the way in which these are used? Have you noticed the frequency of their use? Which pair of words, would you guess, is used with higher frequency?

Our experience and analysis of verbal behavior indicate that *right/wrong* is the pair used with higher frequency when people offer feedback to someone who performs something. We find this disturbing because these terms are meant to attribute moral value, yet they are often used inappropriately.

The primary definitions of *right* and *wrong* in the *Random House Dictionary* (1973) connect these words with morality and ethics. (Subsequent entries suggest colloquial meanings and uses.) Thus, it is inappropriate to say to a child who performed 7 × 3 = 22: "You are wrong." The multiplication exercise has nothing to do with "rightness" or "wrongness." It has nothing to do with morality. The answer is either correct or incorrect. Therefore, the appropriate feedback should be: "Seven times 3 equals 22 is incorrect."

Many subject matter tasks in the school curricula are factual and therefore have correct or incorrect responses. Only when the response by the learner is within the domain of morality (and the moral standards have been clearly specified) could the *right/wrong* pair be used as appropriate feedback.

The connotation of being right or wrong has a rather powerful affective implication to the learner. Consider what it means to a learner who hears these words when spelling, adding, drawing, dribbling, mixing chemicals, pronouncing new words in another language, and so on.

ORGANIZATIONAL FORMATS

One of the questions that confronts every teacher in every class is: How do I organize the learners, the time, the space, the materials? Moreover, how do I organize my class so that we (teacher and learners) can reach the intended objectives? Several guidelines need to be considered when decisions are made about class organization. This organization must accommodate:

a. Best delivery of subject matter
b. Maximum participation by every learner
c. Best conditions for feedback

The overall purpose of class organization is to provide for effective teaching and effective learning. One aspect of this effectiveness is the optimum ratio of number of people : unit of time : unit of space or equipment. Optimum ratio means maximum engagement in the task by each learner per unit of time. This aspect of effectiveness has been termed *time-on-task* or *academic learning time* (ALT).

In the context of the Spectrum, time-on-task varies in accordance with the objectives of each style and the organizational format that accommodates the style.

The Whole Class Format

When the objective of an episode is standardization and synchronization of performance, the most efficient way to achieve the optimum ratio is to engage the whole class in the same task at the same time. The teaching behavior and the learning behavior that will accomplish this is Style A, the command style. (For some tasks, episodes in the canopy of $\widehat{A}$ will accomplish similar results.)

Formats Providing for Individual Differences

When the objective of an episode is to provide for *individual differences* (Styles B–E), four types of organizational format are available. Each is described below.

The Single Station/Single Task Format. In the single station/single task format each learner selects a location or *station*. At this station the learner performs only one task. In the classroom, this organizational format is being used when learners sit at their desks (or at any location they select) reading a number of pages. In the gymnasium, it is being used when each learner does an exercise (as demonstrated) at a location of his/her choice. The assigned task may be different for different learners but each learner is engaged in one task.

The Single Station/Multiple Tasks Format. In the single station/multiple tasks format each learner selects a location and performs more than one task at that location. This format is being used when learners sit at their desks (or other locations) engaged, first, in reading a given number of pages and then, second, in answering questions on a task sheet.

The Multiple Stations/Single Task Format. In the multiple stations/single task format each learner selects the initial location or station and performs the task called for at that station; then the learner moves to the next station and performs the task assigned to that station. This is the format being used in a biology class, for example, when several stations are set up around the room, each containing certain bones of the skeletal system, and the learner moves from station to station identifying the bones at each station and writing his/her name on a task sheet. In the gymnasium this format is used when the learner performs a particular exercise or a skill at one station and then moves on to do the next exercise at the next station. This format teaches learners about traffic flow in the classroom, lab, or gymnasium.

The Multiple Stations/Multiple Tasks Format. The multiple stations/ multiple tasks format is similar to the previous format except that the learner performs several tasks at each station. The tasks at the station can be related to each other representing *sequential* parts of the subject matter, or they can be unrelated because the planning calls for several different objectives at the given station. In a physics class, for example, the learner might have three tasks to perform at the first station:

1. Set up the equipment for Hooke's law
2. Perform the experiment as prescribed
3. Record the results and verify the law

When the learner is done he/she moves on to the next station to perform the tasks assigned to a different piece of equipment. This format is very useful in labs, gymnasiums, shop classes, and home economics classes, where the number of duplicate pieces of equipment may be limited.

Note that these five formats are *not* different styles; they are merely different ways to organize people and their relationship to tasks, time, space and equipment. The purpose is always to be productive by reaching the objectives of the episode.

Using Multiple Stations Formats

In a junior high school a science class is in progress. Twenty-five students congregate in groups of five around five available microscopes. The microscopes are placed on five desks in one area of the room. The task is to identify and label several parts of a leaf.

Now let us analyze this episode and identify what happens under such conditions. Let's assume that it takes an average learner 4–5 minutes to complete this task. That means that the *fifth* learner in the group has to wait 16–20 minutes before the microscope will be available. Moreover, learners who have finished the task must wait until the last person has finished. This is, indeed, an inefficient, wasteful use of time that invites deviant behavior. When this kind of episode is repeated during the week, many hours are lost and that becomes the *learner's perception of what to expect in class.*

Not only is time wasted by this arrangement, but—perhaps more important—the affective climate that evolves is one of goofing off, boredom, and a sense of little accomplishment. Often this is the source of statements like: "We don't learn anything in this class." Such episodes evoke a poor attitude toward the subject matter.

Often one hears teachers blame the situation on the scarcity of equipment ("I have only five microscopes") or the learners ("This is my bad class; these children are undisciplined."). In reality, however, *the teacher's inappropriate decisions* caused the problem.

One way to alleviate this situation is to organize the class by using the multiple stations/single task format or the multiple stations/multiple tasks format. In the science class, for example, it is possible to engage one learner, or two learners at most, at each microscope. The rest of the class will be engaged in other *related* tasks at different stations. The class organization might look like this:

Station 1: Using the miscroscope (5 miscroscopes, 5 learners)
Station 2: Drawing the leaf, its parts, colors, etc. (5 learners)
Station 3: Labeling the parts on a ditto sheet (5 learners)
Station 4: Reading about the structure of the leaf (5 learners)
Station 5: Comparing leaves from different trees (5 learners)

Other solutions are possible, but the guiding principle for efficiency will always be the *optimum ratio* of number of learners : unit of time : unit of equipment. When this ratio is achieved the following benefits result:

1. Each learner has the opportunity to be on-task most or all the time.
2. The task at each station is done *individually*. The learner knows what he/she can and cannot do, and so does the teacher.
3. The potential for deviant behavior is reduced.
4. Considerably more involvement with the same subject matter via different tasks and activities is possible.
5. Efficient use of time, space, and equipment results in better learning.
6. Learners' attitudes about the subject matter and the teacher become more positive.

The multiple stations format can also be used for assigning tasks from different subject matter to different stations. This *learning centers* format is quite prevalent in many elementary schools. It provides for concurrent activities in several subject matter areas. Learners can be engaged in language arts at one station, in math at another station, and in viewing a film strip about science at a third station. At each station the episode is done in a teaching style appropriate for the objectives of the subject matter at that station. In this case the class is characterized by the use of multiple stations, single or multiple tasks, and multiple styles. The rotation system is decided by the teacher by considering the individuals in the class, the schedule for other activities, the plan for the week, and so on.

THE CLASSROOM COMMUNICATION MODEL

The Classroom Communication Model helps answer the questions: How does one deliver the task? What forms and means of communication are available for the delivery of subject matter? It is designed to show the options that exist when communication takes place.

The Six Components of Communication

As shown in Table 9.4, the model identifies six components that are intrinsic to any classroom communication: (1) content, (2) mode, (3) action, (4) medium, (5) direction, and (6) time. Each of these components is described in detail below. Note that the model is descriptive, but does not tell anything about the quality, logic, or truthfulness of the content being communicated.

Content. The first component of any communication is its content. Communication always conveys *something* from one person to another—an idea, a question, a feeling. In the Classroom Communication Model the various items of communication are categorized as information (facts), knowledge (facts plus elaboration of various kinds), and feelings. The category of "Other" is available if another kind of content is identified.

Mode. The second component of any communication is its mode. The model distinguishes three modes of communicating information, knowledge, and feelings: audio, visual, and tactile.

Action. The third component of any communication is the action—that is, the type of activity engaged in when a particular mode is in use. Each mode is represented by two complementary actions:

1. The audio mode is represented by speaking (or other sound systems), which is the output of content, and by hearing, which is the input of content.
2. The visual mode is represented by showing (output) and by seeing (input).

TABLE 9.4. THE CLASSROOM COMMUNICATION MODEL

1 Content	2 Mode	3 Action	4 Medium	5 Direction	6 Time
Information	Audio	→Speaking	Teacher's voice	T → L	Min. ↔ Max.
Knowledge		Other sound systems (output)	Tape recorder	T ← L	Duration
Feelings			Record player	T ↔ L	Frequency
Other		→Hearing (input)	Telephone	L ↔ L	Immediacy
			Other	T ↔ T	
				T ↔ M	
				S ↔ M	
Information	Visual	→Showing (output)	Teacher's performance model	T → L	Min. ↔ Max.
Knowledge			Teacher's gestures	T ← L	
Feelings		→Seeing (input)	Films	T ↔ L	
Other			Television	L ↔ L	
			Books	T ↔ T	
			Computer	T ↔ M	
			Other	L ↔ M	
Information	Tactile	→Touching (output)	Teacher's Touch	T → L	Min. ↔ Max.
Knowledge			Human mediators	T ← L	
Feelings		Being touched (input)	Object mediators	T ↔ L	
Other			Other	L ↔ L	
				T ↔ T	

Adapted from Muska Mosston, *Teaching: From Command to Discovery* (Belmont, California: Wadsworth Publishing Co., 1972).

189

3. The tactile mode is represented by touching (output) and by being touched (input).

Medium. The fourth component of any communication is the medium that is used to convey its content. Somebody or something must deliver the information, the knowledge, or the feelings. The medium is always related to the mode of communication:

Audio Mode	*Visual Mode*	*Tactile Mode*
Teacher's voice	Teacher's performance	Teacher's touch
Learner's voice	model (visual	Learner's touch
Tape recorder	demonstration)	Human mediators (other
Record player	Teacher's gestures	people)
Telephone	Learner's performance	Object mediators (e.g.,
Computer	(visual aspects)	fabric samples, rough
	Films	vs. sanded wood)
	Filmstrips	
	Slide projector	
	Overhead projector	
	Books	
	Charts	
	Television	
	Computers	

Direction. Communication always flows in some direction; it flows from a *source* to a *receiver*. Both the teacher and the learner can serve as either the source or the receiver of information. The resulting directions of flow can be diagrammed as follows:

- T → L (teacher to learner)
- T ← L (learner to teacher)
- T ↔ L (teacher to learner *and* learner to teacher)
- L ↔ L (learner to learner)
- T ↔ T (teacher to teacher, when there are two or more teachers in the same class)

When equipment media (M) are used the directions of flow are similar (e.g., T → M, T ← M, T ↔ M). Information can flow from the teacher or learner to the media—for example, when a teacher talks into a tape recorder. Or information can flow from media to the teacher or learner—for example, when a learner receives information from slides, charts, television, or computer.

Time. The sixth component of any communication is time. All communication takes place at a particular time, and it always takes time to communicate. The time component has at least three dimensions:

1. *Immediacy*. This refers to the amount of time that elapses between the initiation of communication by the teacher and the response by the learner, or vice versa. (The same applies to communication between people and machines.)
2. *Frequency*. This refers to how often communication (or a particular type of communication) takes place.
3. *Duration*. This refers to the length of time required for a given communication.

Immediacy, frequency, and duration can range from minimum to maximum.

All communication has these six components, which can be interrelated in a variety of ways. The *options* are many, but the *sequence* is the same. One must, first, decide about *what* one wants to communicate (content) and then decide about the *mode* of communicating it—whether it will be done by audio, visual, or tactile means, or by some combination of these. Decisions about the subsequent components follow the suggested sequence: action, medium, direction, and time.

The Communication Set

The Classroom Communication Model can aid the teacher during the preimpact set while planning the episode, specifically the *delivery of the subject matter* and the *feedback*. A moment of thought about each of the six components and the relationships among them can enhance the clarity of communication during the delivery of the subject matter. Decisions can be quickly identified by choosing an option for each component and thus establishing the *communication set* for the given delivery of the subject matter. In the communication set shown in Table 9.5, we learn that the teacher made the following decisions:

1. Content: The subject matter to be delivered will be information (facts, dates, names of explorers, etc.).
2. Mode: It will be delivered in the audio mode.
3. Action: It will be delivered by speaking.
4. Medium: It will be conveyed by a tape recorder.
5. Direction: The teacher will be the source and the student will be the receiver.
6. Time: The length of time (duration) needed for the delivery of the taped subject matter is 10 minutes. Since learners will not be asked to

TABLE 9.5. A COMMUNICATION SET

Content	Mode	Action	Medium	Direction	Time
Information ⟶	Audio ⟶	Speaking ↘	Teacher Tape Recorder	T → L	Min. Max. Duration
Knowledge		Hearing	Record Player	T ← L	Immediacy
Feelings				T ↔ L	Frequency
Other					

respond and the tape will not be replayed, no further decisions are required for immediacy and frequency.

Identifying the communication set provides the teacher with the capacity to do three things:

1. Make a reasonable assessment about the efficacy of decisions *before* the episode begins.
2. Do an analysis and make a more accurate assessment *after* the episode has been completed. The analysis will tell whether or not this particular communication set reached the objective of the episode.
3. Vary the delivery of subject matter.

The Classroom Communication Model is descriptive. It offers guidelines for possible options in delivering tasks. The teacher must, in addition to selecting the communication set, decide about the quality, logic, and truthfulness of the content being communicated. These decisions are based on the teacher's knowledge, values, and thinking skills.

By considering the issues discussed in this chapter along with the unique characteristics of individual styles, teachers can enhance their ability to select the style that is most appropriate for a given set of objectives and to use that style in the most effective way.

CHAPTER 10

Style F: The Guided Discovery Style

The first style that engages the learner in discovery is Style F, the guided discovery style.[1] The essence of this style is a particular teacher-learner relationship in which the teacher's sequence of questions brings about a corresponding set of responses by the learner. Each question by the teacher elicits a single correct response that is *discovered* by the learner. The cumulative effect of this sequence—a converging process—leads the learner to discover the sought concept, principle, or idea.

OBJECTIVES OF STYLE F

Like the previous styles we have examined, Style F has both subject matter objectives and behavior objectives:

Subject Matter Objectives	*Behavior Objectives*
To discover the interconnection of steps within a given task	To cross the discovery threshold
To discover the "target"—the concept, the principle, or the idea	To engage the learner in the discovery of concepts and principles representing convergent thinking
	To engage the learner in a unique cognitive relationship with the teacher

---

[1] George Katona used this term and provided examples in his book *Organizing and Memorizing* (New York: Columbia University Press, 1949).

> To teach both teacher and learner
> about *cognitive economy*—that
> is, using *minimal, correct,* and
> *logical* steps to get to a target with
> minimum waste of cognitive output
> To develop an affective climate
> conducive to engagement in the
> act of discovery
> To provide the learner with the
> moment of ''Eureka''

THE ANATOMY OF STYLE F

In the guided discovery style the teacher makes all the decisions in the preimpact set. The main decisions are about the objectives, the target of the episode, and the design of the sequence of questions that will guide the learner to the discovery of the target.

In this style, more decisions are shifted to the learner in the impact set (Figure 10.1). The act of discovering the answers means that the learner makes decisions about parts of the subject matter within the topic selected by the teacher. The impact set is a sequence of corresponding decisions made by the teacher and the learner.

In the postimpact set, the teacher verifies the learner's response to each question (or clue). In some tasks, learners can verify the response for themselves. The roles of continuous, corresponding decisions in the impact and postimpact sets are unique to this style.

IMPLEMENTATION OF STYLE F

The description of an episode here will involve two parts: (1) a delineation of the teacher's and the learner's roles in the preimpact, impact, and postimpact set of decisions; and (2) an example that will illustrate this process.

	A	B	C	D	E	F
Preimpact	(T)	(T)	(T)	(T)	(T)	(T)
Impact	(T) $\longrightarrow$ (L)		(L_d)	(L) $\longrightarrow$ (L) $\longrightarrow$ (T_L)		
Postimpact	(T)	(T) $\longrightarrow$ (L_o) $\longrightarrow$ (L) $\longrightarrow$ (L) $\longrightarrow$ (T_L)				

Figure 10.1. The Shift from Style E to Style F

Teacher's and Learner's Roles

The Preimpact Set. The role of the teacher in the preimpact set is:

1. To make a decision about the specific target of the episode—the concept to be discovered by the learner.
2. To make a decision about the sequence of steps (questions) that will evoke a chain of small discoveries by the learner.
3. To make a decision about the size of each step.
4. To make a decision about setting the scene so that the learner is invited to participate in the process of guided discovery.

In making decisions 2 and 3, the teacher should keep in mind that each step is based on the response given to the previous step. This means that each step must be carefully weighed, judged, tried out, and then established as most efficient at this particular location in the sequence. It also means that there will be an internal connection between steps that is related to the *structure* of the subject matter. In order to design related steps the teacher needs to anticipate the possible responses that the learner may offer to a given question or clue. (See the section below, on "Selecting and Designing the Subject Matter.")

As in previous styles, the learner makes no decisions in the preimpact set.

The Impact Set. In the impact set the teacher's role is as follows:

1. To make a decision about asking the sequence of questions as designed in the preimpact set.
2. To make a decision about the first question that starts the whole journey.
3. To wait for the learner's response.
4. To offer feedback with some frequency (see the section below on "The Postimpact Set").
5. To make a decision about the speed of the questions in relationship to the pace and rhythm of the learner.
6. To acknowledge the achievement of the learner when he/she discovers the target.

The role of the learner in this set is:

1. To listen to the question.
2. To engage in seeking an answer to the question.
3. To discover the answer.
4. To receive periodic feedback from the teacher.
5. To listen to the next question.

Some elaboration is needed here. The direction-of-communication symbol for the impact set in Style F is T↔L. This indicates a continuous and reciprocal relationship between the teacher and the learner. In this set there is a great cognitive intimacy between the two. Each step in the sequence of questions represents a stimulus that triggers a small discovery by the learner that, in turn, prompts the teacher to ask the next question. Now, since the role of the teacher is to offer feedback with some reasonable frequency (offering it after every one of the first few answers usually serves as reassurance to the learner), we face here a unique situation where the impact and postimpact sets are deliberately interwined.

Because feedback is given during the impact phase, it is important for the teacher to exhibit the appropriate verbal behaviors of this style:

1. Never tell the answer.
2. Always wait for the learner's response.
3. Offer frequent feedback (a short "yes"; a nod; "Correct").
4. Maintain a climate of acceptance and patience.

Even if the student's response is incorrect or inadequate, the teacher can behave in an accepting manner by saying: "Let me ask the question in another way"; or "My question must not be clear; let me restate the question." The focus here is on the question, not the learner. A very special cognitive process is being developed and integrated with an emotional process of learning to be accepted and a willingness to speak up. This process must not be diminished by a harsh comment by the teacher. Any such comment not only interrupts the developing process in the responding student, but also curtails the flow of thoughts in the rest of the class. If failure is met with hostility, there is no sense in responding or being involved in discovery. The emotional and cognitive streams are quite visibly intertwined during the process of learning by guided discovery.

The impact phase in guided discovery is a delicate interplay of cognitive and emotional dimensions between teacher and student, both bound intimately and intricately to the subject matter. The tension and anticipation that develop at each step are relieved only when the final discovery has occurred. The student, without being given the answer, has accomplished the purpose, has found the unknown, has learned.

In the impact set, then, the teacher must be aware of the following factors:

1. The objective or the target
2. The direction of the sequence of steps
3. The size of each step
4. The interrelationship of the steps
5. The speed of the sequence
6. The emotions of the learner

The Postimpact Set. The role of the teacher in the postimpact set is to offer feedback to the learner with reasonable frequency. The frequent feedback reassures the learner that his/her answer to each question is acceptable, and that he/she is on the way to the discovery of the target.

The role of the learner in this set is:

1. To accept the feedback when offered by the teacher (or by a surrogate teacher—e.g., programmed materials, a computer, etc.).
2. To engage in self-verification if the feedback is built into the task.

The nature of the postimpact phase in guided discovery is unique to this style. In a sense, feedback is built into every step of the process during the impact set. The success of the learner at each step and the immediacy of positive feedback serve as a continuous motivating force for the learner to seek solutions. The final discovery of the target constitutes the intrinsic reward for the learner.

The immediacy of feedback, consisting of the teacher's accepting behavior in conjunction with approval of correct responses, has a potent social effect in a group situation. When this process begins to develop in a class, the willingness to participate and offer overt responses (verbal or physical) becomes contagious. It seems as if more and more students acquire the feeling of security and are less and less afraid to respond.

It should be kept in mind, however, that conducting an oral guided discovery episode with a group has its drawbacks. Since some students are faster in responding than others, they will become the discoverers of the answers and the rest of the class will remain in the role of receivers and will withdraw from participation. This is one of the hazards of this style. Therefore, guided discovery should not be used too frequently with a group. It is best to use it in a one-to-one situation. Although one feasible alternative is to use the written form of guided discovery, it is difficult to offer feedback after each response in this form unless computers are used. To repeat, this style is more effective when used in a one-to-one fashion.

An Example of Guided Discovery

Let us examine an episode involving children engaged in discovering a particular social concept. The target concept for this episode is *inclusion.* The children will be discovering the concept of "how to include everyone in the same task." In our discussion of Style E we *told* you about this concept. Now, let's follow the interaction between the teachers and the learners during the process of guided discovery.

- *Step 1:* The teacher asks two children to hold a rope for high jumping; invariably they will hold the rope horizontally at a given height (e.g., at hip level).

- *Step 2:* Before asking learners to jump over, the teacher asks the rope holders to *decrease* the height so that everybody can be successful.
- *Step 3:* After everyone has cleared the height, the teacher asks: "What shall we do now with the rope?" The answer is always "Raise it!" (The success of the first jump motivates all to continue.)
- *Step 4:* The teacher asks the rope holders to raise the rope *just a bit.* The jumping is resumed.
- *Step 5:* The teacher asks: "Now what?" The children will respond: "Raise it!"
- *Step 6:* Raising the rope two or three more times will create a new situation, a new reality. Some children *will not* be able to clear the height. In traditional situations, these children will be *eliminated* from the jumping. As the rope continues to be raised, there will be a constantly diminishing number of active participants. Participants will come to a realization of individual differences. However, the *design* that provides opportunity for all has not yet come about.
- *Step 7:* The teacher stops the jumping and tells the group that this design leads to exclusion. Now the teacher asks the group: "What can we do with the rope to create conditions for inclusion of all?" Usually one or both of the following solutions are proposed by the children: (a) Hold the rope higher at the two ends and let the rope dip in the center; (b) slant the rope—hold the rope high at one end and low at the other.
- *Step 8:* The teacher tells the children to slant the rope and asks the participants to jump over it. They will disperse and each individual will select the height where he/she can be successful. The same will occur in subsequent attempts. The results: All learners are included in the activity.

First, let us verify that this episode reached the objective sought. The objective was to create a condition where the learners will *discover* by themselves the way to use the rope for inclusion (not to say the word, but to discover the new condition). And, indeed, in step 7 the concept of the slanting rope was discovered by the learners themselves. The teacher did *not* tell them.

Now, let us proceed step by step to analyze the structure of this episode.

Steps 1 and 2 were used to establish the situation and set the scene. Without being told to do so, the participants held the rope horizontally because this is the way it has always been done. So far the participants relied on recall.

Step 3 called for the teacher to ask a question. The learners, in order to answer the question, had to engage in one of the cognitive operations— recall in this case. The children recalled from previous experiences jumping over a rope that the rope was always raised after every "inning," regardless of success or failure.

Steps 4, 5, and 6 verified the learners' experiences and brought them to a realization of *exclusion*. It set the scene for the next and pivotal step.

Step 7 called for the teacher to ask a question that created cognitive dissonance and engaged the learners in mediation. There is *always* a pause for mediation after this question. Learners are faced with the problem of reversing the condition of exclusion (which is familiar to them) to a condition of inclusion (which is, in this case, new to them). During the mediation period the learners were engaged in the cognitive operation of problem solving. The result of the mediation was the *discovery* of the *new* condition: Slanting the rope reversed the reality of the episode *from exclusion to inclusion*. And all this was performed by the learners, not by the teacher. The teacher was the activator during the first six steps, which set the scene gradually and sequentially. Then, in a moment of "Eureka," the learners discovered the answer.

SELECTING AND DESIGNING THE SUBJECT MATTER

Selecting the Task

As in all styles, the selection and the design of the task must be congruent with the objectives of the episode. In the guided discovery style, the teacher must consider the following five points before selecting the task for the particular episode:

1. Learners can discover ideas in the following categories:
   a. Concepts
   b. Principles (governing rules)
   c. Relationships among entities
   d. Order or system
   e. The reason (cause) for something
   f. Limits
   g. How to discover
2. The topic or the target to be discovered must be unknown to the learner. One cannot discover what one already knows.
3. The target to be discovered must not be a fact, a date, a specific word, a name, or a technical term. These categories of knowledge are learned by being told and/or shown.
4. Some religious, sexual, or political topics may not be appropriate for this style. Since guided discovery prompts learners to see and say things that are selected by the teacher, targets in these areas might conflict with the learner's background or personal preferences. Conflict and embarrassment are not the purpose of the episode and will not enhance the relationship between the teacher and the learner. Sensitive topics can be

discussed when an exchange of views takes place (e.g., in Style H); Style F, however, is not designed for this process.

5. The target must be both discoverable and worthwhile.

Designing the Task

Tasks for guided discovery are designed by adhering to the following principles:

1. The process is precipitated by a very meticulous series of stimuli; some are statements (during setting of the scene) and others are questions that elicit the discovery.
2. Each question is designed to elicit a small discovery, which is a single, correct response.
3. The questions proceed *in a very specific sequence*. This sequence ensures smooth sailing toward the target.
4. The small discoveries build on each other and accumulate until the learner discovers the target—the concept sought. This process represents the model of *convergent thinking*.

Figure 10.2 represents a typical structure for guided discovery. It describes the *sequence* of relationships between each stimulus (the question)

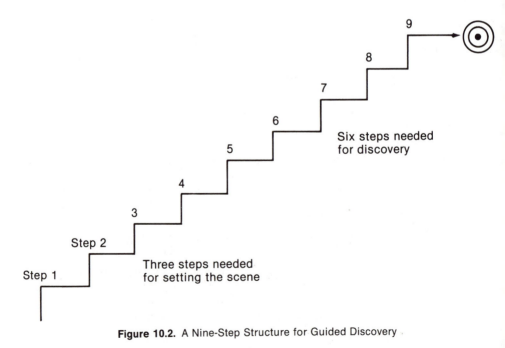

Figure 10.2. A Nine-Step Structure for Guided Discovery

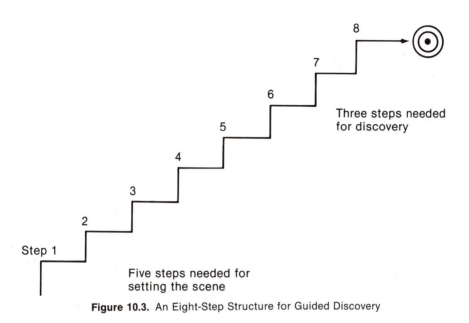

Figure 10.3. An Eight-Step Structure for Guided Discovery

and its corresponding response. The sequence in this case is composed of nine steps. The first three steps set the scene and the next six steps lead to the actual convergent discovery. Other sequences may have fewer or more steps and may have a different *ratio* between the number of steps designed for setting the scene and the number of steps designed for the convergent thinking. Figure 10.3 shows an eight-step sequence where more

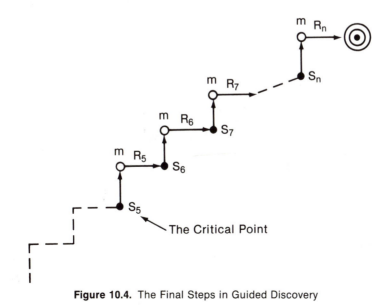

Figure 10.4. The Final Steps in Guided Discovery

steps are required for setting the scene and fewer steps are needed for discovery.

The purpose of setting the scene is to introduce the learner to the episode by starting from the known. This can be done in several ways:

1. By describing a situation or condition
2. By setting up particular equipment
3. By asking questions that invite known information (memory)

Setting the scene within the given subject matter prepares the learner for the next steps in the sequence, the convergent thinking. The *critical point* in the sequence of steps is the point of transition to questions (clues) that elicit discovery. This linkage between the two parts of the sequence occurs with the *first question* that triggers mediation (M). During mediation the learner moves from the known to the discovery of the unknown. From this point on, the teacher-learner relationship is represented by the S→D→M→R model, where at every step the learner is engaged in a cognitive operation other than memory. These steps continue until the final discovery—the "Eureka" moment. They are shown schematically in Figure 10.4.

Now regardless of how meticulously the sequence of questions is designed, there may be times when the student will go off on a tangent (Figure 10.5). This will be manifested by an incorrect response or a tangential response to a given question. The immediate treatment is to repeat the question (offering a second chance) and to wait for the learner's answer. If the second answer is still incorrect, it means that the question

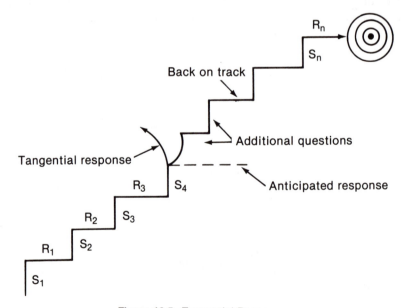

Figure 10.5. Tangential Responses

elicited a tangent. The tangent occurs due to one of two reasons: (1) the question is improperly designed; or (2) the step from the previous question is too large (Figure 10.6). Teachers who have become experienced in this process can at this moment emit an additional question that will bring the learner back on the track and allow the process to continue. If the teacher is inexperienced, the process is usually aborted. There is nothing to be gained by repeating a question over and over again. It will not produce the desired results because the error here is not the fault of the learner, but rather is due to the faulty design of the question. If the teacher persists in asking the question, the learner's cognitive dissonance, which is usually a positive force that induces production, will turn into negative feelings of frustration that will stop the engagement in discovery. It is better to tell the students: "We'll stop now; you have done well so far; I need to review some details for this episode. We'll continue some other time." This, or a similar face-saving device, is safer than continuing with a futile attempt that will only end with feelings of failure by both teacher and learner.

Designing the Sequence of Questions

One of the most difficult aspects of using the guided discovery style is designing the sequence of steps. It should be clear by now that any old questions in any order will not do the job! Four considerations should guide the design:

1. What is my objective? My target?
2. How do I set the scene?
3. What is my first question for discovery?
4. How can I be sure that the size of the steps is not too large?

Figure 10.6. The Ladder of Guided Discovery

TABLE 10.1. FORMAT FOR THE CONVERSION TECHNIQUE

If Taught by Style B	When Taught by Style F
Statement 1	Question 1, which will produce an answer equivalent to statement 1
Statement 2	Question 2, which will produce an answer equivalent to statement 2
Statement 3	Question 3, which will produce an answer equivalent to statement 3
Statement 4	Question 4, which will produce an answer equivalent to statement 4

Working Backwards. One technique for designing the sequence of discovery questions is to work backwards (Polya 1957). Start with the last question—the one that will produce the answer that is on target—then identify the question before the last one, the one before that one, and so on. This is the same technique that is often used for discovering the road from the starting point to the target location in a maze. Often one starts from the target and traces the road back to the starting point.

The Conversion Technique. Another and perhaps easier technique for designing the sequence of questions is the *conversion technique*. First, design a sequence of statements (not questions) as if you were teaching the episode in Style B (i.e., lecturing, telling, showing). Number and list these statements as shown in the left column of Table 10.1. Next, convert each statement into a question whose answer will be equivalent to the statement. Write these questions in the right column.

Table 10.2 shows how the conversion technique was used to develop a sequence of questions for a guided discovery episode in soccer. The target of this episode was *the toes*.

TABLE 10.2. AN EXAMPLE OF THE CONVERSION TECHNIQUE

If Taught by Style B	When Taught by Style F
Statement 1: "When you want to pass the ball to a player who is far from you, you need a long kick." (demonstrate)	Question 1: "What kind of kick is needed when you want to pass the ball to a player who is far from you?"
Statement 2: "When there is a player from the opposing team between you and your teammate, the ball must fly high."	Question 2: "If there is a player from the opposing team between you and your teammate, what must happen to the ball?"
Statement 3: "In order to raise the ball, the foot should be applied to the ball as low as possible."	Question 3: "Where should the force produced by the foot be applied to the ball in order to raise it off the ground?"
Statement 4: "In order to do this, use your toes. It is the most comfortable part of the foot that can get to the lowest part of the ball." (demonstrate)	Question 4: "Which part of the foot can comfortably get to the lowest part of the ball?"

In the same manner, almost *any* sequence can be converted from statements to questions. When you have finished the conversion, invite one student to spare a few minutes and try it out. If corrections or adjustments are needed, make them. Then try the corrected sequence with *another* student. Do not try it with the same student because he/she already knows a part of the sequence and perhaps even the target itself. For each trial engage a fresh mind.

When the sequence goes well several times in a row you will know that the design of steps is clean, and can smoothly guide each *individual* student to discover the target. However, if the process is not smooth, *record* the place where it goes off. If several students go off at the same place, you know that the preceding question needs to be redesigned. If several students in a row do not get to the target and go off at different places the *entire* sequence needs to be redesigned.

Examples of Episodes in Guided Discovery

An Episode in Physics. A classic episode in guided discovery is illustrated in the following process designed to teach a physics student to discover the three classes of levers. This includes the discovery of the role of the axis, the force arm, and the resistance arm in the operation of the lever in each class.

- *The objective of the episode:* To discover the three classes of levers.
- *Equipment needed:* A standard meterstick, a balancing stand, two equal weights (50–100 g), two weight hangers, a string.
- *Step 1:* Place the meterstick on the balancing stand in a balanced position.
- *Step 2:* Question: "How can we upset the equilibrium?" Anticipated answer: "Push one side down or up." ("Correct.")
- *Step 3:* Question: "Can we do the same by use of weights?" Anticipated response: The student usually places one of the weights on one side of the meterstick.
- *Step 4:* Question: "Can you balance the seesaw now?" Anticipated response: The student will place the other weight on the other side of the meterstick and will move it around until it balances (Figure 10.7).
- *Step 5:* Question: "What factors are involved in the maintenance of

Figure 10.7. Balanced Weights

the equilibrium? What keeps the stick in balance?" Anticipated answer: "Equal weights at equal distances from the axis" (Figure 10.8).

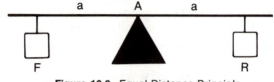

Figure 10.8. Equal Distance Principle

- *Step 6:* Question: "Which factor can we change now to upset the balance?" Anticipated answer: "The distance of either weight from the axis." (The student is asked to do it by moving one of the weights.)
- *Step 7:* Question: "How far can you move it?" Anticipated answer: "Until the end of the meterstick" (Figure 10.9).

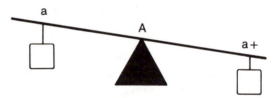

Figure 10.9. Unbalanced Weights

- *Step 8:* Question: "Is this the maximum distance possible between the weight and the axis?" Anticipated answer: "No. It is possible to move farther the place of the axis."
- *Step 9:* Question: "Would you do it, please?" Anticipated response: The student moves the axis to the position shown in Figure 10.10.

Figure 10.10. Weight at Maximum Distance from Axis

- *Step 10:* Question: "Now could you do anything, using the present equipment, to balance the stick?" Anticipated response: More often than not students discover the following solution: They put the string around the stick between the weight (F) and the axis (A) and slowly pull the stick up until it is balanced in the horizontal position (Figure 10.11).

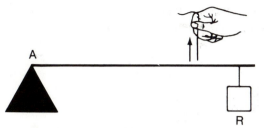

Figure 10.11. Balance with String between Weight and Axis

• *Step 11:* Question: "Among the axis, the weight, and the taut string, what kinds of balanced arrangements have we thus far?" Anticipated response: The student explains verbally and/or demonstrates the two arrangements shown in Figure 10.12.

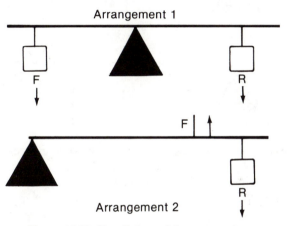

Figure 10.12. Two Balanced Arrangements

• *Step 12:* Question: "Look at the second arrangement. Is it possible to change any factors and have a new balanced arrangement?" Anticipated response: After a short pause student explains verbally and/or demonstrates the arrangement shown in Figure 10.13.

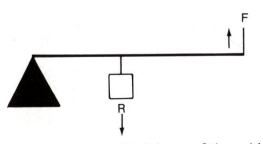

Figure 10.13. Balance with Weight between String and Axis

- *Step 13:* Say to your student: "Indeed, these are the three and the only three possible arrangements of levers. They are called the first-class lever, the second-class lever, and the third-class lever" (Figure 10.14). (Note: The first concern in this episode is the *discovery* of the lever's concept. Then, and only then, *labels* were attached.)

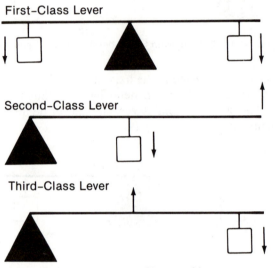

Figure 10.14. Three Classes of Levers

The next episode in teaching the lever could be about *applying* the discovered concept to doors, clocks, muscular action, or any other rotating objects in the world around us. Episodes in application could and should be taught by guided discovery.

An Episode in Physical Education. The second example of an episode in the guided discovery style is designed for a physical education class in which the student is being led to discover the relationship between the application of force and the movement of a flying object.[2]

- *The objective of the episode:* To discover the relationship between the application of a force and the movement of a flying object.
- *Equipment needed:* A soccer ball.
- *Step 1:* Question: "What kind of kick is needed when you want to pass the ball to a player who is far from you?" Anticipated answer: "A long kick." ("Correct.")
- *Step 2:* "Suppose there is a player from the opposing team between

---

[2] Adapted from Muska Mosston and Sara Ashworth, *Teaching Physical Education,* 3rd ed. (Columbus, Ohio: Charles E. Merrill Publishing Co., 1986).

you and your teammate—what must happen then?'' Anticipated answer: "Then the ball must fly high." ("Correct.")

- *Step 3:* Question: "Where should the foot that produces the force be applied on the ball in order to raise it off the ground?" Anticipated answer: "As low as possible!" ("Correct.")
- *Step 4:* "Which part of the foot can comfortably get to the lowest part of the ball without interference with direction of the run and its momentum?" Anticipated answer: "The toes." ("Very good!" proclaims the teacher. "Let's try it!")

This short process of interaction between the questions and the responses produces results that are inevitable. It will always work because there is an intrinsic (logical, if you wish) relationship between the question and the answer in terms of the stated target—application of the toes to achieve a long high kick. Every so often it might be necessary to inject an additional question due to the age of the learner and the level of word comprehension. The basic structure of the sequence, however, remains the same.

Let us examine the sequence design. Notice that it proceeds from the *general to the specific* and each question is related to the specific purpose of the movement. Presenting a situation in which the two players are far apart makes it clear to the learner that a long kick is needed. Now one could produce two kinds of long kicks: one rolling on the ground and the other the high flying kick. In a real game situation the high flying kick will be used to get over the heads of the opponents. Therefore, the condition of an intervening opponent is introduced in the form of a question (step 2) that suggests the need to raise the ball into the air. It is a matter of simple mechanics of forces (which is within the realm of every child's experience) that if you want to raise the ball into the air you must apply the force to the bottom of the ball in an upward direction. Hence the question in step 3, which will inevitably lead to an appropriate correct response. The final question and response practically follow by themselves: When you need to apply a particular part of the foot to meet the conditions that were established in the previous response, this is where the toes come in handy.

An Episode on Systematic Change. The third example of an episode in the guided discovery style is designed for a class in which students are being led to discover the principle of systematic change.[3]

- *The objectives of the episode:* (1). to discover the principle of systematic change, and (2) to apply this principle to learning to create a new model from a previously known one.

---

[3] Adapted from Muska Mosston, *Teaching: From Command to Discovery* (Belmont, California: Wadsworth Publishing Co., 1972).

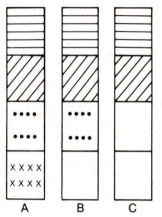

Figure 10.15. Three Rectangles Showing a Pattern of Change

- *Setting the scene:* Draw the three equal-size rectangles each divided into four equal compartments as shown in Figure 10.15.
- *Step 1:* Question: "What is the same about A, B, and C?" Anticipated answer: Young children say: "They are all boxes." Older children say: "They are all rectangles." ("Yes.")
- *Step 2:* Question: "What else is the same?" Anticipated answer: "They are all divided into four compartments (or four equal compartments)." ("Correct.")
- *Step 3:* Question: "What else is the same?" Anticipated answer: "The (or some) compartments have marks in them." (Yes.")
- *Step 4:* Question: "What else?" Anticipated answer: "The top two compartments have the same markings." ("True.")
- *Step 5:* Question: "What's the same about A and B?" Anticipated answer: "The top three compartments have the same markings." ("Correct.")
- *Step 6:* Question: "Now what is the difference among A, B, and C?" Anticipated answer: Young children say: "Each box has one thing less." Older children say: "Each box is different from the previous box by one thing." ("Yes.")
- *Step 7:* Question: "Could you now show what box D should look like?" Anticipated answer: The student draws a rectangle like that shown in Figure 10.16 (D).
- *Step 8:* Question: "If we had box E, what would it look like?" Anticipated answer: "All compartments will be empty." ("True.") The student may draw a rectangle like that shown in Figure 10.17 (E) to illustrate his/her response.

At this point we can assume that the children have internalized the

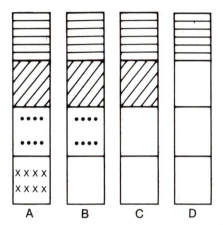

Figure 10.16. Four Rectangles Showing a Pattern of Change

principle of keeping all variables constant except one, which is the idea of systematic change. We could stop here. However, this observation of how a systematic change occurs can be quite useful, so let's continue a few more steps and see where this little exercise in observing, comparing, and contrasting can lead.

- *Step 9:* Question: "So, if we have a model of something and we want to make a new model that is systematically different yet almost the same, what must we do?" Anticipated answer: "Change one thing." ("Correct.")
- *Step 10:* Question: "Let's see how it works with other things. Look at this chair; suppose we wanted to design another chair that looks like this one and yet will be different, what must we do?" Anticipated

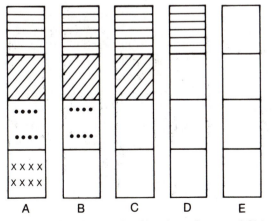

Figure 10.17. Five Rectangles Showing a Pattern of Change

answer: At times, there will be a pause here. Now the learners have to transfer what they have previously learned.

- *Step 11:* Question: "Well? What must we know first?" Anticipated answer: "First we must know the parts of the chair."
- *Step 12:* Question: "Okay, what are the parts that all chairs must have?" Anticipated answer: "A seat." ("Yes.")
- *Step 13:* (When someone else answers "Legs.") Question: "Not quite. Instead of legs a chair must have what? What is it that legs do—what do they give to the seat?" Anticipated answer: "Support." ("Yes, indeed.")
- *Step 14:* Question: "What other parts?" Anticipated answer: "A back!" ("Okay.")
- *Step 15:* Question: "What do we do now?" Anticipated answer: "We'll change one of these."
- *Step 16:* Question: "Which one?" Anticipated answer: "Let's say support." ("Okay.")
- *Step 17:* "What is the smallest support that can be designed for a chair?" Anticipated answer: "One leg." ("Yes.")
- *Step 18:* Question: "What kind of a leg?" Anticipated answer: "One straight leg." ("Okay.")

By adding further steps you can lead your student to identify and design changes in size, color, texture, materials, and so on. All these steps are a part of the focus at hand: *systematic change.* You might even call them a guide for invention. In fact this episode was designed especially to overcome the inhibitions that can prevent children from exercising their creativity. Over the years of working with concepts and theories of discovery processes it became clear that many students seem unable to discover or invent or go beyond the given information. It also became clear that it was not innate inability but rather a variety of inhibitions, both cognitive and emotional, that prevented them from doing so. Students in many classes are literally afraid to produce a response that seems to them to be different from what the teacher expects. (You can also hear from teachers such statements as: "Not everyone can be creative.") But the steps outlined in the systematic change episode help dissolve these inhibitions and encourage students to be inventive and creative. This episode again illustrates the essence, the operation, and the power of guided discovery. It is an example of a worthwhile use of this style because the *objective* is to discover a universal principle, a principle that is useful and that can apply in many situations.

IMPLICATIONS OF STYLE F

The use of Style F implies that:

1. The teacher is willing and capable of crossing the discovery threshold.

2. The teacher includes discovery in his/her education goals.
3. The teacher is willing to invest time to study the structure of the subject matter and to design the appropriate sequence of questions.
4. The teacher is willing to take a chance and experiment with the unknown. In Styles A–E, the onus of performance is on the learner. In guided discovery, however, the onus is on the teacher. The teacher is the one who is responsible for the precise design of the questions that will elicit the correct responses. The performance of the learner is directly related to the performance of the teacher.
5. The teacher trusts the cognitive capacity of the student to discover the appropriate aspects of the subject matter.
6. The teacher is willing to make the changes necessary in his/her teaching behavior.

STYLE-SPECIFIC COMMENTS

It is quite possible that some teachers may feel a degree of discomfort as they read about this style. They may be concerned that Style F, as we have described it, will lock the learner into a very tight and precise kind of thinking. That is exactly what guided discovery does. It has unique objectives and unique ways of reaching them, and this is one of its major assets. Others might argue against Style F on the grounds that each person thinks differently and, therefore, a predetermined sequence of questions cannot equally apply to so many diverse students. If so, they are not taking into account that the power and beauty of guided discovery lies in its *intimacy*. It is the intimacy with the subject matter and the intimacy with the cognitive operation that leads most (sometime all) learners to the expected target. The more perfect the design of the sequence of questions due to profound insights into the *structure* of the task, the greater the number of students who can succeed with it. Adjustments in the size of the step and the wording of the question may be needed for different ages or levels of knowledge, but the intimacy with the subject matter remains the same. Equally powerful is the cognitive intimacy between the teacher and the student. Every cognitive response in the form of discovery is a direct result of what the teacher asked in that step. In this style, the cognitive bond between the teacher and the student is most powerful. No other style comes even close to Style F in this respect.

However, the fact that this elegant and powerful style, when properly designed, always produces results does create a potential danger. When guided discovery is used in universal subject areas such as math, physics, chemistry, and anatomy there is no problem. Students learn to engage in a process of logical sequences and processes. They discover the universal truths of the sciences. But one has to be cautious when using this style in areas such as social studies, religious issues, sex education, political science, and the like. Portions of these areas are often variable and dependent upon personal opinion or cultural mores. They are often related to particular beliefs, a particular morality, or a specific value system. Since the process of Style F guides the learner toward a predetermined target, it is possible to have the learner utter statements, principles, or ideas that are contrary to his/her beliefs and convictions.

It is imperative to realize that Style F is not the "questioning style." Rather, in this style, there is a *particular* way to design and use the sequence of questions. Other styles, as we have seen, have different designs and usages of questions.

Style F is designed for cognitive economy. The particular structure of guided discovery does not invite deviation or cognitive wandering. It gets the learner to the target with maximum efficiency while engaging in the dominant cognitive operation. By "maximum efficiency" we do not mean that guided discovery is the "best" style. Like all other styles, this style has its boundaries and limitations. It is the "best" style only for the objectives that it can reach.

Style F has a considerable impact on memory. When one discovers something for oneself, chances are greater for remembering it (Bruner 1961).

The act of discovery seem to serve as strong motivation for some if not most learners. In guided discovery, because it involves cognitive intimacy with the teacher and the discovered subject matter, there is a reduction of fear, especially the fear of failure. This sense of success induces security and kindles motivation to continue.

Although guided discovery can succeed when used with groups, it produces the best result in a one-to-one situation. In a group, many learners can benefit from this process, but learners *discover* at different speeds. When one learner has discovered the answer (anywhere in the sequence) and utters it in public, the other learners who hear (or see) the response become the receivers. They can no longer discover it. At best, different learners offer their discoveries at different points in the sequence, and thus the discovery experience "belongs" to the group. However, the full benefit of this process is realized when *each* individual learner moves through the sequence and is engaged in discovery *at every step*.

Obviously, this poses a logistical issue. It is difficult to create conditions for a one-to-one process except (1) when the teacher spends time with one learner while others are engaged in other styles or (2) when the learner uses a computer programmed for this task. Another option is to use guided discovery during feedback time in other styles. The teacher can momentarily shift to guided discovery in order to clarify a concept. To do so, in what seems to be a spontaneous behavior, the teacher must be quite skilled in guided discovery.

Note that episodes using the Socratic method are *not* examples of guided discovery. In this kind of episode, although the teacher arranges the questions in sequential manner, the role of the learner is to respond with a

Style F: GUIDED DISCOVERY

The purpose of this style is to discover a concept by answering a sequence of questions presented by the teacher

ROLE OF LEARNER

) To listen to the teacher's question, or clue

) To discover the answer for each question in the sequence

) To discover the final answer which constitute the sought concept

ROLE OF TEACHER

) To design the sequence of questions, each designed for a small discovery by the learner

) To present the questions to the learner, in a sequence

) To provide periodic feedback to the learner

) To acknowledge the discovery of the concept by the learner

Figure 10.18. Style F Classroom Chart

"yes" or "no"; the learner is not engaged in discovery, as described here. These episodes are in Style B.

When using Style F, it is important to consider the issue of wait-time. When a teacher asks a question (expecting an oral answer), the learner needs time to answer it. The teacher, in correspondence, must wait. Depending on which of two clusters of teaching styles we are using, we can look at wait-time in one of two different ways. In situations where a learner is engaged in reproduction tasks and memory is the dominant cognitive operation (Styles A–E), extending waiting will not necessarily produce the expected results. One either remembers (names, dates, events, etc.) or not. Excessive waiting, in fact, can produce frustration. On the other hand, when a learner is engaged in production tasks (Styles F–K), time for mediation and discovery is mandatory. It takes time to engage in discovery within any cognitive operation other than memory (and we are not dealing with delayed recall where after elapsed time the learner says: "Oh, suddenly I remember"). In discovery episodes the teacher must learn to wait for the response. When

TABLE 10.3. THE ANATOMY OF STYLE F: THE GUIDED DISCOVERY STYLE

Decision Sets	Teacher's Decision Categories	Learner's Decision Categories
Preimpact	All decisions	Not involved
Impact	Implementing the preimpact decisions Delivering the sequence of stimuli to the learner and waiting for the learner's response Observing the performance of the learner Restructuring stimuli to guide learner back to focus, if necessary Adjustment decisions	Responding to each question by discovering the answer Discovering the target.
Postimpact	Offering frequent feedback and reinforcing the responses of learner Assessing the teaching style itself	Receiving the feedback

the learner has processed the issue at hand by engaging in the dominant cognitive operation (an/or in the minihierarchy of supporting operations), he/she will be ready to produce the response. Then, and only then, the teacher's role is to continue the interaction by offering feedback and/or proceeding with the next step.

In guided discovery, if the teacher does not wait and, instead, offers the answer, the whole process of discovery by the learner is aborted.

Figure 10.18 and Table 10.3 review the teacher's role and the learner's role in this style.

STYLE F AND THE DEVELOPMENTAL CHANNELS

As with previous styles, we will use the criterion of *independence* to place the learner on the developmental channels when Style F is used (Figure 10.19).

The Physical Developmental Channel. Since the learner is dependent on the specific stimuli given by the teacher, the placement on the physical developmental channel is toward "minimum."

The Social Developmental Channel. Since the learner is so intimately connected to the teacher or a surrogate source, there is no opportunity for

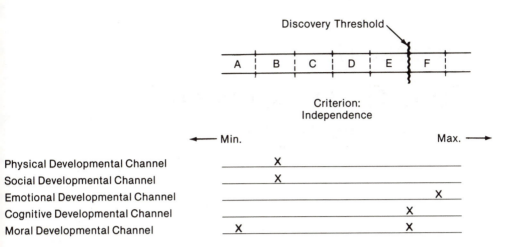

Figure 10.19. Style F and the Developmental Channels

social contact with others. Hence the placement on the social developmental channel is toward "minimum."

The Emotional Developmental Channel. The assumption in Style F is that the learner's self-concept and feeling about himself/herself are positive due to successful engagement in discovery of ideas. The placement on the emotional developmental channel is therefore toward "maximum."

The Cognitive Developmental Channel. The significant change from previous styles occurs in the position on the cognitive developmental channel. Crossing the discovery threshold and engaging in cognitive operations other than memory and recall place the learner toward "maximum" in this channel. However, the learner is not yet *at* the maximum point because an episode in guided discovery usually engages the learner in only *one* dominant cognitive operation.

The Moral Developmental Channel. Placing the learner on the moral developmental channel causes a very interesting situation. The position seems to bifurcate here. If the sequence of questions is designed to get the learner to *state* a predetermined moral position, then the learner is minimally independent in making decisions about his/her moral standing (at least the utterance of the position). If, however, the objective of the sequential questions is to guide the learner to *examine* his/her moral position, then the learner is closer to "maximum" in making independent decisions about the moral position.

CHAPTER 11

Style G: The Convergent Discovery Style

Take a few minutes and solve the following problems:[1]

1. Which word is different from the other three words?
   a. yell
   b. talk
   c. pencil
   d. whisper
2. Which letter is as far away from K in the alphabet as J is from G?
   a. K
   b. M
   c. N
   d. G
   e. I
3. Which pair of words fits best in the blanks? Arm is to wrist as _____ is to
   _____.
   a. leg : foot
   b. thigh : ankle
   c. leg : ankle
   d. leg : knee

---

[1] From Whimbey and Lochhead (1986).

4. Write the two letters that should appear next in the series.
   C B F E I H L K ____ ____
5. One-third is to 9 as 2 is to ____.

The above tasks and thousands like them share in common several characteristics:

1. They represent the flow of convergent thinking.
2. They have one correct answer.
3. The learner by him/herself is engaged in discovering the steps leading to the correct answer.
4. The learner must engage in cognitive operations other than memory.
5. The learner recruits the minihierarchy (see Chapter 2) of cognitive operations needed for the discovery of the correct answer.

In Style G, to which all of these tasks belong, the learner is engaged in reasoning, using rules of logic, and critical thinking. The specific cognitive operations used depend on the structure of the task and its specific cognitive demands. For example, the first task above requires engagement in *categorizing*—grouping together the words *yell, talk,* and *whisper* (all are forms of vocalizing). This operation is followed by *comparing* all the words, and *concluding* that *pencil* is the exception. The minihierarchy in this case will look like this: Comparing → Categorizing → Concluding.

The third task requires engagement in identifying the particular relationship (whole : part) in each optional answer, and then comparing that relationship to the first part of the analogy (Arm is to wrist as _____). The minihierarchy here may look like this: Identifying the relationship → Comparing → Concluding.

The fourth task calls for identifying the interval between any two letters, then discovering the pattern of the intervals and continuing that pattern by adding two letters. The minihierarchy may look like this: Comparing → Sequencing → Extrapolating.

Would you do the analysis of the other two tasks and determine the minihierarchy for each.

The role of the teacher in Style G is to make decisions about the expected cognitive operations and the selection of the tasks that are appropriate for the particular cognitive operations. The role of the learner is to recruit the cognitive operations (the minihierarchy) and to engage in convergent thinking that will lead to the discovery of the single correct answer.

OBJECTIVES OF STYLE G

As with previous styles, Style G has both subject matter and behavior objectives.

Subject Matter Objective

To discover the single correct answer to a question or the single correct solution to a problem

Behavior Objectives

To cross the discovery threshold by discovering the one correct response

To engage in a specific sequence of cognitive operations that comprises the minihierarchy at that time

To become aware of one's engagement in problem solving, reasoning, and critical thinking

THE ANATOMY OF STYLE G

The shift of decisions in Style G occurs in the impact set (Figure 11.1). The learner makes the decision about the steps in seeking to *discover* the one correct answer to a question or the one correct solution to a problem. The learner also makes the decision about the series of questions to ask him/herself—a process that distinguishes this style from guided discovery, in which the teacher made the decision about each step toward the discovery of the answer. Most importantly, the learner makes the decision about the cognitive operations in which he/she will be engaged in the course of discovering the answer. It is reasonable to suggest that skilled learners are aware of the various operations that they call into action. Such learners are engaged in metacognition and proceed in more systematic ways when they are faced with problems, and they are probably more experienced in the use of their cognitive capacities.[2] In addition, the learner makes the decision about how to use an *algorithm* or a *heuristic* that has been presented by the teacher.[3]

	A	B	C	D	E	F	G
Preimpact	(T)	(T)	(T)	(T)	(T)	(T)	(T)
Impact	(T) ⟶ (L)	(L_d)	(L) ⟶ (L)	⟶ (T_L) ⟶	(L)		
Postimpact	(T)	(T) ⟶ (L_o) ⟶ (L)	(L) ⟶ (T_L) ⟶ (L_T)				

Figure 11.1. The Shift from Style F to Style G

[2] Researchers in the newly developing area of metacognition (thinking about thinking) are studying its role and its impact on learning. See Nickerson, Perkins, and Smith 1985; Halpern 1984; Presseisen 1987; and Costa 1984.

[3] An algorithm is a procedure that will always lead to the correct answer—for example, the procedure for solving long-division problems. A heuristic is any rule of thumb used to solve a problem. It does not always produce the correct answer, but it is a useful guide.

IMPLEMENTATION OF STYLE G

Description of an Episode

In any episode utilizing Style G, the teacher presents the question or problem either orally or in some written form (task sheet, assignment in the text, in a manual, on a transparency). The question or the problem is always designed to elicit convergent thinking; that is, it is designed for the discovery of one correct answer.

At this point, time must be provided for thinking to take place. The dissonance and the mediation phases are at work (see Chapter 2), and the teacher must *wait* for the learner's correct response to emerge. When the response appears (orally or in a written form), the teacher offers feedback—either neutral feedback or, if errors in performance are evident, corrective feedback. The episode continues until the learner completes the task. At the end of the episode—during closure—the teacher may offer feedback to the entire class about the learners' engagement in the cognitive operations. If necessary, the teacher demonstrates how to solve a problem of a given kind, explains the procedure, the rationale, the use of the cognitive operations(s), and asks for questions for clarification.

How to Do It

The Preimpact Set. The teacher makes all the decisions in the preimpact set with a focus on:

1. Selecting the cognitive operations for the given episode. (This decision is sometimes made after decision 2.)
2. Selecting the subject matter that reflects these cognitive operations. (This decision is sometimes made prior to decision 1.)
3. Designing the specific questions or problems within the subject matter that will trigger the learner's engagement in the minihierarchy and convergent discovery.
4. Determining the logistics appropriate for the conduct of the episode.

The Impact Set.

1. In the initial two or three episodes in Style G, the teacher addresses the entire class and states the objectives of this style:
   a. To discover the one correct answer to each of the presented questions or problems.
   b. To discover the use of cognitive operations appropriate for the tasks at hand.
   c. To examine the answers for their correctness, by using an answer sheet or answers at the end of the text, or by consulting the teacher.

2. The teacher explains his/her role:
   a. To present the questions.
   b. To provide time for thinking and discovering the answers.
   c. To verify the solutions or, if necessary, to offer corrective feedback.
3. The teacher explains the role of the learner:
   a. To receive the questions or problems.
   b. To engage in *critical thinking* and in discovering the single correct answer to each question.
   c. To engage in verifying the answers and solutions and, if necessary, to call upon the teacher to participate in the verification.
4. In the initial episode in this style or when needed the teacher *demonstrates* the process and procedure of solving a problem by pointing out the steps, the rationale, and the cognitive operations involved in the process (the minihierarchy).
5. The teacher provides time for questions for clarification about the style, the procedures, and so on.
6. The teacher then presents the questions or problems orally or in a written form.
7. The teacher explains the logistics and the parameters (time, space, etc.) that are needed for appropriate class management.
8. The teacher remains available for *learner-initiated* one-on-one dialogue with individual learners after they begin to work. Learners get engaged in the cognitive operations involved in the discovery of the correct solution. The solutions to the problems may be expressed in writing, talking, physical movement, musical notation, or drawing, depending on the subject matter. The learner who needs clarification or an additional explanation has the opportunity to ask the teacher for this information. The teacher, in turn, has a unique opportunity to learn about the student's ways of handling cognitive tasks. The teacher has the opportunity to listen to the student, answer his/her questions, and, if the learner is stuck, to inject a sequence of questions (using Style F) that will guide the learner on the path to discovery. This private and cognitively intimate interaction is *unique* to this style. The teacher can learn a great deal about the way the students think, and the students reaffirm their trust in their teacher.
9. If the teacher detects that a particular error in thinking is occurring in the work of several learners, he/she stops the episode and repeats the explanation of the task, the procedure, and the cognitive operation for the whole class. Alternatively, the teacher can address only the learners who were involved in the common error for the purpose of clarifying the errors and offering guidelines for continued discovery.

The Postimpact Set.

1. The teacher must *wait* for learners to settle into their new role in thinking. It takes time to learn to engage in cognitive operations, to

examine their interrelationships (the minihierarchy), to discover solutions, and to verify their correctness.

2. As the teacher moves from one learner to the next, he/she offers individual feedback about the correctness of the solution and about the cognitive process of arriving at the solution. Note that assessing the cognitive process is possible only in tasks that require the *learner* to specify every step during the discovery of the solution.

3. At times, the teacher can *initiate* the contact with the learner by asking: "How are you doing?"; "Have you verified your solution?"; "How did you do it?"; or "Do you have any difficulty with the task?" In the postimpact phase the teacher has the opportunity to engage the learner in dialogue for the purpose of clarifying and guiding the flow of the discovery. The interaction between the teacher and the learner is similar to that described in the impact set except the teacher rather than the learner initiates the communication.

4. The teacher uses neutral and corrective feedback forms. Neutral feedback acknowledges appropriate thinking and correct solutions. Corrective feedback addresses inappropriate thinking—flaws in reasoning and judgment—and errors in the solutions.

5. At the end of the episode, the teacher may offer feedback to the entire class concerning the way they handled the tasks.

SELECTING AND DESIGNING THE SUBJECT MATTER

Tasks that require convergent thinking and the discovery of one correct solution exist in many forms in all academic areas and in real-life situations. Many textbooks in mathematics, physics, and chemistry contain convergent thinking tasks, and books and articles that specifically deal with reasoning, critical thinking, problem solving, and logic are rich in examples of all sorts. In addition, the latter group of books and articles offers strategies, procedures, and research citings that shed light on issues discussed in this chapter (e.g., Halpern 1984; Lochhead 1986; Nickerson 1986; Hayes 1981; Lipman 1984; Oxman 1984).

As a general guideline for selecting tasks for this teaching style, use the following criteria:

1. Does the task have only one correct response? (The response can be in a form of an answer, a movement, a solution, a construction of real objects.)

2. Does the task invite convergent thinking? (This depends on the structure of the task and on verbal behavior used to introduce the task).

3. Is the discovery process evident?

Let us look again at one of the problems presented in the introduction to this chapter to see how it meets these criteria:

Which letter is as far away from K in the alphabet as J is from G?

Hardly anyone can solve this problem by memory or simply glancing at the question and knowing the answer. The problem requires the learner to proceed through several logical steps before arriving at the one correct solution. The learner has to make a decision about the *representation* of the problem (e.g., G ⎡H I⎤ J | K ⎡? ?⎤ ?), identify the relationships, and draw a conclusion—thereby engaging in discovery process. Regardless of how many attempts a learner may need to find the solution, or how many solution paths the learner devises that lead to a dead end, the process of discovering the one correct answer represents the process of convergent thinking.

Another task that meets the criteria is assembling a mountain tent without having the instruction sheet at hand. You may try to fit the pieces (the connecting tubes, the cords, etc.) in a variety of ways, but there is only one correct solution—after properly fitting each part—that will result in the complete and correct assembly of the tent. The solution is a result of convergent thinking and engaging in the discovery process.

Maze problems, jigsaw puzzles, and, indeed, many exercises in mathematics, physics, and chemistry are further examples of tasks that meet the criteria for Style G.

Whenever you select or design tasks for this style they must adhere to the criteria listed above. Note that not every problem or issue in academic subject areas or in daily life fits these criteria. Many problems that require reasoning and critical thinking are resolved by the opposite process—the process of divergent thinking (see Chapter 12).

IMPLICATIONS OF STYLE G

The successful use of Style G implies that:

1. The teacher is willing to move with the students another step beyond the discovery threshold.
2. The teacher trusts the learner to participate in convergent thinking and discovery on his/her own.
3. The teacher believes that each learner can improve his/her performance in the cognitive operations and in the utilization of the minihierarchies.
4. Each student is willing to engage in the discovery process and develop the skill of convergent thinking. (See Figure 11.2 and Table 11.1.)

TABLE 11.1. THE ANATOMY OF STYLE G: THE CONVERGENT DISCOVERY STYLE

Decision Sets	Teacher's Decision Categories	Learner's Decision Categories
Preimpact	Selecting the problem to be solved or the issue to be discussed	Not involved
Impact	Presenting the problem or the issue Observing (listening) to the learner's process of evolving a solution or a conclusion Offering additional questions, or clues, if necessary	Engaging in examining the problem or the issue Developing a procedure for discovering the solution or conclusion Using the minihierarchy of cognitive operations that leads to the solution
Postimpact	Offering feedback during and after the process of discovery by the learner	Verifying the procedure and the solution by using criteria that are appropriate for the task

STYLE G AND THE DEVELOPMENTAL CHANNELS

As with previous styles, we will use the criterion of *independence* to place the learner on the developmental channels when Style G is used (Figure 11.2).

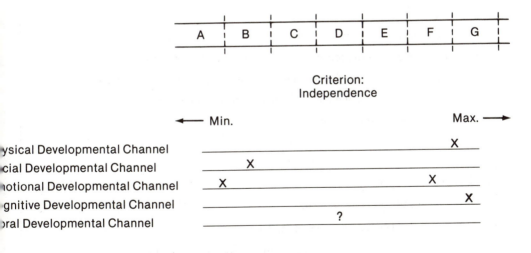

Figure 11.2. Style G and the Developmental Channels

The Physical Developmental Channel. Any student who is successfully functioning in Style G is demonstrating a high degree of independence about his/her engagement in physical tasks. The placement on the physical developmental channel is therefore close to "maximum."

The Social Developmental Channel. Engaging in thought processes and discovering single solutions is a very private experience. Social contact is minimal, except for occasional exchange with another learner. The placement on the social developmental channel is therefore toward "minimum" in Style G.

The Emotional Developmental Channel. The placement on the emotional developmental channel is dual. For those learners who can deal with the emotional stress of doing cognitive tasks the placement is toward "maximum." For others, the placement is toward "minimum."

Style G: THE CONVERGENT DISCOVERY STYLE

The purpose of this style is to discover the solution to a problem, to clarify an issue, to arrive at a conclusion, by employing logical procedures, reasoning, and critical thinking.

ROLE OF LEARNER

o   To examine the problem, the issue

o   To evolve his/her own procedure toward a solution or conclusion

o   To use the miniheirarchy that will lead to the solution or the conclusion

o   To verify the process and the solution by checking them against criteria appropriate for the subject matter at hand.

ROLE OF TEACHER

o   To present the problem, or issue

o   To follow the learner's process of thinking

o   To offer feedback, or clues (if necessary) without providing the solution

---

Figure 11.3. Style G Classroom Chart

The Cognitive Developmental Channel. By definition, a learner who is able to function in Style G is placed toward ''maximum'' on the cognitive developmental channel.

The Moral Developmental Channel. The placement of a learner on the moral developmental channel is a matter of conjecture. The learner might ask the question: ''What is the value of thinking?'' The answer to this question depends on the learner's values, as well as his/her degree of independence using the various thought processes. We shall leave to you the decision about the placement of the learner on this channel.

As we have seen, Style G engages the learner in learner-initiated thought processes that converge on the discovery of a single correct solution. In Chapter 12 we will examine the style that is used when problems have multiple correct solutions and therefore require the learner to engage in divergent thinking.

CHAPTER 12

Style H: The Divergent Production Style

In Style H, the divergent production style, both the description of the task and the structure of the task provide the condition for multiple correct responses. Consider, for example, the following tasks:

1. Walking on a rainy day, you encounter a puddle of water. What options are available to you in getting to the other side of the puddle?
2. Name ten similarities between a bottle of ketchup and a paper clip.
3. Looking at a picture of a woman's hand holding a glass of wine and ready to touch the glass of wine held by a man's hand, write (or tell) three different openings to a story about this picture. Each opening will consist of two sentences.
4. Design five different ways a person facing the broad side of a balance beam can get on the beam and end in a squat position.
5. Offer two different proofs that in a right-angle triangle $a^2 + b^2 = c^2$.

Each of these five tasks asks the learner to engage in divergent thinking—to discover alternatives. None of these tasks has only one correct answer. Each of the tasks triggers a dominant cognitive operation and its accompanying minihierarchy (see Chapter 2). Figuring out ways of getting to the other side of the puddle may call upon memory or involve the discovery of options that one has never tried (e.g., laying a nearby plank across it). Thinking of similarities between a bottle of ketchup and a paper clip instantly engages the learner in comparing and in discovering the many attributes that serve as criteria for comparison. (e.g., both objects are manufactured, both have round parts, both contain hollow spaces, etc.). Generating stories about the touching of wine glasses calls for interpretation and the ability to create different stories about the same event. The gymnastics task invites the learner to discover mounts that may already exist in the experience of others, or to create and design new ones. In the geometry task, the learner faces the challenge of going beyond known information (theorems, etc.) and discovering reasoned solutions to the problem at hand.

All these examples share in common the processes of divergent discovery and/or divergent creativity. They differ from one another in that each requires engagement in a different cognitive operation.

The role of the teacher in Style H is to make the decision about the expected cognitive operation and the selection of the task that is appropriate for that operation. The teacher presents the question, problem, or issue. The role of the learner is to engage in the designated cognitive operation and to make decisions about the discovered or created alternative answers and solutions. In this style, therefore, the learner makes decisions about the specifics of the subject matter.

OBJECTIVES OF STYLE H

As in previous styles, Style H has both subject matter and behavior objectives:

Subject Matter Objective
To produce multiple answers to a
   question or multiple solutions to
   a problem by engaging in
   discovery

Behavior Objectives
To cross the discovery threshold
   by producing divergent responses
To engage in specific cognitive
   operations
To discover alternative possibilities
   while engaging in specific
   cognitive operations
To tolerate others' ideas
To engage in the *reduction process*
   of possible → feasible →
   desirable solutions when
   examining sensitive issues in
   religion, politics, sex, or other
   value-laden areas

THE ANATOMY OF STYLE H

The shift of decisions in Style H occurs in the impact and postimpact sets (Figure 12.1). In the impact set, the learner makes the decisions about the specific discovered answers, solutions, and ideas. In the postimpact set, the

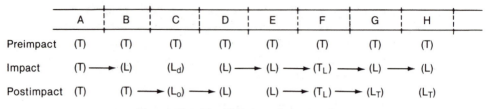

Figure 12.1. The Shift from Style G to Style H

learner makes the decisions concerning the assessment of the answers and solutions. As in previous styles, the teacher makes all the decisions in the preimpact set.

IMPLEMENTATION OF STYLE H

Description of an Episode

In any episode of divergent production the teacher presents the question, problem, or issue at the beginning of the episode. The question is always designed to engage the learner in a particular dominant cognitive operation (see below), and can be presented to the class or to individuals orally or in written form. At this point, time must be provided for thinking to take place. The dissonance and the mediation phases are at work, and the teacher must *wait* for the learners' responses to emerge. As the responses begin to appear, the teacher responds by offering *neutral* feedback. Neutral feedback signals to the learners that their responses are acceptable and encourages them to continue the process of divergent production. The role of the teacher at this stage of the episode is to be accepting and to invite more responses—more divergent production. This attitude creates and maintains a nonthreatening climate that is conducive to the production of alternative ideas. The learners are continuously engaged in the dominant cognitive operation and in making the decisions necessary to produce new responses to the question or problem that governs the episode. In this kind of class climate many answers, solutions, and ideas are produced; some are exciting, some are deviant, and some may be dull. The teacher maintains the flow of ideas by avoiding corrective and/or value feedback to individual responses. The feedback is directed toward the process of production itself: "I see that you have many different ideas"; "You are very good today in producing alternatives."

Later in the episode, treatment of the answers and solutions must take place. Some will need verification, some will need to undergo a selection process, and some will need to be left alone. The decision about which treatment to use is discussed below in the section on "The P–F–D Process."

When a teacher and his/her class become skilled in the process of divergent production and when they develop mutual trust, the flow of ideas becomes rich, varied, and valuable. The climate of discovery always motivates learners to reach for further discovery.

How to Do It

The Preimpact Set. The teacher makes all the decisions in the preimpact set with a focus on:

1. Selecting the dominant cognitive operation for the given episode.
2. Selecting the subject matter for the episode.
3. Designing the *specific* questions or problems within the selected subject matter that will trigger the engagement in the expected cognitive operation.
4. Determining the logistics appropriate for the episode.

Note that there are times when the decision about the subject matter may come first (e.g., quadratic equations, creative writing exercises, etc.). After the subject matter has been selected, the teacher identifies the expected cognitive operation and designs the question or problem accordingly.

The Impact Set.

1. The teacher addresses the entire class and states the objectives of this style:
   a. To discover multiple answers to a question or multiple solutions to a problem.
   b. To engage in a particular cognitive operation.
   c. To examine the answers or solutions for their validity, appropriateness, or value by using a given criterion.
2. The teacher explains his/her role:
   a. To present the question or problem that is within the selected subject area.
   b. To wait for the answers and solutions discovered (created) by the learner.
   c. To accept the answers and solutions offered by the learners.
   d. To assist the learner in verifying the solutions.
3. The teacher explains the role of the learner:
   a. To receive the question or problem.
   b. To engage in *thinking* and in the discovery of multiple answers and solutions.
   c. To engage in verifying the assessing the answers and solutions and, if necessary, to call upon the teacher to participate in this phase.

4. In the initial episode in this style, the teacher *demonstrates the process* (not the responses) by conducting a short episode—for example, an episode in comparing or contrasting. The teacher models waiting and accepting behavior, and offers neutral feedback. The task selected for this model episode does not have to be a part of the subject matter learned at that time. A more neutral task helps learners to focus on the *process* of this style. During the episode the teacher reiterates the roles that are in effect, and reminds the learners about their participation in the particular cognitive operation (initiating metacognitive experiences). At times, the demonstration episode can precede the explanations in steps 2 and 3 above: the teacher creates the experience, and then explains its components. Whenever it is done, the demonstration and the explanation establish the expectations for episodes in style H.

5. The teacher provides time for questions for clarification about Style H. Indeed, learners often need to know what will happen to them when they present their own ideas and solutions because this is a fundamentally different behavior from what was called for in episodes in the preceding styles. Learners need to know and feel that the cognitive and the affective climate will be safe. The accepting behavior by the teacher during the first few episodes in Style H determines the trust level in the class and the climate for productive thinking.

6. The teacher presents the questions to be worked on. They can be delivered orally or in written from, and given to individuals, small groups, or the entire class.

7. The teacher explains the necessary logistics and parameters (time, space, etc.).

8. The learners go to work. They get engaged in mediation and in the production of multiple answers and solutions. These may be expressed in writing, talking, physical movement, musical notations, or drawing, depending on the subject matter and the decisions made by the teacher concerning the mode of communicating the discovered ideas.

The Postimpact Set.

1. The teacher must *wait* for the learners to settle into their new roles as producers of subject matter. Time is always needed for thinking, discovering an idea, and verifying it.

2. When feedback is offered by the teacher, it focuses on the process of divergent production and not on the merit of a particular response.

3. At times, the teacher privately addresses a learner by asking: ''Have you verified that your solutions actually solved the problem?''; ''How did you do it?''; or ''What criterion did you use to verify them?''

4. The way in which responses are treated will depend on the subject matter and/or the nature of the task. Solutions in mathematics may

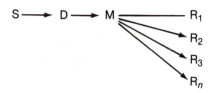

Figure 12.2. A Model for Divergent Production

require only logical verification, while ideas in the social sciences may need to undergo a screening process where values serve as criteria. In the arts, ideas produced in some tasks may be subjected to personal preferences, while those produced in other tasks may be judged by a committee, an audience, or the culture at large. Procedures for the treatment of multiple responses in various areas are discussed below in the section on "The P–F–D Process." Knowing these procedures is vital for the selection of feedback about the discovered solutions.

The process in Style H is represented in Figure 12.2. The teacher presents the stimulus (S) in the form of a question or problem. The learner moves into a state of cognitive dissonance (D), engaging in mediation (M) via a dominant cognitive operation. Within time, the responses begin to emerge. The learner produces different answers, different solutions, diverse ideas.

Operational Suggestions

There are several ways to implement episodes in Style H. They vary mainly in organizational procedures, the time-on-task provided for each individual, and the degree of privacy provided during the production of ideas. Seven options are described below, and the assets and liabilities of each are listed.

Option 1. The teacher conducts the episode with the entire class via individual oral responses. In this option, the teacher moves in the class from row to row and calls on individual students.

Assets	*Liabilities*
Learners hear every learner's idea.	Time-on-task per student is low.
Learners hear an abundance of ideas.	Waiting time is high.
The teacher can set the climate of acceptance.	Some learners may not yet be ready to risk divergent responses in public.

Option 2. The entire class is engaged via individual oral responses. Learners volunteer to respond.

Assets	*Liabilities*
Same as above.	Some learners may not participate.
Pressure to respond is reduced.	Some learners may monopolize the
No one is put on the spot.	time.

Option 3. Half the class is engaged in Style H while the other half is in a different style. The learners in Style H provide their responses orally.

Assets	*Liabilities*
Each learner has more time-on-task.	Pressure to come up with ideas is increased.
There is more time for each learner to produce more divergent responses.	Some learners may be inhibited.
The teacher can set the climate of acceptance.	

Option 4. The class is divided into small groups of four to five learners each. In each group, responses are recorded on a large sheet of paper.

Assets	*Liabilities*
Time-on-task is considerably increased.	Domineering students may take over the conduct of the exercise.
There is more intimate socialization within the context of the task.	The teacher cannot attend all the groups at the same time and monitor the verbal behavior.
There is more communication about the subject matter.	
Learners get to see the diversity or similarity in responses.	
Learners' work is highly visible.	
If each group is working on a different question, lots of subject matter evolves.	

Note than in option 4 the large sheets with the responses written on them can be used for further development and treatment of the ideas. This can be done in a subsequent episode.

Option 5. The bulletin board is used for an ongoing exercise. For example, in an exercise that requires students to write divergent interpretations of a picture, the picture can be tacked onto the board for a few days. The learners post their responses whenever they are available. These slips of paper can be unsigned or learners can sign on the back of the paper. Using option 5 for this exercise will produce a considerable number of written interpretations. Once the climate of Style H has been established, students enjoy this kind of exercise.

Assets	*Liability*
It is fun. There is very little pressure.	When the response is inappropriate, the teacher may not know to whom feedback should be offered. (Writing the name on the back will eliminate this liability.)
Divergent responses are highly visible.	
The activity can continue for quite a while.	
Acceptance of different responses develops.	
It can be used as an interval activity.	

Option 6. Each learner produces written responses.

Asset	*Liabilities*
The teacher will know how each learner produced ideas in a written form.	The teacher does not know the responses immediately.
	It is awkward for those who have difficulty in writing.

The techniques of handling the responses are:

- Each learner reads the responses aloud.
- The teacher collects the papers and reads the ideas to the class.
- A learner collects the papers and reads the ideas to the class.
- The responses are posted on the board

Each of these techniques has its own assets and liabilities. Have you identified any?

Option 7. While the rest of the class is engaged in another episode (probably another task in another style), the teacher conducts a short episode in Style H with one student.

Asset	*Liabilities*
The teacher knows specifically how each learner thinks in a given cognitive operation.	It requires classroom organization that accommodates this process.
	It occupies a great deal of the teacher's time.

Any of these options can be conducted while the class is organized in many different ways: in circles or rows, on the floor, outdoors, and so on.

The *focus*, however is on *the question* that produces divergent responses, not the organizational formats.

If the episode deals with a controversial issue, sometimes it is better for learners to hear a multitude of responses. Therefore, the teacher should start the episode in small groups (option 4). Once the responses are recorded on a large sheet in each group, collect the sheets, paste them on the board, and move on to another episode with the entire class. Everyone can then see *all* the responses. The teacher's alternatives now include reviewing the ideas, asking the students to elaborate, or allowing others to ask questions for clarification or offer counterideas (with or without a reason).

Regardless of which option is used, the teacher must be in charge at all times. This is an organized activity of investigating an issue in a systematic way. It is *not* a so-called free discussion where statement are uttered without a focus.

If necessary, the P–F–D process can be used with any of these options. In controversial issues the P–F–D is mandatory.

SELECTING AND DESIGNING
THE SUBJECT MATTER

Style H is a very rich style. The brain always stands poised to engage in the many cognitive operations that are available to us. Indeed, because the human capacity to participate in divergent production is virtually infinite, it is not possible for us to fathom here the structure and function of all the cognitive operations.

Therefore the discussions offered below are intended to serve primarily as entry points to understanding and designing Style H experiences. The examples we give are by no means exhaustive of the many types of experience that are available in this style. Each example represents an episode that engages the learner in a dominant cognitive operation— comparing, contrasting, categorizing, problem solving, or interpreting—and its accompanying minihierarchy. Both concrete and abstract subject matter are addressed.

Comparing

Comparing is a prevalent cognitive operation used by humans in daily life. It gives us the information we need to establish preferences, to say: "This is better than that," or "This is more beautiful than that." We compare when we buy things, when we meet people, when we select a mate, when we elect officials, when we read books, and when we listen to music.

Comparing (and the adjoining operation of contrasting) involves identifying the attributes that are shared by the compared items. Attributes vary, depending on whether we compare concrete objects or abstract ideas. When we buy a car, we compare makes, sizes, colors, gadgets, prices, and so on. When we compare two symphonies, we compare keys, themes, structures, and methods of orchestration. The *process* of comparing, however, is the same: identifying and discovering the attributes that will offer us knowledge about the things we compare, and will give as the basis for making a *preference* decision.

An Episode in Comparing. In order to design an episode that will engage the learner in comparing, the teacher must make two major decisions:

1. A decision about the task, ascertaining that it will indeed provide for discovery of divergent responses.
2. A decision about the stimulus, ascertaining that the specific question will indeed engage the learner in the cognitive operation of comparing for the duration of the episode.

The following is an example of an episode in comparing. Holding up a pipe in one hand and a book of matches in the other, the teacher asks the students: "What are five things that are the same about these two objects?" After a slight pause, the responses begin to emerge:

- They are both manufactured.
- They both produce smoke.
- They are both made of parts.
- They both have some color on them.
- They are both used for smoking.

After each response, the teacher offers feedback by nodding or saying "Yes." The teacher continues: "You have the idea. Let's have five more." The participants respond:

- They are both held in your hands.
- You hold both between your thumb and the index finger.
- Both have writing on them.
- Both have weight.
- Both occupy space.

The teacher provides further encouragement: "You are doing well in comparing these objects; please continue."

- Neither one is used by everyone.
- Both need oxygen.
- Both depend on an operator to function.
- Both can give pleasure.
- Both can produce pain.

- Both are used in this task.
- Both are not to be used by young children
- Both are purchased with money.
- Both can hold other things inside.
- Both get smaller when used.
- Wind can put out both.
- Both can have more than one use.
- When both are wet they won't work.

The teacher provides more feedback and asks the students to continue: "Yes." "These are correct responses." "Five more."

At times one hears a light sigh at this point. The teacher pushes for more responses and more people enter the activity:

- Both are made from wood.
- Both are connected with fire.
- Both are bought in a store.
- You are holding them at the same height from the floor.

"You are doing well identifying similarities. Let's hear five more."- Often one hears a grunt at this point: "Oh, no!" Although the teacher presses for more, a pause ensues. The flow of ideas seems to stop. (If *you* are participating now in this exercise, can *you* identify five more?) The teacher waits. The pause may continue a bit longer. The pipe and the matches are still held in front of the students. The responses continue at a slower pace:

- Both are in this room.
- Both are useful in some way.
- Both can comfort.
- Both can be harmful.
- Both belong to you.

"Yes!" "All these are correct responses." And with a smile the teacher says: "Let us have five more!"

The process continues for a while. The teacher can stop the exercise before all the ideas are exhausted. There have been groups where all the members contributed and produced 40, 45, or 50 different responses within a period of a few minutes.

The objective of the episode—to engage in divergent production in the cognitive operation of comparing—has been accomplished. It was accomplished because of the two decisions that the teacher had made before the episode began: (1) The task of using two objects was conducive to the discovery of multiple similarities (divergent production), and (2) the design of the question invited participation in the act of comparing.

The teacher's verbal behavior is crucial in episodes of this sort. "Any" wording, "any" question *will not* produce the desired results and will not reach the objective of episodes in Style H. Each dominant cognitive operation can be triggered only by a particular stimulus. It is possible to vary the words in the question but they must remain within the domain of the cognitive operation in focus.

It is possible, then, to ask a student the following question: "What are the common attributes of object X and object Y?" For younger students a more appropriate verbal behavior is: "What is the same about these two objects?" Another way of saying it is: "Compare X and Y." (Note that the instruction says "compare," not "compare and contrast.")

All these forms of verbal behavior accomplish the same thing: They trigger a search for the common attributes. Suppose the exercise is to compare a pencil with a straw broom. Any of the above questions will trigger the brain to conjure up images and to search for the *first* common attribute. Since both objects are visible, the participant starts by looking at them and identifying the obvious. There could be one, two, or more attributes that are obvious and can serve as a starting point—for example:

- Both have a long shape.
- Both are painted with some color.
- Both are manufactured.
- Both are bought in a store.
- Both are operated by hand.
- The main functional part is at one end.
- The length of the object serves as a handle.
- Both have more than one part.

Did you come up with the same or a similar list? Or are the attributes that seem obvious to you different from these? It really does not matter. The entry point may differ, but the triggering *question* will always produce the same end results: engagement and practice in the cognitive operation of comparing. After some practice in comparing, the learner begins to realize that the question activates the search for *common attributes*—shape, color, size, function, structure, material, use, source, content, and many others— that are relevant to the task at hand.

Contrasting

A cognitive operation that usually pairs up with comparing is the operation of contrasting. Contrasting, as the *dominant* operation during an episode, can be activated by the following questions: "What is different about these two objects?" "Contrast X and Y." Engagement in contrasting will produce multiple responses referring to attributes that are similar to those identified and discovered in the comparing exercises.

Initially, exercises in comparing and exercises in contrasting should be done in separate episodes. These episodes can be adjacent or separated by time. It takes time to become adept at each operation, and during this learning phase they should be presented one at a time.

After the learners have had reasonable practice in each of these operations, they will be able to approach the combination of comparing and contrasting in a systematic way. They will first engage in comparing, and when they exhaust the attributes, they will move on to contrasting. Approaching the task systematically may help organize the information derived from engagement in these cognitive operations.

Concrete Objects and Abstract Ideas. We have suggested the use of concrete objects as the initial step in doing exercises in these operations because:

1. Objects are nonthreatening. In fact, it is fun to compare and to contrast a pencil with a broom, a book with a lamp, or a shoe with a bike. The focus is one and the same: practicing the operations of comparing and contrasting.
2. Objects are visible. They provide many clues. They offer many attributes.
3. Responses can be readily verified, if necessary, by looking at the objects closely, by touching, by turning them around.
4. No real previous knowledge is needed in order to participate in the exercise. One gets the necessary knowledge by looking, touching, and hearing.
5. Many objects are always available at no cost. Almost any two objects can set the scene and serve as a stimulus for comparing and contrasting.

In time, episodes in comparing and in contrasting expand to poetry, literature, events in history, current events, and so on. The purpose is to transfer the skill of systematic comparing and systematic contrasting to abstract ideas.

Categorizing

The next cognitive operation that is extremely important in daily life is categorizing. Placing things into categories is a very popular and frequent behavior. Just as the ability to engage in comparing and in contrasting satisfies the need for establishing preferences, the ability to categorize satisfies the need to establish *belonging*.

We, as humans, must know where things belong. We engage in categorizing many times every day. Whenever we organize things, whenever we look for things, whenever we differentiate things, we first seek the category to which they belong. To make this procedure easier and more functional, we have names for the established categories of things, events, people, institutions, and ideas. *Socks, shirts, chairs, cars, pencils, radios, clocks,* and *dishes* are all designations for categories of things. *Conferences, trips, wars, concerts,* and *meals* are designations for categories of events. *Americans, Spaniards, Italians, Germans, French, Finns, English, Israelis, Chinese,* and *Arabs* are designations for categories of people. *Churches, banks, schools, professional organizations,* and *theaters* are designations for categories of institutions. *Science, social studies, political science, history,* and *industrial arts* are designations for categories of school courses. The need to categorize is pervasive and universal. It is probably a necessary skill for survival. Without knowing where things belong, without having the language that supplies names for the categories, there would be chaos in our perception of the reality around us.

Categories can be large and all-inclusive (e.g., people, animals, building, mountains, etc.) or they can be smaller and represent a subcategory. For example, within the category of *mountains,* which includes all the mountains in the world, there are subcategories that include only those mountains of a particular region—the Appalachians, the Alps, the Himalayas. Regardless of the size of the category, it serves the human need to categorize.

Although humans have an intrinsic ability to engage the brain in the operation of categorizing, categorizing is also a skill that must be cultivated during schooling. It requires practice, just like any other skill, in order to reach a degree of proficiency.

An Episode in Categorizing. The following exercise is one of many that could be used to provide practice in categorizing.

The teacher gives the students an assortment of small objects, in this case a variety of buttons, some coins, a paper clip, several rubber bands, an assortment of nails, a couple of pebbles, and a pencil. The students are asked to perform the following task. (If you wish to participate in this exercise from its inception, stop reading now, take a few minutes to collect these items, and then come back to the task.) The task is: Arrange these objects in two groups, so that the objects in one group will have something in common and the objects in the other group will not have that something.

Here is what participants always do and say: First, they take a few seconds to look at the objects and then one student reaches out and arranges them in two groups, saying: "These have metal and these don't." The objects are grouped like this:

Metal Objects	*Nonmetal Objects*
Coins	Plastic and other nonmetal buttons
Paper clip	Rubber bands
Nails	Pebbles
Metal buttons	Pencil

A quick glance at these two groups can *verify* that what the student has said is, indeed, true. Now, since in Style H we seek to develop the ability to discover divergent ideas in the particular cognitive operation, the teacher says to the students: "This is one possible way to arrange these objects."

Then the teacher proceeds by saying: "Put all the objects together again and let's see another arrangement where the objects in one group will have something in common, while the objects in the other group will not have it." The response is usually readily available: "These objects are round and these are not round." This statement produces the following grouping which is different from the first arrangement:

Round Objects	*Nonround Objects*
Round buttons	Oblong buttons
Coins	Paper clip
Rubber bands	Nails
Pebbles	Pencil

The teacher continues: "Put all the objects together again and make another arrangement!" The third attempt may produce the following statement: "This one is flexible and can change its shape, but these are solid and have a fixed shape." The objects are arranged like this:

Flexible Objects	*Inflexible Objects*
Rubber bands	Buttons
	Coins
	Paper clip
	Nails
	Pebbles
	Pencil

The fourth attempt may produce:

Objects That Hold Things Together	*Objects That Do Not Hold Things Together*
Paper Clip	Coins
Rubber bands	Pebbles
Nails	Pencil
Buttons	

A fifth attempt may produce:

Blue Objects	*Nonblue Objects*
Rubber bands	Coins
Pencil	Pebbles
Blue button	Nonblue buttons
	Nails
	Paper clip

A sixth attempt may produce:

Objects with Writing on Them	*Objects without Writing on Them*
Pencil	Buttons
Coins	Paper clip
	Rubber bands
	Nails
	Pebbles

Not all groups of students who do this exercise will produce exactly the same sequence of categories. The categories they discover will be similar, but the sequence of discovering the attributes will vary because different students employ different entry points into the categorizing process. Whatever the sequence, however, the students will have participated in categorizing the objects and will have done so in many different ways. In other words, they will have engaged in *divergent production*.

Moreover, in each attempt the participants will have discovered another reason for grouping the objects in that particular way. They will have discovered the common attribute around which they clustered the particular objects, and they will have learned that, as the attribute changed, so did the objects in the respective groups. For example, in the first attempt described above the participants categorized the object by the attribute *type of material* (metal or nonmetal). In the second attempt the attribute was *geometric form* (round or nonround); in the third it was *flexibility* (flexible or nonflexible); and so on.

The Categorizing Skill in Various Subject Matter Areas. The examples offered thus far have illustrated the use of categorizing with concrete objects. This is the first step for all learners. Many students, of all ages, are not adept at this cognitive skill and an introduction through the manipulation of concrete objects will teach students a *systematic approach* to this operation.

Because concrete objects are visible and touchable, the results of categorization can be verified instantly. These objects can be used to teach people the *skill itself* with minimum pain. When the teacher begins with objects that do not pertain to the subject matter at hand, it reduces the students' anxiety about producing divergent ideas. The application of categorization to various subject matter areas takes time and patience.

The following example in biology (human anatomy) will illustrate one way in which categorization can be applied to a subject matter area. The task is to categorize the following muscles: triceps, quadriceps, gluteus maximus, splenius, semispinalis, the gastrocnemius, biceps, and brachialis.

Obviously, this task is different from the exercise using the various objects. Here prior knowledge is necessary. The student must know certain things about each muscle *before* he/she can begin to categorize. Specifically, the following information is needed:

1. The general location of each muscle
2. The specific joint that each muscle spans
3. The side of the joint on which the muscle is located
4. The specific bones to which each muscle is attached
5. The specific points of origin and insertion of each muscle

This information can be obtained by a Style B episode where the task is to identify these muscles on a skeleton and/or by the use of an anatomical atlas. When students have learned where each muscle is located (item 1 on the list above), they can categorize them as follows:

Muscles of the Upper Arm
Triceps
Biceps
Brachialis

Muscles of the Pelvis and Thigh
Quadriceps
Gluteus maximus

Muscles of the Back of the Neck
Splenius
Semispinalis

Muscle of the Calf and Foot
Gastrocnemius

This categorization is based on the criterion *location.*

If information items 2 and 3 are used, the categories will look like this:

Extensors
Triceps
Quadriceps
Gluteus maximus
Splenius
Semispinalis
Gastrocnemius

Flexors
Biceps
Brachialis

All the muscles in the extensor category are used for extension movements. For example, the gastrocnemius is used when the foot is extended, as when the toes are pointed in gymnastics. The common attribute in the second category is flexion. Both muscles in this category are used for flexing the forearm. This categorization is based on the criterion *function.*

If information items 2, 3, 4, and 5 are used, the following categories will emerge:

Class I Levers
Triceps
Splenius
Semispinalis
Gastrocnemius

Class III Levers
Biceps
Quadriceps
Brachialis
Gluteus maximus

Information item 5—namely, the specific points of origin and insertion of each muscle—helps in identifying the class of lever that is in operation when these muscles activate the bones at the given joint.

The criterion for this categorization is *type of leverage*.

This example is concerned with semiabstract subject matter. It deals with a combination of concrete data (about muscles and bones) and some abstract knowledge (about the laws of levers). A source of verification is readily available in anatomy and kinesiology books. The focus of this exercise, however, is the use of *categorizing* for furthering one's knowledge about the workings of the muscular system.

When an exercise in categorizing results in understanding the interrelationship of different types of information as well as understanding concepts in a given field, the exercise is particularly worthwhile. Teachers can conceive and design such exercises in social studies, math, music, home economics, chemistry, physical education, art, English composition, or in any other area of the curriculum.

How to Implement the Categorizing Sequence.

- *Step 1:* Offer your students a succinct explanation about the cognitive operation of categorizing: "When we categorize we assemble in a group only the items that share a common attribute." This step identifies the purpose of the episode.
- *Step 2:* Identify the subject area in which categorizing will be done—for example, social studies—the states; or biology—the muscular system.
- *Step 3:* Identify the *specific* items to be categorized. If it is "the states," name them, show them on a chart, or mark them on a map. If it is the muscular system, list the muscles that will be categorized.
- *Step 4:* Ask the students to gather specific information about the items. The students must, first, know the facts about each item if they are to develop a categorization system of any value.
- *Step 5:* Identify the attribute that is intrinsic (or relevant) to the subject matter at hand. For example, some intrinsic attributes of states are location, size of population, major cities, major natural bodies (lakes, mountains, etc.), industries, agricultural products, and so on.
- *Step 6:* Identify the first attribute. For example, the attribute *location* will provide the criterion (in step 7) for assembling the states that share a common location into a particular group such as all the states that are east of _____ and also north of _____ .
- *Step 7:* Assemble the items that share the attribute and establish the first category. The actual operation of categorizing begins here. The students do the exercise.
- *Step 8:* Identify the second attribute.

- *Step 9:* Assemble the items anew. Based on the second attribute you will have a *new* category. For example, if the attribute is production of a particular agricultural product, the states that belong to this category will, in all probability, be different from the group in step 7. The students do the exercise.
- *Step 10:* Identify the third attribute.

And so on. You will need to make a decision about the number of attributes and the duration of the exercise. When the final categorization process is complete, offer your group feedback about their participation and production in this cognitive operation.

Interpreting

Interpreting is a very commonly used cognitive operation. We interpret virtually everything we hear or see. The *expression* of one's interpretation can take many forms: It can be done by talking, by writing, by painting, by composing music, and so on. The first four definitions of *interpret* in the *Random House Dictionary* allude to the close connection between interpretation and expression: (1) "To set forth the meaning of; explain; explicate; elucidate"; (2) "To construe or understand in a particular way"; (3) "To bring out the meaning of (a dramatic work, music, etc.) by performance or execution"; and (4) "To perform or render (a song, role in a play, etc.) according to one's understanding or sensitivity."

The following are two examples of divergent production episodes that engage the learner in interpreting. One is an episode in art and the other is in creative writing.

An Art Episode. This episode occurred in a fourth-grade class. Both teachers and students were familiar with Style H, which they had experienced several times before. It was Halloween time and the subject matter involved the production of clay masks.

The teacher gave each student a glob of clay, took a few minutes to explain and demonstrate the techniques for working with clay, and then delivered the task: "Make a mask that represents a human face." Time parameters were set at seven minutes. The students dispersed to their locations and began to work. While each individual student was molding the clay to represent his/her interpretation of the human face, the teacher moved about from one student to another and offered two kinds of feedback: corrective or value feedback about the *technique* of dealing with clay, and neutral feedback about the *design* of the mask.

Within the prescribed time parameters, the students finished their task. At this point the teacher said: "Your next task is to produce a second mask that is similar to the first one, but different by one aspect. When you finish that one, move on to produce a third mask that will be different from the first two by one aspect. You have 20 minutes to complete both masks."

The students took some more clay and proceeded with the design and production of the second mask. (It was clear that they were familiar with Style B routines concerning the materials, tools, etc.) The second mask produced by each student was different from the first one by one aspect— ears were a different shape or the nose was different, and so on—and represented a *different interpretation* of the human face.

As students finished the second mask, they continued with the third one, which represented still another interpretation. By the end of the 27 minutes allotted for this Style H episode, each student had designed and produced three different masks. In total, 19 students had designed and produced 57 different masks. The divergent production called upon the cognitive operation of interpreting, and it was manifested by individuals and by the whole class.

A Creative Writing Episode. An important goal of language arts is to reach some level of skill in creative writing. Yet many people, both young and old, feel considerable discomfort whenever they have to express a thought in writing. One possible reason may be that they remember past experiences when they were criticized for poor spelling, improper use of grammar, or unclear handwriting. Of course, the ability to handle these components of writing must be developed in language arts—but not as the point of entry to creative writing experiences. It is proposed here that when a teacher introduces students to the experience of creative writing the focus should be, first, on helping them feel comfortable about expressing their ideas and feelings. Corrections of spelling and grammar should be done in separate episodes. The first few creative writing episodes should promote a climate of comfort in expressing one's ideas. Corrections of mechanics and other aspects of writing should not come into play until a later time.

The following episode serves as a point of entry and is based on the assumptions that:

1. It is easier to talk than to write. (Most people express their thoughts all the time by talking to friends, neighbors, colleagues, etc.)
2. Talking is a passing experience. Writing establishes a permanent record in which errors can be detected more readily.
3. Focusing on the expression of the ideas induces a climate of safety and acceptance. Knowing that details of grammar and spelling will be dealt with separately invites students to participate more readily in the expression of ideas.

At the beginning of the episode the teacher shows the students a picture that offers various interpretations. This picture serves as the stimulus. The teacher states the task: "Look at this picture and come up with two connected sentences that can serve as an opening to a story about this picture."

The teacher waits while the students look at the picture for a minute or two. Meanwhile the content of the picture conjures up images in the students' minds. Since they were asked simply to say two sentences, the *risk* to the students is small. The teacher asks the students, one by one, to *tell* the class the two sentences they chose as an opening for the story. Almost without exception students will utter their sentences. The acceptance by the teacher, manifested through *neutral* feedback ("Mm. . . ," "Yes," "Next"), sends the students a clear message: It is all right to express your reactions to the picture your way!

It is interesting to see how the students will relax a bit and will exhibit patience. They, indeed, want to hear what their peers have wrought. After the last student has responded, the teacher offers value feedback to the whole class: "You have the idea. You did very well in designing openers to a story. We have 28 students here, and we have now 28 ways to open a story about this picture. Your next task is to design *two different* openers that we have not heard, each composed of two sentences."

The teacher shows the picture again and again waits to give students time to engage in interpreting. At this point, they will start reacting to each other's ideas, wit, humor, and somber statements and will offer feedback to one another: "That's clever." "That's good!" "That's really different."

When all this happens, the students are on their way to being able to interpret and express their ideas. The episode, with its nonthreatening, uncritical approach has broken through the emotional barrier of embarrassment and a sense of withdrawal. The exercise can end at this point (it is often enough for an initial episode) or it can continue as described below.

Meanwhile, let's review what has happened so far:

1. The picture served as the stimulus.
2. Learners entered the state of cognitive dissonance when they looked at the picture.
3. The specific verbal behavior of the teacher—the wording of the task—reduced the risk for the participants.
4. The task triggered engagement in the operation of interpreting.
5. Responses began to come forth.
6. The teacher exhibited accepting behavior by using neutral feedback.
7. The students relaxed as more and more ideas were accepted.
8. Peers began to react overtly to the ideas.
9. The flow of ideas increased.

As the next step (in the same or a different episode) the teacher gives a new task: "Design two sentences that will be the ending of the story about this picture." The flow of ideas will continue as before. The teacher then asks the students to repeat the task by designing two different endings. The production of ideas will be endless.

It is generally easier to start with the openings and closings of a story. After two or three episodes the teacher can ask the students to start working on the middle of the story. The results of these episodes will be an array of stories developed by *each* student, which is the essence of divergent production.

After a few episodes in ''talking'' the story, the task shifts to writing. The sequence of events is the same: creating an opening to the story, then an ending, and then the middle. When the teacher reads these creative writing exercises, the feedback focuses on the expression of ideas. One teacher who used this approach pinned the slips of paper on a display board (the names of the students were on the back of the paper) so that each student could see the collective products of the class. These included dozens of openings, endings, or full stories, resulting from interpreting the same picture.

In the same manner, episodes in interpreting can be designed in different subject matter areas. The stimulus for the interpreting exercises can be pictures, objects, events, people, poems, music, human situations, and so on. Regardless of the stimulus that is used, the principle of developing the skill of interpreting is the same: *Each* student offers several *different* interpretations to the *same* stimulus.

Problem Solving

This section includes examples of problems that have more than one correct solution. The multiple solutions—divergent production—are the results of engaging in discovery or in creativity. Again, the line of demarcation between these two processes may be blurred at times, but the process in focus is divergent production of solutions to a single problem.

The focal issues confronting the teacher are:

• Determining what parts of the subject matter lend themselves to problems or questions that invite the discovery of multiple solutions.
• Identifying and designing a problem that will engage the learners in the discovery of multiple solutions.

An Episode in Human Movement. Among the richest subject matter areas for designs of problems that elicit multiple solutions are human movement, sports, and dance. The variability and versatility of human movements are so vast that many problems can be identified and designed for divergent production—the discovery of multiple solutions. In the following example the teacher asks two volunteers to stand behind one of the lines marked on the floor (Figure 12.3.) They stand in the space designated as area 1. The teacher says to the participants: ''Your task is to move your body from area 1 to area 2 three times. Each time move between the lines in a different way.'' Almost instantly, the following movements are produced;

• Walking across
• Hopping across
• Skipping across

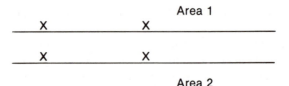

Figure 12.3. Layout for Human Movement Exercise

The teacher offers feedback and expands on the tasks: "Well done! You are performing the task correctly. Continue three more times, using three different ways for crossing." Movements such as these are often produced at this stage:

- Spinning around while crossing the lines
- Taking long steps
- Running across

The teacher continues: "You are doing well in producing different movements. Three more!" The following movements may now occur:

- Walking backward
- Running backward
- Walking sideways

This process of adding ideas continues for a while (and it differs from one individual to another) until a *pause* occurs. Until this point the participants were, indeed, producing divergent responses, each in his/her own way. But these responses were mainly the products of recall and thus were *safe* responses. One could even call them *common* responses because most people use similar movements in the first several attempts. Everyone remembers walking, running, skipping, and so on.

After the pause, however, many participants will begin to produce movements that are less common, although some of these are still the product of recalling previous experiences. But then, as responses continue past the second or third pause, learners will cross the discovery threshold or creativity threshold. At this point, the teacher will actually see the learners steeped in thinking. They are in the state of cognitive dissonance. It is as if each one is saying to him/herself: "My problem is to move across the two lines in a different way. I have already done it in several different ways. *How else* can I do it?" As they seek alternative solutions, some will fidget, some will shake their heads, others will grunt. But soon new solutions will evolve and the process of divergent production will continue.

While all this is gong on, the participants are reinforced by receiving periodically neutral feedback and value feedback about the divergent production (not the individual solution).

While the two volunteers engage in this production of alternative movements, two things happen to the rest of the class as they observe. First, most (if not all) of the observers become active participants in the cognitive production of alternatives. They enter the state of cognitive dissonance at the same time as the demonstrators. The teacher can facilitate participation by halting the active demonstration for a moment and asking the other students: "Who has another alternative solution?" Invariably the great majority of hands go up. It is very difficult *not* to get engaged. Second, members of the class will begin to respond to the solutions performed by the two demonstrators. They'll say: "That's great!" "Oh, that *is* different!" They'll applaud, they'll cheer, and sometimes they'll jeer. Peer approval or disapproval, at this stage, is acceptable. There is no need for the teacher to stop the process. It is all new to the participants.

At this point, the teacher invites the whole class to participate in the process of divergent production. The following movements may be produced:

- Crawling on the belly, no hands
- Rolling in different ways
- Moving on one knee and one foot
- Frog leaping
- Walking on toes while the trunk and arms move all over
- Jumping cross-legged
- Long jumping
- Dancing using various steps
- Stomping
- Moving heavily
- Moving lightly
- Moving with bent knees
- Twisting

In 10–15 minutes, dozens of alternative solutions will evolve. In order to enhance and intensify the engagement in discovering or in creating divergent solutions, the teacher can put parameters on the exercise: "For the next five solutions, while you move from area 1 to area 2, have only three points of contact between the body and the ground." Solutions abound:

- Two feet, one finger
- Two fingers of the same hand, one foot
- Two fingers, one of each hand, and one foot
- A foot and a knee of one leg and the foot of the other leg
- Two knees and the forehead
- Two feet and an elbow (some flexibility!)

While the learners perform their solutions, the teacher periodically verifies (but does not evaluate) the solution by actually counting the number of points of contact that were designed by one student or another. This verification is done swiftly and in good spirit.

After a while, the teacher can change the parameters: "This time, use five (or eight, or eleven) points of contact." As the new combinations evolve, cognitive inhibition is reduced and often disappears in such episodes. It changes to joyful production. Episodes like this often evoke laughter, enjoyment, and intense interest in this process. It becomes very real. People realize in a relatively short time that they can, indeed, produce new ideas in an area in which they were not accustomed to do so.

Note that this episode conforms to the model for divergent production that was shown in Figure 12.2. The stimulus (S), in the form of a problem, moved the learner to a state of cognitive dissonance (D). During the mediation phase (M), the learner was engaged in solving the problem (a dominant cognitive operation in this episode), resulting in the production of multiple solutions ($R_1 . . . R_n$).

The field of human movement is particularly conducive to processes of divergent discovery and divergent creativity because a considerable portion of the subject matter does not represent *fixed knowledge;* the content of the field is varied and variable. Therefore, teachers can be quite prolific in designing problems in this field.[1]

Problem Solving in Other Subject Matter Areas. Poetry, music, dance, fashion design, home economics, and some parts of social studies are subject matter areas that more readily provide for divergent discovery and creativity. There is always another way to express one's feelings about a stormy sea in a poem; there is always a new combination of movements to go beyond the ritualistic patterns of folk dance or the patterns of classical ballet; there is always a new stroke of the pen in designing clothes; there is always a new combination of sounds that expand the tradition in musical composition. In these subject matter areas, the teacher has a wider range of options in the design of problems that, when solved via divergent discovery or divergent creativity, enlarge and enrich the very content of the subject matter itself.

On the other hand, most aspects of the subject matter in science and in mathematics constitute concrete facts, specific laws, and particular relationships. These aspects of knowledge represent, in general, fixed knowledge that is not conducive to divergent production. There is only one Hooke's law, there are only three specific classes of lever, and there are particular rules for balancing algebraic equations. These and many other examples in scientific knowledge can be taught in episodes of convergent discovery where a single correct statement of a principle, relationship or theorem is

---

[1] See Chapter 10 in Muska Mosston and Sara Ashworth, *Teaching Physical Education,* 3rd ed. (Columbus, Ohio: Charles E. Merrill Publishing Co., 1986).

sought; they cannot, however, be taught by divergent discovery. It is, indeed, possible to discover multiple ways to prove a particular mathematical concept or theorem, but the concept itself is singular and fixed (until disproven).

However, *uses* of scientific principles and mathematical concepts are conducive to multiple possibilities, and therefore problems can be designed for the discovery of multiple applications of a principle and multiple inventions that are based on the same concept. Any high school science fair is rich with examples in the category of discovery and creative thinking.

In summary, a teacher planning for episodes in divergent production or divergent discovery is faced with the challenge of discovering which parts of the subject matter are conducive to the design of problems that invite multiple solutions.

THE P–F–D PROCESS

The Treatment of Solutions

Since the essence of the experiences in Style H is the discovery of multiple solutions, certain questions arise: What does one do with all the solutions to a problem? Are they all valid? Are they all acceptable? Is there one "best" solution?

The treatment of the discovered solutions depends on the subject matter and the implications of the solutions. Although multiple solutions can be discovered for many problems, at times only one, or even none, is selected as the final step in the problem-solving process.

How, then, does this reduction or filtering process take place? By what criteria are some solutions accepted and others rejected? Consider the following example.

The board of an automobile company assigned its engineers and inventors to come up with new car designs. Their initial task was to produce different designs that could be used for future cars. Some time later the designers came back for a meeting with the board to present their ideas. At this meeting the designers presented their *possible* solutions, regardless of how "far out" a solution might seem. (The dots in Figure 12.4 represent the

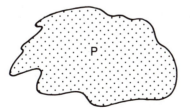

Figure 12.4. P (Possible Solutions)

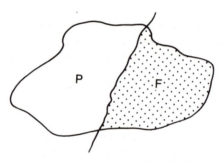

Figure 12.5. F (Feasible Solutions)

variety of their ideas.) At this stage, the goal was to generate and exchange all possible ideas without any criticism or evaluation (a procedure known as brainstorming).

The designers presented a total of 23 designs. The board examined all of these and decided that, although it would theoretically be possible to produce any of them, some would be too expensive to produce. By applying the criterion of *cost,* the board reduced to 15 the number of designs that it deemed *feasible* (Figure 12.5). The other designs were shelved.

This step of going from the *possible* to the *feasible* level is called the *reduction* (or filtering) process. It can be represented schematically as follows:

$$\text{Feasibility criterion: cost } \frac{P}{F} \rangle$$

The process of reduction by a criterion (cost, in this instance) ensures a rational selection of feasible designs from all the possible ones.

The next step involves further selection—a reduction from the *feasible* to the *desirable* level. This reduction is done by applying another criterion. The board of the automobile company used *marketability* as their criterion in this stage. Each of the feasible designs was judged against specific aspects of marketability (color, style of upholstery, etc.) and a decision was made to put 8 of the 15 feasible designs into production. These 8 designs represented

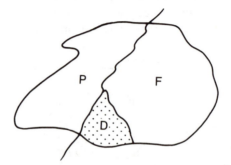

Figure 12.6. D (Desirable Solutions)

the *desirable* solutions (Figure 12.6). Schematically, the board's reduction process now looked like this:

Feasibility criterion: cost   P
                                               F
Desirability criterion: marketability   D

This process ensured that many different designs were presented and examined and that the cars finally selected for production were the best in terms of cost and marketability.

Solutions to other economic, social, or moral issues can be treated in the same manner. Possible solutions are offered first. Then a feasibility criterion for reduction is established. Each idea is then examined against this criterion and the nonfeasible solutions are eliminated. Then a desirability criterion is selected, the feasible solutions are evaluated against this criterion, and the nondesirable solutions are eliminated. The P–F–D process provides for a rational selection of "best" solutions, and—because agreed-upon criteria are used—reduces the potential eruption of emotions when solutions to a sensitive issue are pitted against each other.

We have all experienced the tension and, at times, anger that often develops in group problem-solving situations whether in faculty meetings, club meetings, family discussions, or even social gatherings. Without a procedure like the P–F–D process, people tend to present their own "best" solution (i.e., each person starts with his/her desired solution) and then must protect and defend that solution. Flexibility and acceptance of other solutions becomes difficult, conflict may develop and, at times, the whole problem-solving effort stops.

One way to prevent this kind of occurrence (assuming that the people involved really want to solve the problem at hand) is to avoid the use of pronouns. Instead of asking: "What is *your* solution?" ask: "What are some *possible* solutions to the problem confronting us?" This question gives permission to any participant to generate several solutions (even conflicting ones) without the need to defend or own any particular one. It also encourages participants' verbal behavior to shift from "*I* think that . . . ," or "*My* solution is . . ." to "A possible solution is . . . ," or "Another possible solution is . . ."

When a reasonable number of possible solutions have been produced, one or more feasibility criteria can be identified for the examination of the validity, merit, or usefulness of suggested solutions. Then the process continues through the selection of one or more desirability criteria and the elimination of all but the most desirable solutions. At times, there is no need to conclude the reduction process with one desirable solution for all involved. The reduction-to-the-desirable step can be done by judging the offered solutions against one's own values or standards; thus, the process of seeking solutions (particularly in social issues) usually ends with many individually desirable solutions. The important aspect of the experience is learning to go through the process of examining alternatives against criteria, and developing patience and tolerance in dealing with other people's ideas.

In solving problems with inherent divergent solutions (mainly in social, religious, political, and sexual areas, but also in some areas of the sciences), some people tend to have a position or solution almost instantly. In responding to a presented problem, the brain instantly functions on *one* of the three levels—P, F, or D. People who respond to the problem with their opinion are responding on level D. Opinion, whether it is a spontaneous response or a result of previous dealings with the issue, is a sort of conclusion. It always represents the desirable level for the individual—a solution that he/she already owns.

Selecting Criteria

A major issue in using the P–F–D procedure is the selection of criteria for the reduction process. Several categories of criteria that can be used for this purpose are described below.

Functionality. Solutions can be evaluated against a functional criterion— that is, by how well they serve a given purpose. For example, in the problem of crossing the puddle presented at the beginning of the chapter, "allows me to keep dry" would be a functional criteria. Then, although there are many possible options, the only functional solutions will be those that enable you to avoid getting wet. For many people, this criterion might eliminate all options except walking around the puddle. For the more agile, however, jumping over the puddle would also be a functional solution. Wading through the puddle—a possible and feasible solution—would not be desirable when evaluated against the functional criterion of staying dry.

Rules and Standards. In solving mathematical problems, the verification and acceptance of solutions is always based on mathematical rules and standard procedures. The same is true in subjects like physics and chemistry where the verification of solutions is subjected to the present governing rules of the given field of knowledge. The discovery of new knowledge, however, is often accompanied by the creation of new models, new rules, or new criteria for the verification of solutions. Another kind of rule is found in the domain of sports. It is, indeed, possible to discover (or create) a new way of performing a particular event in sport, but its validity and acceptance depends upon whether it adheres to the "rules of the game." Examples of this abound in high-jumping, discus throwing, pole-vaulting, and gymnastics, to name but a few. The rules in mathematics and science represent the universality of certain logical procedures, and they may remain permanent. The rules of sports, however, are the product of consensus and agreement by committees, and are subject to change.

Aesthetic Values. Discovered solutions and creative ideas in the arts are always subjected to the aesthetic values of a given culture (or subculture) at a given time. These values serve as criteria for acceptance. The discovered or created product in the arts is often (if not always) subjected to the judgment of experts (critics, curators, publishers, etc.) and/or of the public. Painting, writings, and musical creations have been known to be rejected at one time and hailed in another. The fluctuations in aesthetic values determine the fluctuations of acceptance.

Commercial Concerns. An invention may be unusual, useful, and even crucial to the solution of a problem, but it will never see the light of day if it does not satisfy the commercial goals of some producer. In the example of the automobile company, both the cost and marketability criteria were based on commercial concerns.

Tradition. Traditional ceremonies, rituals, and codes of behavior serve as powerful criteria for determining what is acceptable and what is not in various aspects of religious, social, and political life. Individuals and groups may discover new solutions to problems and issues in these domains, but they are always subjected to scrutiny and curbing by the traditional ways and powers of the social institutions.

Legal Requirements. Many solutions to social issues, although they may be possible, are deemed undesirable because they conflict with the prevailing law at a given place and time.

When the teacher designs an episode in divergent production he/she must answer the following questions.

1. Does the problem at hand require the P–F–D treatment of the generated solutions?
2. Does the problem require the use of all three steps (P, F, and D) or would it suffice to move directly from the possible to the desirable level?
3. What criterion (or criteria) should be used for the reduction of the solutions when moving from one level to the other?

Using the P–F–D Process in the Classroom

In the classroom the P–F–D technique is very useful when solving problems either in various subjects or in class conduct. It helps maintain the safety and integrity of the teacher and the students.

One fourth-grade teacher used a divergent production episode that

SOLUTIONS

Figure 12.7. Possible Solutions to Playground Discipline Problem

incorporated the P–F–D process to resolve discipline problems on the playground. The teacher pointed out to the students that problems arose whenever the class went outside. The teacher asked: "What are the *possible* ways that can be used to reduce or even solve these problems?"

As the children offered their solutions, the teacher listened to the ideas and wrote them on the board (Figure 12.7). Some solutions dealt with

Feasibility Criterion:
Using only school personnel

SOLUTIONS

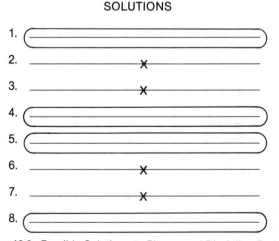

Figure 12.8. Feasible Solutions to Playground Discipline Problem

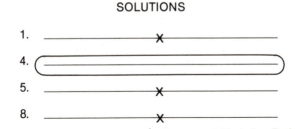

Desirability Criterion:
Can go into effect immediately

Figure 12.9. Desirable Solution to Playground Discipline Problem

long-range treatment; some were immediate remedies; others suggested employing additional personnel to enforce rules; and still others called for self-monitoring procedures.

The teacher then asked the students: "From all these possible solutions, if we consider the criterion 'using only school personnel,' which ones are feasible? Which solutions can be implemented by using only school personnel?"

Each solution written on the board was evaluated against the criterion, and those that met the criterion were circled. The others were crossed out (Figure 12.8). The results indicated that solutions 1, 4, 5 and 8 qualified as *feasible*.

The teacher then continued with the reduction process by asking: "Which of these four solutions can go into effect *immediately*?" After evaluating each remaining solution (1, 4, 5, 8) against this criterion, the learners concluded that only solution 4 qualified as *desirable* (Figure 12.9).

The students followed through in putting this solution into effect and problems on the playground were significantly reduced.

This example shows an interrelationship and an integration of the *cognitive, emotional* and *social* domains. The process of producing solutions and the use of the P–F–D technique was the cognitive part. Accepting this process, dealing with peers' ideas, and learning to be ready to act upon the selected solution was the emotional part. Putting the solution into effect by engaging in new behaviors on the playground was the social part. The entire process was conducted by the students, led by the appropriate questions from the teacher.

When they are given an opportunity to use the P–F–D process students realize very quickly that it is fair, productive, and efficient. They learn that it does not exclude anyone nor does it pit one student against the other. Two of the important results of this process are the development of patience with peers and the enhancement of respect for other people's ideas.

IMPLICATIONS OF STYLE H

The successful use of Style H implies that:

1. The teacher is willing to move with the students another step beyond the discovery threshold.
2. The teacher is willing to take a risk of encountering responses and ideas that are new to him/her without judging.
3. The teacher can accept the notion that each cognitive operation is a skill that can be cultivated by practice.
4. The teacher believes that each student can improve his/her performance in these cognitive operations.
5. The student is willing to take the risk of producing divergent responses.
6. The student understands that certain problems and issues have more than one solution or point of view.
7. The student trusts the teacher not to embarrass him/her during the production of ideas.
8. The student learns to tolerate solutions and ideas presented by peers.

STYLE-SPECIFIC COMMENTS

The following comments are reminders of "dos" and "don'ts" for episodes in divergent production. They are quite specific to this style and enhance its implementation. To being with, let us reemphasize how important it is to use the appropriate verbal behavior for Style H. In order to maintain the *integrity* of the participants and the divergent process, the verbal behavior that starts the process must always be devoid of *pronouns*. Do not ask: "What do *you* think we should do?" or "What is *your* opinion?" There are three reasons why these questions should be avoided in Style H:

1. The pronoun *you* instantly invites the solution that is already on the *desirable* level for the individual.
2. These are Style B questions. Opinions are always anchored in previous experiences or positions. Therefore, the learner *recalls* the opinion. The learner is *not* engaged in *discovering* solutions.
3. Whenever a person states an opinion, he/she "owns" it and is obliged to protect and defend it. Whenever several opposing opinions are expressed in a group that is attempting to solve a problem, conflict is likely to arise and often the mutual problem is not solved.

Starting the process with the discovery of *possible* solutions takes the onus off the individual responder, who is now free to offer two or more solutions that are different or even opposite to each other. The problem at hand is thus addressed with the broadest array of possible solutions. The pressure to defend one's opinion is drastically reduced and often eliminated. When criteria are applied for the reduction process, no one gets upset or offended that his/her solution does not qualify. Hence the solution that is selected as most desirable can more readily be accepted by most or all participants.

The verbal behavior that is appropriate here is: "What are *possible* solutions to the problem?"

Teachers who use the P–F–D process in their respective subject matter areas are invited to follow the following steps:

1. Identify a problem that is suitable for this process. Consider the potential tension the problem will trigger. If it is a "hot" problem, then the P–F–D process should be applied.

2. Identify the specific verbal behavior that you will use in stating the problem.

3. In the first few episodes *do not* announce that you are looking for the *desirable* solution. Take your students through the entire process. Remember that it is new to them. They will see no point in producing divergent ideas on the P level if they think you are looking only for D-level solutions. They need time to experience the entire P–F–D process both cognitively and emotionally. Then they will understand that even though some issues have desirable solutions, it is important to examine the many possible ones and learn to select the desirable ones.

4. Direct your class to the *possible* level first. Take enough time to give every student an opportunity to participate and to let the class exhaust the possibilities.

5. Proceed to the *feasible* level. Ascertain that the *criterion* applies—that it will, indeed, reduce the possible to the feasible. Announce the criterion and write it on the board. The verbal behavior is: "Using the criterion of _____, which of these possible solutions are feasible?" Do not erase the ideas that do not qualify; just mark them with a line or an X. Erasure may mean to students that their ideas don't count.

6. Go on to the *desirable* level. Again, ascertain that the criterion applies and announce it to the students.

Another important issue in Style H is to give students sufficient "air time." In divergent production episodes the majority of time (both in oral and written episodes) should be occupied by the learners. The teacher uses minimum time for the presentation of the question or problem and the rest of the time is devoted to the production of ideas by the learners. Feedback from the teacher is periodic and short. This time ratio may sound obvious, but some teachers have the tendency to interrupt students' flow of ideas by getting involved in tangential discussions or expressing their own ideas. These interludes usually disrupt the smooth flow of ideas developed by the learners. In episodes of divergent production it is mandatory for the teacher to *wait* and listen; otherwise the teacher violates the very objective of the episode. If the teacher wishes to participate in the episode as a member of the group, he/she must declare this in advance and adhere to the rules of the game.

An interesting phenomenon occurs quite often in Style H episodes: After the production of several ideas (or solutions) either by an individual learner or by a group, everything comes to a stop. A long pause ensues, and it feels as if the participants have exhausted their ideas—that they are stuck. In fact, this is not so at all. Usually, the first few responses in the beginning of an episode are based on recall. When a pause occurs, the learners have reached the discovery threshold and are really in a state of cognitive dissonance. The teacher must wait, respect the learners, and wait some more. Additional ideas will start to emerge. Cognitive production takes time and patience. Subsequently, another pause will take place, and then another. Such pauses always occur in divergent production—whether the episode involves one person, a small group, or an entire class. The teacher must develop the skill of being patient, waiting, and *not* contributing his/her ideas. In addition, the teacher must be sensitive to the degree of frustration that may develop when the pauses become too long or too frequent. Before this happens, it is time to end the episode. If necessary, the individual learner or the group may continue to deal with the issue in a subsequent episode.

Another way in which Style H is fundamentally different from all the previous styles is that is requires some degree of courage. This style, for the first time, introduces the dimension of *risk*—risk for both the teacher and the learner.[2]

In Styles A–D the subject matter is stated in advance and the learner's performance is either correct or incorrect. Since the focus is on *reproduction* of extant knowledge, the risk to both learner and teacher is relatively low. In Style E the choice of an appropriate degree of difficulty requires some risk taking by learners but is not as risky as the production of ideas. In Style F, if the questions are appropriate, success in responding is practically guaranteed and requires little risk taking on the student's part.

In Style H, however, many of the discovered and divergent responses produced by learners may supersede the teacher's present knowledge. At times they may even infringe on the teacher's standards and value system. The risk for the *teacher* may be high and the risk for the *student* may be equally high. In previous styles, the student knew the boundaries and

---

[2] See Doyle (1983) for the relationship between risk and different types of tasks.

responded within the range of clear expectations. In Style H the student is invited to produce the *unexpected*. This is risky and not all students are prepared or willing to take this risk. The need to be safe is quite powerful. As a result, *cognitive inhibition* sets in and the process of divergent production is terminated. This can trigger frustration and ill feelings about episodes in this style. We have, at times, heard students say to the teacher: "I don't want to do that; just *tell* me what you want!"

Therefore, the teacher should allow time to *enter* this style slowly, focusing on questions and problems that are more concrete and do not involve strong beliefs or moral judgments. The initial episodes should be *safe*. Both the teacher and the students need time in order to learn the following:

1. How the process of divergent production works.
2. How to handle waiting time.
3. How to *trust* each other in a new way. It is this trust that enables the offering and accepting of the utmost private possession—one's thoughts.

Since Style H focuses on thinking processes, one question that is frequently heard in classes is: "What do you think about _____ ?" Seemingly, this is an innocent question laden with good intentions. But, what happens when this question is asked? Since "think" is a general word it does not focus on any particular cognitive operation. As a result each student calls upon different operations in dealing with this question. Some students will invoke recalling as their cognitive activity and will respond by offering factual data. Others may engage in comparing or contrasting and will offer comparative data to shed light on the issue at hand. For them, this *is* thinking. Still others may utilize interpretation as their approach to the issue.

If the question is in reference to specific subject matter area such as "What do you think about this poem?" or "What do you think about the change of government in _____ ?" the teacher then should be prepared to accept any answer whether it is factual, comparative, interpretive, or whatever. In order to clarify the nature of these unspecified thinking experiences, each responding student should be asked to explain the source or reason for the answer.

The charts shown in Figure 12.10 and Table 12.1 can be used as classroom aids to remind both teacher and learners of their roles in Style H. Table 12.2 can serve as a guide for selecting and practicing a single cognitive operation in a given episode. It includes operational definitions for a variety of cognitive operations and suggestions for appropriate verbal behavior that will trigger each operation.

Style H: DIVERGENT PRODUCTION STYLE

The purpose of this style is to engage in producing (discovering) multiple responses to a single question.

ROLE OF LEARNER

o To make the 9 impact decisions of Style B

o To produce divergent responses (multiple responses to the same question)

o To ascertain the validity of the responses

o To verify responses in some subject matter tasks

ROLE OF TEACHER

o To make the decision about the question to be asked

o To accept the responses

o To serve as source of verification in some subject matter tasks

---

Figure 12.10. Style H Classroom Chart

TABLE 12.1. THE ANATOMY OF STYLE H: THE DIVERGENT PRODUCTION STYLE

Decision Set	Teacher's Decision Categories	Learner's Decision Categories
Preimpact	All decisions	Not involved
Impact	Implementing preimpact decisions Delivering the stimulus: the question, problem, etc. Observing the performance of the learner Providing criteria for the reduction process (when the issue requires the P–F–D process) Adjustment decisions	The nine decisions as in Style B Producing divergent responses to the stimulus question, problem, etc. Engaging in the reduction process (when the issue requires the P–F–D process)
Postimpact	Acknowledging the responses of the learner Serving as source of verification in some subject matter tasks Assessing the teaching style itself	Ascertaining the validity of the responses Verifying responses in some subject matter tasks

TABLE 12.2. COGNITIVE OPERATIONS AND VERBAL BEHAVIOR

Operation	Operational Definition	Suggested Verbal Behaviors[a]
Comparing	Examining and identifying specific characteristics that are the same about various items (X, Y, Z).	1. What is the same about _____ ? 2. What is alike about X, Y, and Z? 3. Compare items X, Y, and Z.
Contrasting	Examining and identifying specific characteristics that are different about various items (X, Y, Z).	1. What is different about _____ ? 2. How do these items differ? 3. Contrast items X, Y, and Z.
Categorizing	Arranging items in different groups, where each group shares a common attribute.	1. Arrange these objects in two groups so that the objects in *one* group will have something in common and the objects in the *other* group will not have that something. 2. Categorize these items.
Problem solving	Doing something about an obstacle, an issue, an irritant, a problem.	1. What can be done about _____ ? 2. What are 5 possible ways to answer _____ ? 3. What are the possible feelings about _____ ?
Interpreting	Explaining, performing, or bringing out the meaning of something.	1. What are 3 possible things the poem says? 2. What feelings does the author project?
Hypothesizing	Making assumptions about events, happenings, issues in reference to the past or the future.	1. What if _____ happened? 2. What could be the possible outcome of _____ ? 3. What caused _____ to happen?
Imagining	Forming a mental image of something.	1. What are possible ways that this item can be redesigned? 2. Draw three different seafront scenes.

[a] Avoid using a pronoun in the question. It puts the responses on the D (desirable) level. This exercise seeks the P (possible) level.

STYLE H AND THE DEVELOPMENTAL CHANNELS

We have come a long way since the beginning of the Spectrum. Let us see what happens to a person who is in Style H when *independence* is the criterion for placement in the developmental channels (Figure 12.11).

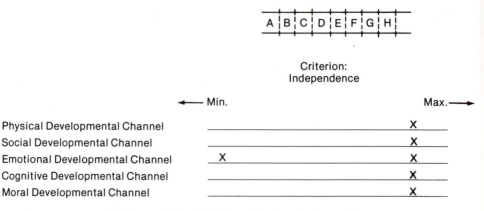

Figure 12.11. Style H and the Developmental Channels

The Physical Developmental Channel. Any student who is successfully functioning in Style H is demonstrating a high degree of independence about his/her physical development when engaged in physical tasks. The placement on the physical developmental channel is therefore very close to "maximum."

The Social Developmental Channel. The very process of developing different ideas in the presence of peers and learning to accept other people's ideas requires considerable independence in social interaction. The placement on the social developmental channel is therefore close to "maximum."

The Emotional Developmental Channel. As with some previous styles, placement on the emotional developmental channel is dual in Style H. Since the emotional state of the learner dictates the degree of risk he/she is willing to take in facing the unknown, the position on this channel depends upon how independent the learner is in his/her emotions. Some learners will remain toward "minimum"; others will approach "maximum."

The Cognitive Developmental Channel. By definition, a student who is able to function in Style H demonstrates independence in the production of divergent ideas. This student is therefore placed almost at "maximum" on the cognitive developmental channel.

The Moral Developmental Channel. The ability to be independent on the emotional and cognitive channels suggests that trust and honesty are also evolving. Thus, the student is moving toward "maximum" on the moral developmental channel.

The divergent production style engages the learner in making decisions within the dominant cognitive operation. The consequences of the decisions made by the learner constitute the subject matter created in the episode. In this style, the learner achieves a high level of cognitive independence and is on his/her way to becoming an autonomous thinker and learner. Teachers who use Style H frequently and diligently will enjoy the experience of leading their students beyond the discovery and creativity thresholds, and will join them in the joy of producing divergent ideas.

CHAPTER 13

Style I: The Learner-Designed Individual Program Style

Style I represents another step beyond the discovery threshold, which has been crossed thus far in Styles F, G, and H. In Style F, the guided discovery style, the specific response at each step of the process was discovered by the learner, but the learner's responses depended upon the meticulous sequence of stimuli (questions, clues) presented by the teacher. Style G, the convergent discovery style, called for greater independence on the part of the learner in the process of discovering the one correct answer. The dependency on the teacher (or surrogate source) decreased because the learner did not require a separate stimulus from the teacher at each step. The structure and the reality of this style, though, still maintained a powerful bond between the learner and the teacher because the teacher designed the question or problem. In Style H, the learner was even more independent in producing divergent ideas, but the teacher continued to make the decisions about the design of the specific problems.

In Style I, the learner's independence becomes even more pronounced. In this style the teacher designates the general subject matter area (a particular period in history, a particular phase of physics, a particular aspect of shop, a particular aspect of physical education, etc.). The learner discovers and designs the questions or problems within the subject matter area *and* seeks the solutions.

It is imperative to understand that Style I is not an "anything goes" or a "do whatever you want" style. On the contrary, this style is a *highly disciplined* approach to evoke and develop the creative capacities of the individual learner. It is a model for a systematic way to explore and examine an issue in order to discover its components, the relationships among the components, and a possible order or sequence for these components. In a word, Style I enables the learner to discover the *structure* of the issue at hand. It requires the learner to know some facts, to be able to identify categories, to engage in analysis, and then to construct a schema. It requires an integration of the skills—cognitive and others—learned in all the previous styles. Although Style I is highly disciplined and focused on structure, it does not require that spontaneous ideas and random discoveries be excluded or rejected. These can always be woven into the rest of the structure and find their proper place in juxtaposition to other ideas.

This style is most fruitful with students who have successfully experienced Styles A–H. It is for the student who is ready for this expansion of discovery but is also well-versed in the decisions and the processes learned in the other styles. Without the background of the previous styles, students may face difficulties in organizing both the questions and the answers into a reasonable, rational, and workable structure. Raising random questions and finding random answers is not enough. In order to understand an issue and the relationships of its components, one needs the skills learned in previous styles. Style I provides the learner with the opportunity to practice all of these skills and find ways of interrelating them over a *longer* period of time. This style cannot be done in one episode; it requires a *series* of interconnected episodes.

The very nature of Style I is the development of an idea or ideas. Style I is a process of discovering and creating series and sequences of questions and problems that inquire into the very essence of the issue at hand. It is a process of discovering and creating multiple and alternative solutions to each of the problems, and developing a structure that binds them together.

OBJECTIVES OF STYLE I

Like each of the previous styles, Style I has both subject matter objectives and behavior objectives:

Subject Matter Objectives

To discover, create, and organize ideas on one's own

To set standards of performance and evaluation on one's own

To develop subject matter that deals with a complete topic over an extended period of time

Behavior Objectives

To accommodate individual differences in thinking and in performance

To provide an opportunity for the learner to demonstrate expanded independence over a relatively long period of time

THE ANATOMY OF STYLE I

The shift of decisions in Style I is represented schematically in Figure 13.1. In this section we will describe the roles of the teacher and the learner in each decision set as governed by this anatomy.

	A	B	C	D	E	F	G	H	I
Preimpact	(T)	(T)	(T)	(T)	(E)	(T)	(T)	(T)	(T)
Impact	(T) $\longrightarrow$ (L)		(d)	(L$_d$) $\longrightarrow$ (L) $\longrightarrow$ (T$_L$) $\longrightarrow$ (L) $\longrightarrow$ (L) $\longrightarrow$ (L)					
Postimpact	(T)	(T) $\longrightarrow$ (o) $\longrightarrow$ (L$_o$)		(L) $\longrightarrow$ (T$_L$) $\longrightarrow$ (L$_T$)			(L$_T$) $\longrightarrow$ (L)		

Figure 13.1. The Shift from Style H to Style I

Teacher and Student Roles

The Preimpact Set. As was true in all previous styles, the anatomy of Style I calls for the teacher to make the decisions in the preimpact set:

1. The teacher makes the decision about introducing this style to the learners and inviting them to participate in a new degree of independence.
2. The teacher makes the decision about the general subject matter area within which the learner will evolve the questions and the answers—for example, the historical period to be investigated, the general area of activity in physical education (ball games, water environment, aerial apparatus, etc.), a general law or a cluster of laws in physics.

The Impact Set. The role of the learner in the impact set is as follows:

1. To collect available general data about the subject matter area.
2. To make a decision about which topic will be the *focus* of his/her study.
3. To discover and evolve questions or problems related to this topic.
4. To categorize those questions that can be clustered together.
5. To keep single or unattached questions available for investigation.
6. To identify sources from which answers can be derived.
7. To seek multiple answers to each question. Some answers will come from previously available knowledge; others will be discovered by the learner's cognitive production.
8. To discover new uses of available tools and instruments and, if necessary, design new ones that aid the evolvement of solutions.
9. To categorize and organize the answers or solutions into a reasonable, rational, or workable structure.
10. To communicate with the teacher about his/her progress in discovering and organizing the questions and the answers. The learner does not "check in"; rather he/she informs the teacher.

The role of the teacher in the impact set is:

1. To introduce the style and identify the general subject matter area.
2. To listen to the learner's periodic presentations of questions and answers.
3. To observe the progress of the learner.
4. To offer answers only when directly asked by the learner.
5. To alert the learner to any discrepancies between the learner's intent and action.

The Postimpact Set. In the postimpact set the role of the learner is:

1. To check out and verify the answers or solutions by criteria that are conducive to the particular subject matter area. For example: In physics, solutions can be verified by means of experiments. In mathematics, logical procedures serve as criteria for validation of solutions. In physical education or shop, functional criteria ("Does it work?") can be used to verify newly discovered and designed ideas. Each field of knowledge or subject matter area has evolved, over the years, its own criteria for solutions or for performance. The learner needs to be familiar with the established criteria although at times he/she may need to broaden the criteria or create new criteria.
2. To communicate (to inform the teacher about) the progress of the solutions by talking; writing; creating models, pictures, or drawings; or using instruments.
3. To assess the total success of the experience.

The role of the teacher in the postimpact set is:

1. To listen to the learner's presentations and assessments.
2. To acknowledge the congruity between the assessment and the selected criteria, and/or alert the learner to existing discrepancies.
3. To offer feedback. In reality it is indeed difficult to refrain from the use of value feedback. When a teacher follows the work of a student for several weeks (or months), sees the progress, observes the attempts, the struggle, and the achievements, it is impossible to remain neutral—nor is it necessary. The crux here is to teach the learner him/herself to engage in the assessment and self-verification of the solutions.

The final product of the discoveries can be presented in a variety of different forms. It can be a written or a verbal presentation; an expression in drawings or photographs; a film, videotape, or model made of various materials; or any combination of these. It can be presented to the teacher, to peers, or to any audience.

IMPLEMENTATION OF STYLE I

Let us examine an example in which a learner engages in Style I to design a program in aquatics, within the general subject matter area of human movement. Note that we have chosen an example from the field of human movement because this field is very rich with possibilities for Style I.[1] Moreover, because human movements are very visible, it is relatively easy to visualize the steps that the student goes through.

How to Do It

The Preimpact Set.

> **1.** The teacher makes the decision that time will be devoted for some (or all) students to engage in Style I.
> **2.** The teacher makes the decision that the general subject matter area will be aquatics. In this context, the preimpact decisions serve as a prelude to all the ensuing episodes that constitute a series of impact and postimpact sets.

The Impact Set.

1. The learner makes the decision about selecting a particular topic within the subject matter area of aquatic activities—in this case, ''Transportation and Aquatic Games.''
2. The learner makes the decision about the environment in which to examine and discover the possibilities of this topic. In this case, the environment will be a little island on a pond, reasonably close to the surrounding land. This island is strewn with some rocks and half covered with tall trees. Rocks jut out from the water between the island and the surrounding land, which is covered by bushes.
3. The learner makes the decision about the tools and equipment that are necessary for dealing with the issues involved in this topic.
4. The learner makes decisions about designing the questions and problems that need to be examined in this topic. In this case:
   a. What are the possible uses of the waterway between the island and the surrounding land? (Is it conducive to swimming? diving? walking through? floating objects around the rocks?)
   b. What are possible land and water games that can be designed at the narrow part between the island and the surrounding land?
   c. What are possible uses for various materials to serve as means of transportation?

---

[1] See Chapter 12 in Muska Mosston and Sara Ashworth, *Teaching Physical Education*, 3rd ed. (Columbus, Ohio: Charles E. Merrill Publishing Co., 1986).

   d. What are the differences between daytime and night-time transpor-
      tation?
5. The learner makes the decision about the plan for evaluating the process
   and the solutions. The evaluation decisions will take place in the
   postimpact.
6. The learner begins to respond to each problem by experimenting with,
   examining, and discovering the multiple movements that will, in fact,
   solve the problems. Some of the responses will remain within the
   cognitive domain alone; others will be the product of the cognitive
   process expressed in physical performance. These will be the responses
   to the questions previously designed, and will include *instances* of
   swimming activities, floating possibilities, games on the land, in the trees,
   and so on.
7. The learner organizes the discovered movements into categories as
   required by the parameters established by the learner, by the teacher, or
   by prevailing school conditions. These categories might be:
   a. Ways of transporting the body through and over the water without
      implements.
   b. Ways of transporting the body with implements (log for flotation, rope
      for swinging over the water, etc.)
   c. Ways of moving through an obstacle course using the jutting rocks.
   d. Methods of propulsion under water.
   e. Games utilizing small stones.
   f. Games utilizing the rocks on the island's bank and a rock in the water.
   g. Possibilities for shallow diving and deep diving.
8. During the experimentation, the learner makes adjustments in the design
   of the problem, reorganizes the order and sequence, checks the validity
   for the intended categories, and slowly builds up the entire schema—an
   entire integrated program of movements possible and suitable in this
   environment.

   It must be remembered that Style I can only be done when time is
allotted for a series of episodes. It is, indeed, a kind of involvement that
requires several weeks or more, so that one can immerse oneself in the
process of discovering, creating, and organizing ideas.

The Postimpact Set

   1. The learner makes decisions every time he/she verifies a response by
      performing the movement, checking its validity as a solution to the
      problem, and ascertaining its membership in a category.
   2. The learner records the solutions in an organized way during the
      entire process, so that the total written product reflects the relation-
      ships between the problems and the categories of solutions.
   3. At the conclusion of this process, the learner has the option of

presenting the program via different media. It can be presented to the observing teacher or at times to an audience of peers and guests.

SUBJECT MATTER CONSIDERATIONS

The same process and the same procedures can be used to discover and organize other individual programs in human movement by examining the relationships between body movements and other environments, various kinds of equipment, objects, and/or other people.

In the same manner a series of Style I episodes can be conducted in various subject matter areas. Areas that offer opportunities in this style include industrial arts, some aspects of home economics, some aspects of

---

Style I: THE LEARNER'S DESIGNED INDIVIDUAL PROGRAM

The purpose of this style is for the learner to design, develop and perform a series of tasks organized into a personal program.

ROLE OF LEARNER

o   To select the topic that will be the focus of his/her study

o   To identify questions and issues appropriate for the topic

o   To organize the questions, to organize the tasks, and design a personal program—a course of action

o   To collect data about the topic, to answer the questions and organize the answers into a reasonable framework.

o   To verify his/her procedures and solutions based on criteria intrinsic to the subject matter at hand

ROLE OF TEACHER

o   To select the general subject matter area from which the learner selects his/her topic

o   To observe the learner's progress

o   To listen to the learner's periodic presentation of questions and answers.

Figure 13.2 Style I Classroom Chart

advanced music composition, art expressions, some aspects of creative writing, and student science fairs.

Areas that deal with basic information are not conducive to Style I. These include elementary courses in math, physics, chemistry, computer science, and language fundamentals, as well as the factual areas of social studies. Most preliminary knowledge in these area is anchored in factual data and, therefore, requires the use of Styles A–E. (It is interesting to note in this regard that one of the paradoxes we have observed in schools is the dichotomy that divides the curriculum into "academic" and "nonacademic" courses. Most of the areas that are conducive to Style I—and also to Style H—are usually considered nonacademic. The areas that are more conducive to Styles A–E are usually considered academic. Maybe it is time to reexamine the ways we stigmatize curricular activities in our schools.)

Note that the procedure we have outlined for Style I has been called by various names, such as *project, research project, independent study, creative work,* and so on. The particular name given to the procedure is irrelevant. What is important is to adhere to the decisions that will get the learner (and the teacher) to the objectives of Style I. On the other hand, the use of one of these names may seem to imply a Style I experience, while the analysis of the decisions yields a different picture. For example students engaging in some *research projects* may be merely searching in library books for correct answers to questions given by the teacher. This is a Style B episode, which will reach *only* the objectives of Style B. See Figure 13.2 and Table 13.1.

TABLE 13.1. THE ANATOMY OF STYLE I: THE LEARNER-DESIGNED INDIVIDUAL PROGRAM STYLE

Decision Sets	Teacher's Decision Categories	Learner's Decision Categories
Preimpact	Selecting the general subject matter area	Not involved
Impact	Identifying the general subject matter area Observing the learner's progress Offering information when asked by the learner	Selecting the topic within the subject matter area Identifying the questions and the issues Collecting data about the issues Designing a personal program, a course of action Performing the task
Postimpact	Acknowledging the congruity between the learner's self-assessment and the selected criteria, or alerting the learner to existing discrepancies in the process of thinking and the achieved results	Verifying the results and conclusion based on criteria intrinsic to the field of study

IMPLICATIONS OF STYLE I

At this stage, the learner and the teacher have traveled a long way from the beginning of the Spectrum. It takes time to learn to make the specific decisions that define the behavior in each style. Both teacher and learner have experienced the weaning process—the process of shifting decisions from the teacher to the learner and its ramifications. If *autonomy of the learner* is, indeed, one of the goals of education, then the process of becoming an autonomous learner must be manifested in the teaching-learning process. Both the teacher and the learner need to know and accept this goal, both must be deliberately engaged in the weaning process, and both must accept the consequences of becoming autonomous.

The Spectrum of Teaching Styles is a framework that defines the process of shifting decisions and their impact on the learner. When teacher and learner reach the learner-designed individual program style, it implies that both have experienced all the previous styles, both accept the "non-versus" basis of the Spectrum, and both have been able to be flexible in their mobility along the Spectrum. It implies that both know the place of each style in the teaching-learning experience and are ready, now, for a period of time to be devoted to further development of the autonomous learner.

STYLE I AND THE DEVELOPMENTAL CHANNELS

When we use the criterion of *independence* to place the learner on the developmental channels in Style I, we find the position of the learner is very close to the "maximum" on all five channels (see Figure 13.3). It is

Criterion:
Independence

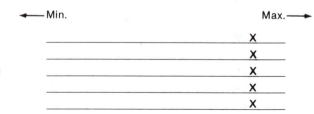

←——Min.   Max.——→

Physical Developmental Channel   X
Social Developmental Channel   X
Emotional Developmental Channel   X
Cognitive Developmental Channel   X
Moral Developmental Channel   X

Figure 13.3 Style I and the Developmental Channels

interesting to note that on the social developmental channel, the learner is independent to choose whether or not to come in contact with others.

As we have seen, Style I engages the learner in a great deal of independent decision making in the impact and postimpact sets. In Chapter 14 we will encounter the first style, Style J, in which the learner is engaged in the preimpact decisions as well.

Style J:
The Learner-Initiated
Style

As we approach the far end of the Spectrum, we find the learner making preimpact decisions for the first time. Style J differs from Style I in these two major respects:

1. The learner *initiates* the style.
2. The learner makes the decision of how to use the teacher.

OBJECTIVES OF STYLE J

The primary *subject matter objective* of Style J is to provide the learner with the opportunity to discover, create, and develop ideas in the area of his/her choice. The primary *behavior objective* is to provide the learner with the opportunity to *initiate* his/her learning experience, design it, do it, and evaluate it.

THE ANATOMY OF STYLE J

The shift of decisions in Style J is shown schematically in Figure 14.1. The roles of the teacher and the learner in the three decision sets are those described below.

Teacher and Learner Roles

The Preimpact Set. The learner's role in the preimpact set is as follows:

1. To initiate the series of episodes.

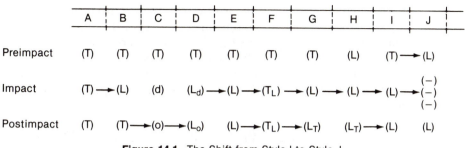

Figure 14.1. The Shift from Style I to Style J

2. To make decisions about the general subject matter area, the specific topic to focus on within this area, and the plan of study.
3. To makes all the remaining preimpact decisions.
4. To make the decision of how to use the teacher in various episodes.

Because the learner makes all the decisions in this set, the teacher has no preimpact role to play.

The Impact Set. The role of the teacher in the impact set is as follows:

1. To accept the decisions initiated by the learner and to provide the most general conditions for the learner's plans.
2. To ascertain the broadest possible parameters for the learner's plans. If the plans call for activities and conditions that are beyond the capabilities of the school to provide—for example, in terms of time, money, administrative, or judicial factors—the obvious conclusion is that this plan cannot currently be pursued.
3. To redirect the learner to other sources within or outside the school if the teacher does not know the subject matter area that the learner wants to work on. Again, this can be done within the parameters mentioned in item 2.
4. To follow through with the request of the learner.

The learner's role in this set is as follows:

1. To make all the impact decisions in every episode. This includes decisions that follow from the decision made in the preimpact phase about how to use the teacher. The learner thus decides which style the teacher will use when the teacher is invited to conduct an episode with the learner. For example, the learner can say to the teacher: "Teach me this skill by Style A," or "I need to understand a particular concept; teach me by Style F." This explains the designation (−) in Figure 14.1. It shows that during the impact set (indicated

by the outer parentheses) the learner can request from the teacher any style for a given episode (the inner brackets). It is quite obvious that Style J can be used to its fullest *only* when both the learner and the teacher are thoroughly familiar with the Spectrum.

2. To decide how long the impact phase will last and how it will be divided over a period of time into a series of episodes all initiated by the learner.

The Postimpact Set. The role of the learner in the postimpact phase is as follows:

1. To make all postimpact decisions concerning his/her performance in the selected subject matter. These evaluation decisions are made by using the criteria previously selected by the learner.
2. To make postimpact decisions about his/her learning behavior.
3. To make the postimpact decisions about the attainment of the objective of all the episodes.

The role of the teacher in this phase is as follows:

1. To receive and accept the decisions made by the learner.
2. To alert the learner to any discrepancies between the learner's intent and action.

In the postimpact phase, since the learner makes all the evaluation decisions, it is the learner who evaluates the O–T–L–O relationships. Therefore, when the teacher is invited to conduct an episode (or several) in a style requested by the learner, it subjects the teacher him/herself during that episode to the evaluation done by the learner.

IMPLEMENTATION OF STYLE J

The implementation of this style is similar to that of Style I. The major difference is that the learner *initiates* the experience; the learner is the one who states: "I am ready to do. . . ." This means that for the first time on the Spectrum, the learner makes all the preimpact decisions. The role of the teacher in the preimpact is quite subtle in accepting the reality that the learner, in fact, is ready to make all the decisions in the ensuing series of episodes. The teacher, then, assumes the role of a stand-by resource—a guide or advisor who is available to be called by the learner.

The implementation of this style takes a considerable amount of time; it may last for weeks or even longer. It takes time to identify an area for investigation, to develop a plan, to identify issues and questions, to search for information, to construct knowledge, and to organize all this into a

---

Style J: THE LEARNER INITIATED STYLE

The purpose of this style is to provide the learner with the opportunity to initiate his/her learning experience, design it, do it, and evaluate it.

ROLE OF LEARNER

o   To initiate the style

o   To design the program for him/herself

o   To do it

o   To evaluate it

o   To decide how to use the teacher

ROLE OF TEACHER

o   To accept the learner's decision to initiate his/her learning experience

o   To provide the general conditions for the learner's plans

o   To accept the learner's procedures and products

o   To alert the learner to any discrepancies between the learner's intent and action.

Figure 14.2. Style J Classroom Chart

meaningful framework. In addition to personal motivation and intellectual curiosity, it requires emotional endurance to follow through with the plan, to grapple with the obstacles, and to wait for the final product to emerge.

IMPLICATIONS OF STYLE J

The reality of the learner-initiated style speaks for itself. The learner's degree of independence is very high. Learners who can function in Style J for a portion of the time must, by definition, have the ability to make many decisions about themselves and for themselves in all the developmental channels. If we accept the notion that the Spectrum is cumulative, then a person who can function in Style J, indeed, demonstrates the ability to move

TABLE 14.1. THE ANATOMY OF STYLE J: THE LEARNER-INITIATED STYLE

Decision Sets	Teacher's Decision Categories	Learner's Decision Categories
Preimpact	Not involved	Initiating the style Selecting the subject matter area, the specific topics Organizing the plan of study
Impact	Accepting the learner's decisions Providing the most general conditions for the learner's plans	Performing the tasks that he/she had designed Deciding how to use the teacher in various episodes
Postimpact	Accepting the learner's evaluation Alerting the learner to any discrepancies between the learner's intent and action	Engaging in evaluating his/her performance and the process of making all the decisions

along the Spectrum in both directions and to benefit from the contributions of all the styles. See Figure 14.2 and Table 14.1.

STYLE J AND THE DEVELOPMENTAL CHANNELS

When we use the criterion of *independence* to place the learner on the developmental channels, we find in Style J, as in Style I, the position of the learner is very close to "maximum" on all five channels (Figure 14.3). The learner is highly independent in making decisions *about* him/herself in reference to all the developmental channels.

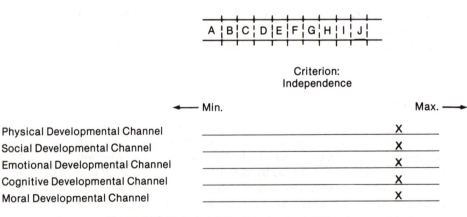

Criterion:
Independence

← Min.   Max. →

Physical Developmental Channel	X
Social Developmental Channel	X
Emotional Developmental Channel	X
Cognitive Developmental Channel	X
Moral Developmental Channel	X

Figure 14.3. Style J and the Development Channels

CHAPTER 15

Style K:
The Self-Teaching
Style

Only a little needs to be said about Style K. In this style, *all* decisions in each of the three decisions sets have been shifted from the teacher to the learner. The internal logic of the Spectrum leads us to the realization that it is, indeed, possible for a learner to make all the decisions. Obviously, however, the pure self-teaching style does not exist in the classroom. It exists only in situations when an individual is engaged in teaching him/herself. In such situations, the individual takes on the roles of both teacher and learner. (In Figure 15.1, which shows the shift in decisions from Style J to Style K, the self-teaching individual is still designated as L, the learner, since his/her teaching role is a function of the primary learning role.)

This interplay of roles usually occurs in the privacy of one's mind and one's experiences. It does not need an audience, an outside receiver, or an outside appreciator. Under some circumstances, however, it could move outside the individual's private domain. This style can occur anytime, anywhere, and in any social context, environment, or political system. It is a testimony to the unfathomed human capacity to teach, to learn, and to grow.

Who is the self-teaching individual? It could be the person who fathoms the intricacies of a complex hobby or the scientist who is propelled to understand the unknown. It could be the writer, the architect, the composer, the painter, the choreographer, the sculptor, or the explorer who is bold enough to push back boundaries, tenacious enough to endure obstacles, and romantic enough to march to a different drummer.

The ability to engage in Style K may seem like the ultimate in human development. In education, certainly, it has been perceived at times as the apex of development, the stage where one becomes a truly *free* person. But our study of the Spectrum has led us to a somewhat different view of

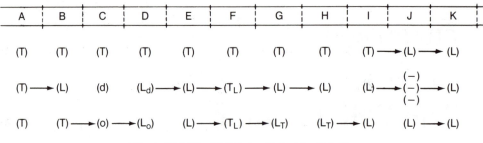

Figure 15.1 The Shift from Style J to Style K

freedom in respect to educational goals. As we saw at the beginning of the Spectrum, when Style A *stands alone* there is a limitation on the goals that can be met. With all its assets, Style A represents only a portion of human existence. Similarly, Style K, despite its assets, has limitations when *it* stands alone. A person who makes all the decisions about everything all the time may function well in Style K but be unable to adapt to conditions that bring him/her into conflict with other people, social mores, traditions, and perhaps progress. Thus Style K, like Style A or, indeed, any of the styles on the Spectrum, represents only a portion of the human experience. Therefore, a unified theory of teaching must take into account the relationships among and the integration of *all* the styles. It is the full Spectrum of Teaching Styles—not a particular style used in isolation from the others— that will serve as a cornerstone for an expanded pedagogy. Such a pedagogy involves a different vision of human development: a vision of a free person who can function in all the styles and be mobile along the entire Spectrum.

CHAPTER 16

Discipline

Every teacher, at one time or another, has experienced what is commonly known as discipline problems. The issues of maintaining control and keeping a climate of productive learning are universal. To deal with these issues effectively we need to address the following questions:

- What is discipline?
- What is nondiscipine?
- How can these be identified?
- What are the interventions for nondisciplined conduct?

DISCIPLINE AND NORMS

In this chapter, when we use the term *discipline* we are referring to something that is based on adherence to an established, accepted, or aspired-to set of *norms*. The teacher promotes discipline by making these norms clear, by requiring students to adhere to them, and by noting and treating instances of nonadherence. Students exhibit discipline when they can and do adhere to the norms. *Nondiscipline,* on the other hand, is manifested by violating these norms. When the teacher does not make the norms clear, does not enforce them, and/or does not note and treat instances of nonadherence, what is commonly referred to as a "discipline problem" results.

Sources of Norms

Where do norms come from? Who makes the decision about which norms are acceptable? There are at least three levels of sources from which norms emanate: (1) national, state, and local governments, (2) institutions, and (3) individuals.

Governmental Norms. Norms established by a government pertain to all citizens living under its jurisdiction. These norms are published in the form of laws, regulations, or codes, and they remain fixed until changed by repeal or modification of the law or code itself. Everyone is expected to adhere to these norms, and is subjected to the established system of rewards and reprimands for adhering to or violating the norms. Adhering to governmental norms requires a particular kind of discipline.

Institutional Norms. At the institutional level, norms are established that apply only to those associated with the institution. These norms reflect the rules, the "dos" and "don'ts," that characterize that particular institution, whether it is a family, a school, a military organization, a church, a social club, a corporation, a professional association, or a sport club. Only those who belong to the institution are expected to adhere to the norms and are subjected to the reward and reprimand systems of the given institution.

Adhering to institutional norms requires a particular kind of discipline that differs from that required in adhering to governmental norms.

Individual Norms. Norms can be established by and for an individual. Individual norms are rooted in one's set of values and beliefs, and in one's goals—which may be professional goals, athletic aspirations, weight-loss goals, a code of ethics one aspires to, and so on. Only the individual who establishes these norms is expected to adhere to them and respond to the systems of reward and reprimand that he/she has set up. Adhering to one's norms requires a particular kind of discipline that differs from that required in adhering to governmental or institutional norms.

Congruent and Incongruent Norms

All conduct reflects a relationship to all three levels of norms, but in varying degrees. At one theoretical extreme, the governmental, institutional, and individual norms would mesh—they would all be congruent with one another. This condition would create minimal disciplinary discrepancies. At the other extreme, the gulf between any two sets of norms would be so great that adhering to a norm at one level would always involve violating a norm at another level. This anarchic condition would cause maximum disciplinary discrepancies. In reality, of course, most situations involve some combination of congruent and incongruent norms.

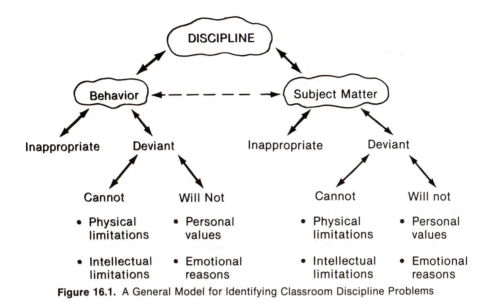

Figure 16.1. A General Model for Identifying Classroom Discipline Problems

Schools and school personnel have an especially important role to play in respect to norms. They must adhere to governmental norms; they must—as institutions—establish institutional norms; they must guide individual students who are beginning to establish their own norms; and they must deal with issues of discipline and nondiscipline that arise from each of these sources.

A GENERAL MODEL FOR IDENTIFYING DISCIPLINE PROBLEMS

The model shown in Figure 16.1 identifies the areas in which discipline problems are visible in the classroom, and the kinds of behaviors that are commonly identified as discipline problems.[1]

In this model, discipline problems always occur in relationship to *two* components: (1) the performance in the subject matter, and (2) the behavior vis-à-vis the "rules of the class" (the norms of the given classroom and/or school). Although subject matter and behavior are shown as two separate entities, the broken arrow that connects them indicates there is always a reciprocal influence between the two.

A learner is considered disciplined when he/she adheres to the procedures and techniques of performing the tasks in a given subject area (e.g., doing mathematics according to the rules of mathematics, playing basketball according to the rules of basketball). In addition, the learner must adhere to

---

[1] The term *discipline problem* as used in this text is not a reflection of a moral position, but rather a means of identifying a problem that needs a solution or treatment.

the rules of classroom behavior: staying within the prescribed role by making the decisions that he/she may make in the classroom.

Discipline problems in subject matter and in behavior are manifested in two forms: (1) inappropriate behavior and (2) deviant behavior. Inappropriate behavior and deviant behaviors have distinct characteristics. Observable signs of each type of behavior are listed below:

Subject Matter

Inappropriate Behavior

The learner does not know how to do the task.

The learner is off task.

The learner forgot the procedure or technique for performing the task.

Deviant Behavior

The learner *cannot* do the task due to physical limitations or intellectual limitations.

The learner *will not* do the task and demonstrates defiance by refusing to deal with the entire subject matter (e.g., uses verbal behavior like: "I hate math!"; "Why are we studying these names and dates—who cares?"; etc).

Note that deviant behavior ("I will not . . .") usually stems from either a clash of values between the learner and the teacher (or institution), or from an emotional condition that prevents the learner from adhering to the norms.

Behavior

Inappropriate Behavior

The learner is making decisions not shifted to him/her.

The learner is not making the decisions shifted to him/her.

The learner is testing a parameter.

The behavior is temporary and is responsive to immediate treatment.

The learner seems to be saying, in effect: "I forget!"; "I am only testing you"; or "I don't know; tell me."

Deviant Behavior

The learner is unable to behave as expected due to personal values and beliefs.

The learner is unable to behave as expected due to emotional stress and resistance to the expectations.

The behavior is longer lasting and is often manifested through anger and overt defiance of authority.

The learner seems to be saying, in effect: "I will not!"; "You can't force me!"; "I don't know and I don't want to know"; or "All this is ridiculous!"

DISCIPLINE AND THE SPECTRUM

Since each style on the Spectrum is defined by the decisions made by the teacher and those made by the learner, each style, by definition, has its own norms and its own discipline. For example, discipline in Style A (the command style) means adhering to all the decisions that are made by the teacher. Not following the decisions constitutes either inappropriate or deviant behavior, depending on the nature of the digression. In Style B, discipline means making the nine decisions that are shifted from the teacher to the learner—decisions that the learner could not make in Style A. Discipline in Styles A–E means adhering to the task as prescribed by the teacher, while discipline in divergent production means producing alternative ideas.

In classrooms conducted by the Spectrum, where episodes flow from one style to another, multiple forms of discipline are exercised by the learners and the teacher. Each episode is designed and practiced within a given style, with its unique discipline, in order to reach the particular objectives of that episode. Different objectives require different styles and different forms of discipline. There is no one style nor one form of discipline that can accommodate the multiplicity of objectives that are sought during the school day.

TECHNIQUES FOR INTERVENTION

When discipline problems are apparent in the classroom, the teacher must make a series of decisions in order to remedy the discrepancy. This section describes approaches to intervention, and steps in carrying out the intervention. There are two major approaches that are available to the teacher: (1) punishment and (2) treatment.

Punishment

Punishment by the authority figure is usually carried out in response to a breach of a rule, a code, or a strongly held tradition. Punishment is usually manifested by the removal of privileges or by curtailing the number and kind of decisions that the offender can make. Punishment procedures can be established and executed on the governmental, institutional, or individual level. Punishment, in order to be effective, must operate on a clear "one-to-one" basis; that is, there must be a clear identification of the possible violations *in advance,* and a clear statement of the corresponding punitive measures: "If you do this, your punishment will be that." Many systems of law and many institutional codes operate in this manner. Under such conditions, the expectations and the punitive measures are clearly stated in advance and serve as a control mechanism for the participants. The reason for stating norms (expectations) in advance is *accountability*. A person can be held accountable to a set of norms (on any level) only when the person is aware of and understands the expectations.

In the classroom, therefore, before punishment is exercised there must be a clear statement of how various punitive measures correspond to specific kinds and degrees of violation. This view of the use of punishment seems simple and clear in principle, but it is difficult to carry out in the complex reality of schools, particularly in public schools that serve a pluralistic society. In the public schools, there is always the potential for conflict between the institutional norms or expectations and those of individual students, who come from diverse cultures. The establishment of universal norms in a public school or even a single classroom is, indeed, a difficult and challenging task for both the school authorities *and* for the individual teacher who has his/her own values and idiosyncratic code of behavior.

In private schools, religious schools, and military schools the potential for conflict is less. The values of the institution and those of the students are more congruent, and the institutional norms are less subject to fluctuations in the norms of the community at large, and to scrutiny by community members.

In any school setting the use of punishment as a mean of intervention is a powerful tool for protecting the institution and its participants. It is a tool that forces the individual to cope with the norms and adhere to the rules of conduct. It is a tool that ensures the perpetuation of the code itself. On the other hand, it is a tool that must be subjected to scrutiny and judgment by the members of the institution in order to maintain the gentle balance between use and abuse.

Treatment

Treatment of discipline problems means focusing on the individual him/herself rather than on the institution. Treatment means understanding what norm was violated, why it was violated, and how the *learner* can internalize the process of correcting the violation.

It must be stated at this point that some people view these two approaches to discipline problems—punishment and treatment—as representing two distinctly opposing philosophies. Teachers who hold this view may choose and value one approach over the other. However, the two approaches may coexist in a school and in the classroom. The issue is one of achieving balance—the subtle and difficult balance of knowing when to punish and when to treat a violator. Let us proceed, then, to analyze the process of treatment and suggest some rational steps for implementing it.

Steps for the Treatment.

1. Locate the discipline problem. Using the model in Figure 16.1, identify specifically *what* has been violated.
   a. Identify whether the problem is in behavior or in subject matter.
   b. Identify whether the apparent discipline problem should be characterized as inappropriate behavior or deviant behavior.
   c. If, to the best of your judgment, it is in the deviant behavior category, decide whether the violation is the result of "I cannot" or "I will not."
2. Identify the specific, single *decision* that is preventing the learner from accomplishing the objective of the episode.
3. Make contact with the learner in order to verify that the learner knows that there is a discrepancy between the expectation of the teacher and the conduct of the learner.
   a. Ask *specific* questions. For example: "What is your role in this style?" "What decisions are shifted to you in this style?"
   b. Wait for the learner's answer.
   c. The learner's answer will indicate whether he/she knows the decisions or not.
      i. If the learner knows the appropriate decisions, reinforce the learner and say: "I see that you know your role; let me see how you make the decisions in the episode." Wait and observe the learner's behavior.
      ii. If the learner does not know the decision, provide the correction: "Your role in this style and in this episode is to make the following decisions: . . . Let me see you make the decisions." Wait, observe, and offer feedback once more. This kind of verbal behavior focuses on the specific decision, reestablishes the expectations, and provides the learner with the opportunity to practice appropriate decision making.

This approach is generally useful when the learner exhibits inappropriate behavior. The treatment is succinct and focused. A change in the learner's behavior is likely to occur in a short period of time. When the teacher is quite certain that the learner exhibits deviant behavior, these few steps may have to be repeated over a longer period of time. Meanwhile, the teacher must exhibit patience and understanding of the origin of the deviation. If the deviation is a result of "I cannot," obviously some modification of the expectation for that individual learner must be introduced.

If the deviation is a result of conflicting values or an emotional difficulty ("I will not"), a one-on-one session holds the most promise for potential change. One or more sessions in private, without a public confrontation in front of the rest of the class, can provide the proper climate for discussing expectations, discrepancies, and consequences. A series of such sessions provides the teacher with the opportunity to understand the difficulties encountered by the learner. The learner, on the other hand, can experience the teacher's patience and compassion that are needed in order to resolve the difficulty. In both the "I cannot" and "I will not" categories, it is imperative for the teacher to be aware of the temptation to stigmatize the learner. Stigma is the inhibitor of treatment and potential change. Understanding and compassion are healers; they open the door for new possibilities in the relationship between the learner and the teacher.

The same three steps are useful when the violation occurs in the performance of the subject matter. In this case inappropriate behavior is usually manifested by technical errors—for example, by forgetting the rules of the subject matter—which are temporary in nature. The correction can be accomplished by identifying *specifically* where the individual learner went off course and by reviewing with him/her the specific procedure, techniques, or idea of the task at hand.

Deviant behavior is usually manifested by rejection of the subject matter itself, and it often stems from continuous failure in the subject matter. The spirit of the treatment is the same as previously described. The specifics of the treatment begin with a diagnosis of where the failure began. Is the failure in recent tasks? Or is the present condition a result of cumulative failures in understanding the subject matter over a long period of time? Once the teacher has identified the original point of failure it becomes the entry point for that individual learner in the given subject matter. At times, this diagnosis and reintroduction of the learner to the subject matter is beyond the realm of the individual teacher. It may require a coordinated effort with other school personnel—for the purpose of testing, assigning a tutor, identifying an individual program, and so on. The point here is that it is possible to intervene and remedy deviant behavior in the performance of subject matter.

While the steps just delineated serve as a workable framework for intervention in discipline problems, the teacher must consider two important issues that affect the intervention decisions. The first is the issue of fairness—that is, applying the treatment (or punishment) in a judicious fashion. This issue involves:

1. Establishing the rules of the class
2. Establishing procedures for reconciling the rules of one class with the rules of another (i.e., what do the learner and the teacher do when the rules differ from class to class?)
3. Establishing procedures for reconciling differences between the rules of the school and the rules of the individual class

The second issue is that of privacy. As a rule of thumb, most discipline treatments should be done privately. The teacher must go over to the learner and conduct the entire transaction with minimal or no public display. Respecting the learner's integrity helps prevent retaliation from the learner and the beginning of combative relationships.

Each teacher will need to struggle with these difficult issues within his/her understanding of the entire issue of discipline problems.

Examples of Inappropriate Behavior and Its Treatment. The following are random examples of discipline problems that occur in classes, and examples of the verbal behavior involved in the treatment.

Example 1. In the first situation, the learner is not engaged in the task. He/she is moving all about the room. The learner goes to one spot, stays there for a few seconds, moves to another and checks it out, moves again, and so on. No place seems "right" to this learner. Meanwhile, time is passing, the rest of the class is on-task.

Treatment

1. Observe the behavior.
2. Identify as much as possible the *single decision* (or the major decision) that is preventing the learner from accomplishing the objectives. In this case, it is the location decision.
3. Make contact with the learner. Ask a question to find out if the learner understands what he/she is supposed to be doing. Possible questions: "What is your role in this style?" "What decisions are shifted to you in this style?"
4. The learner's answer will be either correct or incorrect.
   a. If the response is correct, reinforce it: "Yes, I see that you know what you are supposed to do. I'll observe how you make these decisions."
   b. If the response is incorrect, provide the correction by reminding the learner of the role/decisions. Then say: "I'll observe how you make these decisions."
5. Wait and observe. Is the learner's behavior appropriate or not?
6. Offer feedback. If the behavior of the learner is inappropriate, identify the specific decision that prevents the performance. Place parameters on *that* decision: "I see that you need more time to learn to make a location decision. Find *one* location within *this* part of the room and begin your task."
7. Step back and observe. If the learner can find a location, give feedback. If he/she continues to hesitate, reduce again the number of choices. "Find *one* location among these three chairs. Let me see you make this decision."
8. If the learner now finds a location, give feedback. If he/she doesn't,

reduce again the number of choices: "For the rest of this episode, sit in *this* chair. You are ready to make your next decision about starting the task. I'll be back in a couple of minutes to see how you are doing"; or "Let me see how you do one problem."

9. Observe.
10. Before the next episode, privately speak to the learner. Since he/she showed some difficulty, begin by saying: "In this next episode make a location decision among these three spots"; or "In the next Style B episode, the location decision will be shifted to you again. It is all right for you to make this decision. I'll be watching to see how you make this decision."

Note that the treatment is about *one* decision, not a generalized statement about the student. It gives the student no options to respond to other things. It reduces the opportunity for the student to make the excuses that he/she has *learned* to use in the past to get out of a jam. Some of these are: "He took my place"; "I don't like to sit in the sun"; "They are too noisy." The minute you hear the student moving into this kind of verbal behavior, privately bring him/her right back into focus: "Right now your *role* is to make *one* decision—the location decision. Let me see how you make this decision."

Do not respond to the stated excuse. It rarely works. You will only get more and more entangled with the learner's network of manipulations. Students who have repeatedly demonstrated inappropriate behavior are very skilled at manipulating others. Focus on the *single decision* and persist in the request to see it made.

The premise, again, is that the learner who has difficulty making a location decision has *learned* that behavior; that is, has learned *not* to make the appropriate decision. The treatment provides a concrete opportunity *to learn* to make it.

Example 2. In this situation the learner takes advantage of the right to work individually and privately. He/she spends time at another student's location for one of the following purposes:

1. To talk and socialize
2. To avoid doing the task
3. To copy
4. To annoy and disturb the peer

If this behavior is allowed to persist, then not only is the talking learner off-task, but the other student is deprived of his/her *privacy* and the opportunity to do the task.

Treatment
1. Observe.
2. Identify the specific decisions: location, starting time, and not maintaining privacy.
3. Make contact: "What is the objective for the learner in this style?"
4. If the learner's answer is incorrect, proceed by saying: "The objective of this style is to work individually and privately. Let me see you do that."
5. Observe.
6. Offer feedback. If corrective feedback is needed, offer it. (If excuses are offered by the learner, do not get engaged.) Say: "In this style, each learner has *private time* to do the task. I cannot let you interfere with his/her private time. If you need to make another location decision that will facilitate privacy, you may make this decision."
7. Observe.
8. Offer feedback. If corrective statement is needed, offer it: "I see you need more time to learn to work individually and without interfering with other people's private time. For the rest of this episode make a location in this empty area of the room."
9. Observe.
10. Before the next Style B episode you may say: "If you think you are ready to work individually and privately, you may make your own location decision," or "For this episode sit here. When you think you are ready to make your own location decision where you can work individually and privately, let me know."

When talking occurs *during* the performance of the task, the talker interferes with the pace and rhythm decision of the other person and hence disrupts his/her productivity.

Avoid using statements such as:

- "Sh . . . sh."
- "Do not talk."
- "Stop talking."
- "You only talk to me in this style."
- "You cannot talk in this style."
- "This style is the no-talking style."

These statements may temporarily correct the behavior, but they are not inviting the learner to internalize the parameters of the appropriate behavior. They are all negative and often annoying statements. Instead, focus on the concept of privacy.

Example 3. In this situation the learner does not start working on the task. Anything, any distraction, delays him/her from getting to it. Sharpening a pencil, drinking water, roaming, fiddling in the desk looking for an eraser, playing with the caged gerbil—all precede the performance of the task.

This inability to make a starting time decision obviously affects the learner's time-on-task. This student usually does not have enough time to finish the task, and this in turn affects achievement. Unsatisfactory achievement elicits and builds up ill feeling about the subject matter, which leads to further procrastination, and on the cycle goes.

Treatment

1. Identify the decision. In this case it is the starting time decision.
2. Make contact and acknowledge the difficulty: "I notice you have difficulties starting the task. I'll stay next to you while you start working on one problem in case you need my assistance."
3. Offer feedback, then move away.
4. Observe. Watch to see if the learner can stay on task or if he/she also has difficulty with another decision—pace and rhythm.
5. Offer feedback. If the learner stays on task, offer reinforcing feedback.
6. Observe.
7. Lead into the next episode: "When we do spelling this afternoon, I'll come to you first to see how you start the task," or "Tomorrow, when you work on the algebra exercises, I'll come to see how to start the task." The learner knows what the focus is, and that you are available to deal with this particular discrepancy.

Note that delay in starting the task is occasionally exhibited by a bright student who does not need the entire time allotted for the episode because he/she can finish the task in a few minutes. In this instance, it is not inappropriate behavior; it is not an example of inability to make an appropriate starting-time decision. Rather, the teacher should make a subject matter adjustment for the learner.

Example 4. In this situation the learner does not pace him/herself and finish the task within the allotted time parameters. The learner periodically stops doing the task and gets engaged in off-task activities, talks to neighbors and interrupts their performances, and/or begins to daydream. Even if the learner is able to finish the task, he/she has not yet learned to persist in continuous performance of the task. Usually, however, this learner will not get the work done.

Learners who exhibit this type of inappropriate behavior have been accustomed to doing the task at their own speed, reflecting their mood at that moment. If the task is not completed, these learners know how to get the teacher to extend the time without being penalized. This behavior can be very contagious and often, as if by agreement, the entire class adopts a slower speed that becomes the average group pace and rhythm. The extraordinary aspect of this phenomenon is not the pace and rhythm itself, but the way the students manipulate the teacher. By slowing down the pace and rhythm, they "force" the teacher to extend the time parameters. It is a subtle manipulation, but some teachers fall into the web. They often attempt to justify their response by saying: "I want to accommodate individual differences," or "I don't want to put pressure on them." The fact is, however, that the resulting pace and rhythm are often less than optimal for their students, the time-on-task is less than satisfactory, and productivity is less than desirable. All of these outcomes are the result of previously learned behaviors.

The treatment for this condition is an extension of the treatment in the previous example. Once you have watched the learner do one problem, time how long it takes before the learner becomes distracted. Move in after the disruption with more feedback. Move to other students. Then return to the learner *before* the next distraction occurs. Return frequently to offer feedback.

This feedback process will provide a legitimate pause point for the learner and will help focus his/her attention on the task. The feedback should identify the amount of work done between visits: "You did these three problems in the last two minutes." After several episodes of frequent feedback, tell the learner you will be back to offer feedback "in three minutes" and you will check five problems. What you are teaching the learner is the relationship between time and the quantity of work. The goal is to slowly reduce the frequency of feedback statements and distractions and to increase the quantity of work (without, of course, sacrificing quality).

Note that when setting time parameters, it is better to give less time rather than more. It is always easier to expand time, should that become necessary, than to reduce it. When you allot too much time for each task you may be teaching your learners to manipulate and waste time rather than helping them learn an appropriate relationship between time and doing the task.

Example 5. In this situation, the learner attempts to divert the teacher's focus. There are classes where subtle manipulations go on. Students are quite adept at sizing up the teacher's personality and ego needs. They seem to know what question to ask that, as if by magic, will take the teacher on a tangent. They have subtle ways of flattering the teacher and reinforcing the teacher's needs. Teachers who become victims of this kind of manipulation often exhibit the following pattern of behavior:

1. They remain the focus of class activities. They are the main actors in the class.

2. They repeat and elaborate the explanations, examples, or interpretations.
3. They answer their own questions. All the students have to do is wait for a few seconds and pretend that they are engaged in thinking, and the teacher will answer the question and continue with the next step.
4. They interrupt student answers by saying: "Yes, but . . . ," or "It reminds me of . . . ," and they keep going, carried away with their own verbosity.

Teachers who behave in this way are perfect targets for students who know how to trigger the teacher and divert the direction of the class. Such teachers are rarely aware of the dynamics of this process. The students patiently sit through it, knowing well that it is they who have made the decisions about pace and rhythm and the rate of production. Some are amused; others may be upset with the waste of time. The one, however, who is responsible for changing this situation is the teacher.

Example 6. In this situation the learner needs excessive feedback from the teacher. Every time the teacher turns around, the learner is requesting feedback. Competency in the subject matter is not the issue; the emotional demand is.

Treatment
1. Since the learner needs feedback, give it to him/her. Do Style B a lot for a few days and saturate the learner with you and your feedback. Try to be there *before* the learner calls you.
2. After a while, speak privately with the learner: "For the last several days I've had the opportunity to spend lots of time with you and to offer you lots of feedback about your work. I see that you are doing well in your work and in your decisions. There are 20 other students in the class. For this episode I will need to offer other students the same kind of feedback I offered you during the last few days. For this episode I'll be spending more time with other students. I will also be back to offer you feedback. I just won't be here as often. I'll be back to you to see how you are doing in a few minutes."
3. Move on and offer feedback to a few others.
4. Go back to the learner. Depending on the severity of the dependency, you may need to return with some frequency.

The principle on which these treatment steps are based is the weaning process: In each episode, slowly and gently, you wean the learner from the excessive dependency.

Example 7. In this situation, when the class is engaged in a Style C episode, a learner who is observing a doer is not providing feedback to the doer.

Treatment

1. Observe.
2. Identify the specific decisions. In this case the observer is not providing feedback to the doer.
3. Make contact. Ask: "What is the observer's role?"
4. The observer either knows or doesn't know the role.
   a. If the observer knows, say: "Yes, you understand your role very well. Let me see you do it."
   b. If the observer does not know, say: "Your role is to give feedback to the doer. How is your doer doing on the task?" When the observer responds (e.g., "Fine!"), ask: "Have you told him/her?" The observer will answer "No." Say: "Then let me see you do it."
5. Observe the observer offering feedback to the doer. Then offer your own feedback to the observer: "Yes, now you are letting your doer know how well he/she is doing."
6. After the initial episodes in Style C, remind the observer about the use of corrective, value, and neutral forms of feedback.

Example 8. In Style C a special condition arises periodically—that is, the *doer* comes to the teacher and initiates communication. This behavior may result from any of the following needs:

- A need to ask questions for clarification
- A need for feedback and reinforcement
- A need to complain about the observer

The need to come to the teacher, despite the explanations of the roles, is rooted in past experiences. The teacher has always been the source of information and reinforcement. The teacher has always been the arbiter when conflict developed between learners. The teacher has always been the source of comfort and feedback.

In Style C, however, the *reality* is different and the teacher must therefore respond to the doer in congruence with the *purposes* of this style. The appropriate verbal behavior is crucial at this point. It can either enhance the expected behaviors or it can prevent their inception.

You should begin the treatment in this situation by privately asking the doer: "In this style with whom does the teacher communicate?" "With the observer," the doer will answer. Then say: "Let's go back to your observer and see what the question is."

If the doer comes to you to complain about the observer, regardless of the nature of the complaint, do not get involved in dialogue with the doer. Listen to what he/she has to say and then ask the doer to join you and the observer. It is possible that as you get there the observer, too, will shower you with statements. After all, the doer went to you to complain. A conflict is in the making. Both the doer and the observer must protect their positions.

What do you do? Here are some recommendations for how to proceed: *Do not* start by asking: "Who started it?" or "What's the problem?" These questions beg for trouble. They are as ambiguous as the answers you'll get, they invite conflict and contradiction, and they will force you to be the arbiter and to sit in judgment.

Instead, since you listened to the doer, ask the observer to tell you his/her version. Then say to both: "Apparently there is some misunderstanding here," and continue by reminding them that Style C provides new conditions for learners to work with each other. Then ask: "What are the roles of the doer and the observer in this style?"

Note that through this entire process you ask the learners specific questions focusing on their roles; you do not *tell* them what to do. When you *tell,* the focus is on you. The learners do not have to get involved. When you ask specific questions, the learners must respond and think about their roles. After they review with you their respective roles, you say to them: "Continue with your roles and tasks; I'll be back in a few minutes to see how you are doing."

This kind of verbal behavior is suggested as a point of entry. It does not resort to accusations or personal comments; rather, it redefines the behavior sought and its boundaries. It reinforces the new roles for the learners.

In order to ascertain that this pair is functioning and benefiting from the style, visit them a few minutes later and address yourself to the observer only. *Your* behavior will demonstrate that you adhere to the structure of the style and that you, indeed, *trust* your students to learn the new behaviors.

DISCIPLINE ISSUES IN STYLES D–J

The following is a list of difficulties and discipline issues that appear in classes when the Styles D–J are in use. It is hoped that you'll be able to extrapolate from the previous descriptions, and evolve the appropriate ways to deal with these potential problems:

In Style D
• Some learners may copy, or cheat.

In Style E
• Some learners may find it difficult to make a decision about the level at which to enter the task. They are used to having the teacher tell them at what level they belong.
• Some learners may exhibit laziness and select a level below their abilities.
• Some learners may insist that everyone know the level they are on.

• Some learners who are at the top level may find it difficult to accept the legitimacy of other levels of difficulty.

In Style F
• Some learners may resist the target. This may happen in sensitive subject matter areas.
• Some questions (designed by the teacher) may not lead the learner to discover precise answers. Frustration and inappropriate behavior may result.

In Style G
• Some learners may not understand the task.
• Some learners may not be able to enter the discovery process by themselves. They may need a clue or two.
• Some learners may not be able to recruit the appropriate minihierarchy of operations. They may need a few experiences in guided discovery in the same kind of problems or issues.

In Style H
• Some learners may have difficulty producing divergent ideas.
• Some learners may be unable to accept other people's ideas.
• Some learners may express their thoughts as if these the only desirable answers to an issue.
• When the P–F–D is used and a desired response is identified, a learner may declare that this was his/her original idea.
• Some learners may put down other people's ideas.
• Some learners may not risk being wrong.
• Teachers may discard answers that *they* did not think about.
• Teachers may favor answers that *they* did not think about.

In Style I
• Some learners may produce way below their ability.
• Some learners may have aspirations that exceed their ability.
• Some learners may copy.
• Some learners may say: "That's all I can do!"

In Style J
• A learner who initiates the process may not follow through.
• A learner with good ideas who initiates this style may not be able to organize his/her activities in order to produce.
• A learner with good ideas may fail to initiate this style.

It is assumed at this point that the issues involved in discipline problems are somewhat clarified. Inappropriate behavior and deviant behavior can take a multitude of forms and may stem from many diverse reasons. The foregoing analysis and suggestions were presented to offer you some entry points and some techniques to deal with these problems regardless of the form in which they arise.

CHAPTER 17

Implementing the Spectrum in the Classroom

The implementation of the Spectrum in your classes can be divided into four processes:

1. Introducing the Spectrum to your students
2. Selecting the most appropriate style for each episode
3. Organizing the day
4. Maintaining the behaviors of the styles and their impact as time goes on

This chapter will discuss each process in detail, offering specific guidance to the teacher, and will suggest some ways in which use of the Spectrum impacts selected educational variables.

INTRODUCING THE SPECTRUM TO YOUR STUDENTS

Although the preceding chapters contain considerable information about the operation of each style, it is important to know how to introduce the *idea* of the Spectrum to your students. Because the behaviors implicit within each style may be new to them, students need to be familiar with the concept of the entire Spectrum and its basis *before* a specific style is implemented. Understanding why your teaching behavior is changing is very important for your students and will create a climate that is more conducive to changes in their behaviors. The same metacognitive behavior—the awareness of one's thinking—that is necessary to enhance the use of the cognitive operations is called upon for the awareness of one's decisions in every style.

There are a variety of ways to introduce the idea of the Spectrum. Different teachers have experimented with different techniques, settings, and sequences. Regardless of the individual approach, however, the crux of the Spectrum is the organization of decisions and their specific place in the roles of the teacher and the learner. Therefore the introduction of the idea of the Spectrum calls for *focusing on decisions*. The following steps are an effective way of doing this:

1. First and foremost, students need to be aware that a part of human behavior always involves a process of *making decisions*. So, explain to your students that people make decisions all the time.

2. The next step is to focus on decisions that the students themselves have actually made. Ask: "This morning, before you came to school, what decisions did you make?" Your students will offer a myriad of answers. These will span from decisions about which shirt to wear to decisions about whether or not to come to school. Do not comment about their statements; just jot them down on the board.

3. Next, focus on the decisions other people in their lives have made. Ask: "What decisions did your father or mother make?" "Other people?" Again, jot the responses on the board.

4. Next, focus on decisions that are made at school. Ask: "In school, what other decisions are made?" You will get quite a list.

5. At this point, reiterate that when human beings interact, they always make decisions for and about each other.

6. Now, bring the focus to decisions that are made in the classroom by the teacher and the students.

7. Explain that one arrangement is a condition where the teacher makes *all* the decisions and the students follow and obey. (At times you'll hear a grunt at this point.)

8. Proceed to ask the students if they know situations in life where one person makes all the decisions for others. Listen and record their responses. You will be amazed to see that they will produce a list similar to the one you read in Chapter 4 (Style A). They will talk about certain sports, a band, an orchestra, fire drill, traffic guard, and so on. Your role is to focus on the prevalence and importance of this kind of behavior. Say: "Some situations call for this kind of behavior."

9. Move on to clarify the *objectives* of such behavior. *You* start the list on the board (review the objectives cited in Style A) and after three or four objectives, ask your students to contribute.

10. Now you are ready to do a *short* episode in Style A. Tell the students that for the next three to five minutes you'll make all the

decisions for them (except, perhaps, location—since they are already seated—and attire and appearance).

11. Select an activity that is relevant to your class. *Do not* use a silly activity or a game. It will create a giddy mood and will tarnish the initiation of Style A. Your students must see the usefulness of the style in order to engage in it productively.

12. Review for yourself the procedure and the verbal behavior before you conduct the episode.

13. Conduct the episode swiftly and pleasantly. Do not dwell on small errors. The purpose of the episode is to convey to your students the *essence* of the decisions made in Style A.

14. Move on and introduce a short episode (10 minutes) in Style B. Your students will experience the first *deliberate* shift of decisions. Prepare the decisions chart, explain the shift in the nine decisions, and follow through with a short episode in B.

15. At the end of *each episode* tell the students how they did.

16. Be prepared for questions like these: "Why are we doing this?" "Are we going to do it all the time?" "Do we have to do it?" "What will happen if we don't?" "Why can't you teach the way you did before? We liked it better."

17. On the following day, review the details of Style A, and again conduct a short episode in this style. At the end of the episode, offer the students feedback about the way they performed the roles.

18. Explain the concept of an *episode*. Explain that different styles will be used in different episodes, for different purposes.

19. Review the shift of decisions in Style B, and conduct an episode in Style B. This time the episode should be longer so that you will have the opportunity to offer individual feedback to at least half the students.

20. On the third day, review the styles by asking your students questions about each of the styles learned. Their awareness and knowledge of the decisions is the key to successful implementation of any style.

21. On subsequent days there is no need to review the entire style. An abbreviated form will suffice. Call it by name or by the designated letter and the students will know the expected behavior.

22. When you and your class are ready, proceed to introduce other styles in a similar manner.

Note that during the implementation of each style, some students will exhibit testing behavior. They will test you to see if you really mean what you say; they will test the boundaries of the style. Have patience. It is as new to them as it is to you. The more they see the purpose of the styles and their contributions, the more willing will your students be to learn the new behaviors.

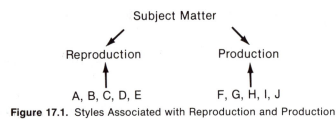

Figure 17.1. Styles Associated with Reproduction and Production

SELECTING THE MOST APPROPRIATE STYLE FOR EACH EPISODE

"How will I teach my students in this episode?" A teacher who is aware of students, the subject matter, and the objectives of education is always considering this question. How does one make the decision about which style to employ in a given episode?

The major factor in selecting the teaching style is the *objective* you seek to reach in the given episode. In determining the selection ask the following questions:

1. Do I want the learner to engage in reproduction or production of ideas? (See Figure 17.1.)
2. Do I want the learner to engage in memory, discovery, or creativity? (See Figure 17.2.)

The answers to the first two questions will place the selection in one of the three clusters: A–E, F–G, or H–J.

3. Do I want the learner to engage in convergent or divergent thinking within the cluster?
4. Which cognitive operation will be the dominant one in the episode?
5. What behavior do I want to elicit from the learner?
   a. Precision in performance
   b. Synchronization and replication of a model
   c. Beginning of independence in learning
   d. Socialization
   e. Self-assessment
   f. Initiating discovery
   g. Developing options in the subject matter
   h. Other

The answers to questions 3, 4, and 5 will provide much of the information you need to make your selection of the most appropriate style. The last set of questions should enable you to pinpoint it exactly.

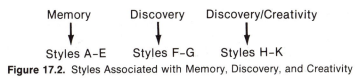

Figure 17.2. Styles Associated with Memory, Discovery, and Creativity

6. What tasks in the subject matter are congruent with information derived from the previous answers?
7. How do I design the task?
8. How do I design the appropriate questions?
9. Which style will best suit this design?

These steps for selecting a style follow the model offered in Chapter 1; they represent the *pedagogical unit* (Figure 1.5), in which the identification of an objective determines the teaching behavior that will elicit the learning behavior leading to the expected outcomes.

ORGANIZING THE DAY

As we have seen, an episode is designed for the accomplishment of a particular objective by the use of particular style. A lesson that will last 45–60 minutes can be organized as a series of episodes, each of which has a different objective, a different or same subject matter, and a different style. For example, a lesson could be organized as shown in Table 17.1.

When planning a lesson, identify *one* objective per episode. Select the style that will accomplish it (using the guidelines in the previous section) and then estimate the length of time that will be needed for the episode. In the model lesson plan in Table 17.1, the "Objective" and "Style" columns represent the O–T–L–O. The "Time" column provides a reasonable idea of the time distribution needed for the efficient flow of the lesson.

This model is one way of thinking about the organization of a single lesson. As you gain experience in conceiving the flow of your classroom events as a series of episodes, you'll be able to expand your planning for the whole day. Teachers in elementary schools have used a corner of the blackboard to identify the plan for the day (see Table 17.2).

This kind of general planning for the day provides the teacher and the learner with *clear* expectations for the day. Everyone knows where they are going and how they are going to get there. It is more specific and informative variation than the technique that teachers often use to identify the subject

O ⟷ T ⟷ L ⟷ O

Figure 17.3. The Pedagogical Unit

TABLE 17.1. A LESSON PLAN

Episode	Objective	Style	Time
Episode 1	To review	A	5 minutes
Episode 2	To introduce	B	10 minutes
Episode 3	To practice the new material	C	20 minutes
Episode 4	To summarize and check the knowledge	A	10 minutes

matter for the day (or half the day) by writing lists such as this on the board:

- Reading
- Spelling
- Math
- Snack

This list tells the learners, in general terms, what areas will be studied. In some classes, one can see time parameters also identified on the board, which tells learners even more about expectations. But when the style is identified as well, learners know specifically the role of the teacher and the role of the learner in each episode. This a priori knowledge of the style makes a significant difference in the climate, conduct, and productivity of the class.

MAINTAINING THE SPECTRUM

An appropriate introduction of the Spectrum, combined with several well-planned episodes and lessons and consistency in the teaching behavior, produces awareness and readiness in most students. In such cases, the early stages of implementation are quite joyous and productive. Generally, students are very amenable to adopting and internalizing the behaviors prescribed by the various styles.

Once the students understand the purpose of the decisions and the

TABLE 17.2. A PLAN FOR THE DAY

Time	Subject Matter	Style
9:00– 9:15	Pronouncing new words	A
9:15– 9:35	Practicing the new words	B
9:40–10:00	Reading	B
10:00–10:30	Math	C
15	Math: new concept delivery (lecture)	B̂
	Social studies (pg. ___)	D

reasons for shifting decisions, they learn to use the styles rather rapidly. Usually two to three episodes in a given style are needed for efficient functioning in that style. Teachers, in these *initial* episodes, must take the time to explain the roles, the decisions involved, and answer questions for clarification. When the initiation is done with precision and care, the students benefit from the style rather quickly. This success breeds motivation to continue and maintain the appropriate behavior.

After the initial two or three episodes in a given style, there is no need to repeat the entire introduction to the style. Mentioning the name of the style or its letter designation is sufficient. The name or letter serves as a shorthand. The students instantly know which behaviors are expected in the ensuing episode. The verbal behavior that teachers may use is: "Our next episodes will be in Style C. The materials are in the usual place. Time parameters are 20 minutes. You may begin when you are ready."

In the long run, however, maintenance of the Spectrum requires an additional step. Even the best of teachers and the best of students need periodic reminders. After several months of using the Spectrum, it is advisable to review the structure of the styles in detail and see if, indeed, the behaviors of the teacher and the students reflect fidelity to the styles. Each review session on the features and benefits of the styles will involve the students in *self-awareness* and will offer the teacher feedback about his/her performance.

This periodic interaction and exchange of insights not only maintains the Spectrum but also maintains and further develops a process that began many months ago: the process of learning to make decisions that lead to the accomplishment of specific objectives.

IMPACT OF THE SPECTRUM ON EDUCATIONAL VARIABLES

When investigating the relationship between teaching and various educational variables (e.g., time-on-task or ALT, discipline, feedback, management techniques), the more refined the differentiation and description of the teaching behavior, the more differentiated and precise the information concerning the impact of that behavior. Since the Spectrum offers a schema for differentiated styles, each defined by its intrinsic O–T–L–O, the implications for the educational variables must also be differentiated. For example, feedback behavior in Style B *must* be different from that in Style D or in any other style. Therefore, the study of feedback must be related to the particular style in use. In the same manner, discipline cannot be generalized as an educational variable when the Spectrum is used because each style has its own discipline requirements and expectations. Definitions and treatments of discipline problems vary from style to style and are always related to the particular style (O–T–L–O) in use in a given episode. The same is true for

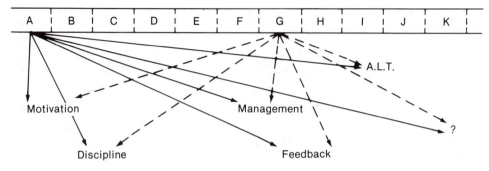

Figure 17.4. Implications Network for Each Style

time-on-task, asking questions, management procedures, cognitive development, and any other variable that has an impact on learning.

The information and data about *any* of the educational variables change
from style to style. The realization that each style has a unique set of
relationships with each educational variable can help the teacher see a wide
network of implications to each teaching act (Figure 17.4). Seeing the
implications in advance or after the fact can enrich the teacher's awareness
of the power and responsibility of his/her work. Seeing the relationships
between the Spectrum and a wide range of educational variables may open
new vistas for research on teaching that could enrich the very conduct of
the profession itself.

EPILOGUE

Teaching is, indeed, a complex human activity. It requires considerable
knowledge and skill in many areas of human development. It requires not
only a wide range of subject matter knowledge, but also the sensitivity and
insight to understand the state of each learner as a human being who moves,
thinks, feels, judges, ponders, creates, and connects with other humans. It is
quite a challenge to a teacher to integrate all these dimensions during the
moments of contact with the evolving learner. It is quite a challenge to be
flexible and mobile along the full Spectrum of Teaching Styles, and thus be
able to exercise the many options on the road from command to discovery.

References

Ashworth, S. (1983). "The Differences of Feedback Behavior between Teachers Trained by the Spectrum and Those Not So Trained." Unpublished doctoral dissertation, Temple University, Philadelphia.

Berliner, D. C. (1984). "The Half-Full Glass: A Review of Research on Teaching." In P. L. Hosford (Ed.), *Using What We Know about Teaching*. Alexandria, VA: Association of Supervision and Curriculum Development.

Berliner, D. C., & Gage, N. L. (1976). "The Psychology of Teaching Methods." In N. L. Gage (Ed.), *The Psychology of Teaching Methods*. Chicago, IL: National Society for the Study of Education.

Bohm, D., & Peat, D. F. (1987). *Science, Order, and Creativity*. New York: Bantam Books.

Burke Guild, P., & Garger, S. (1985). *Marching to a Different Drummer*. Alexandria, VA: Association for Supervision and Curriculum Development.

Center-on-Teaching. (1977). In *Educational Programs That Work*, L. White-Stevens. Trenton, NJ: Division of School Programs, Department of Education, State of New Jersey.

Chamberlin, J. R. (1979). "The Effects of Mosston's Styles B and E on Motor Skill Acquisition and Self-Concept of Fifth Grade Learners" Unpublished doctoral dissertation, Temple University, Philadelphia, PA.

Costa, A. L. (1984). "Mediating the metacognitive." *Educational Leadership, 42,* 57–62.

Dillon, J. (1984). "Research on Questioning and Discussion." *Educational Leadership, 42,* 50–56.

Doyle, W. (1983, Summer). "Academic Work." *Review of Educational Research.*

Fergusen, M. (1980). *The Aquarian Conspiracy*. Los Angeles, CA: J. P. Tarcher.

Festinger, L. (1957). *The Theory of Cognitive Dissonance*. Evanston, IL, Row, Peterson, 1957.

Goldberger, M., Gerney, P., & Chamberlain, J. (1982). "The Effects of Three Styles of Teaching on the Psychomotor Performance and Social Skill Development of Fifth Grade Children." *Research Quarterly for Exercise and Sport, 53,* 116–124.

Good, T. L., & Brophy, J. E. (1987). *Looking in Classrooms* (4th ed.). New York: Harper & Row.

Guilford, J. P. (1950). "Creativity." *American Psychologist, 5,* 444–454.

Guilford, J. P. (1959). "Three Faces of Intellect." *American Psychologist, 14,* 469–479.

Guilford, J. P. (1970). "Creativity, Retrospect and Prospect." *Journal of Creative Behavior, 4,* 149–168.

Halpern, D. F. (1984). *Thought and Knowledge: An Introduction to Critical Thinking.* Hillsdale, NJ: Lawrence Erlbaum Associates.

Hunter, M. (1979). "Teaching Is Decision Making." *Educational Leadership, 37,* 62–67.

Joyce, B. (1981). "A Memorandum for the Future." In B. Dillon-Peterson (Ed.), *Staff Development/Organization Development.* Alexandria, VA: Association for Supervision and Curriculum Development.

Lipman, M. (1984). "The Cultivation of Reasoning through Philosophy." *Educational Leadership, 42,* 51–56.

Lipman, M. (1985). "The Seed of Reason." In R. T. Hyman (Ed.), *Thinking Processes in the Classroom.* New Jersey Association for Supervision and Curriculum Development.

Mosston, M. (1966). *Teaching Physical Education.* Columbus, OH: Charles E. Merrill.

Mosston, M., & Ashworth, S. (1985). "Toward a Unified Theory of Teaching." *Educational Leadership, 42* (8), 31–34.

Mosston, M., & Ashworth, S. (1986). *Teaching Physical Education* (3rd ed.). Columbus, OH: Charles E. Merrill.

Nickerson, R. S., Perkins, D. N., & Smith, E. (1985). *The Teaching of Thinking.* Hillsdale, NJ: Lawrence Erlbaum Associates.

Oxman, W. G. (1984, May). "Thinking, Basic Skills, & Learning." *American Education,* pp. 17–21.

Oxman, W. G., & Michellli, N. M. (1981). "Analysis of Teacher Perception of In-Service Training in the Use of the Spectrum of Teaching Styles." Unpublished eight-year follow-up study. Glen Ridge, NJ: Gemini Educational Services.

Pichert, J. W., Anderson, R. C., Armburster, B. V., Surber, J. R., & Shirley, L. L. (1976). "Final Report: An Evaluation of the Spectrum of Teaching Styles." Laboratory for Cognitive Studies in Education, University of Illinois, Urbana.

Presseisen, B. Z. (1987). *Thinking Skills throughout the Curriculum.* Bloomington, IN: Pi Lamda Theta.

Rothenberg, A., & Hausman, C. R. (1976). *The Creativity Question.* Durham, NC: Duke University Press.

Roueche, J. E., & Baker, G. A., III. (1986). *Profiling Excellence in American Schools.* Arlington, VA: American Association of School Administrators.

Shavelson, R. J. (1976). "Teacher's Decision Making." In N. L. Gage (Ed.), *The Psychology of Teaching Methods.* Chicago, IL: National Society for the Study of Education.

Shirey, L. L., Anderson, R. C., & Pichert, J. W. (1978). "Active vs. Passive Time on Task of Spectrum and Non-Spectrum Students," Research Report, Laboratory for Cognitive Studies in Education, University of Illinois, Urbana.

Whimbey, A., & Lochhead, J. (1986). *Problem Solving and Comprehension.* Hillsdale, NJ: Lawrence Erlbaum Associates.

Bibliography

Adler, Mortimer J. *The Paideia Proposal: An Educational Manifesto*. New York: Macmillan, 1982.

Allport, G. W. *Becoming*. New Haven: Yale University Press, 1955.

Anderson, J. *The Architecture of Cognition*. Cambridge, MA: Harvard University Press, 1983.

Anderson, R., Hiebert, E., Scott, J., & Wilkinson, I. *Becoming a Nation of Readers*. Report of the Commission on Reading. Washington, D.C.: National Institute of Education, 1985.

Ausubel, D., Novak, J., & Hanesian, H. *Educational Psychology: A Cognitive View*. New York: Holt, Rinehart & Winston, 1978.

Babad, E. "Some Correlates of Teachers' Expectancy Bias." *American Educational Research Journal, 22,* 175–183, 1985.

Bandura, A. *Social Learning Theory*. Englewood Cliffs, NJ: Prentice-Hall, 1977.

Bereiter, C. "How to Keep Thinking Skills from Going the Way of All Frills." *Educational Leadership, 42,* 75–77, 1984.

Berliner, D. C., & Rosenshine, B. "The Acquisition of Knowledge in the Classroom." In R. C. Anderson & R. J. Spiro (Eds.), *Schooling and the Acquisition of Knowledge*. Hillsdale, NJ: Lawrence Erlbaum Associates, 1977.

Biddle, B., & Anderson, D. "Theory, Method, Knowledge, and Research on Teaching." In M. Wittrock (Ed.), *Handbook of Research on Teaching* (3rd ed.). New York: Macmillan, 1986.

Bloom, B. *All Our Children Learn*. Hightstown, NJ: McGraw-Hill, 1980.

Bloom, B. "The Search for a Method of Group Instruction as Effective as One-to-One Tutoring." *Educational Leadership, 41,* 4–17, 1984.

Bloom, B., Englehart, M. D., Furst, E. J., Hill, W. H., & Krathwhol, D. R. *Taxonomy of Educational Objectives: Handbook I—Cognitive Domain*. New York: David McKay, 1956.

Brainin, S. S. "Mediating Learning: Pedagogic Issues in Improvement of Cognitive Functioning." In E. W. Gordon (Ed.), *Review of Research in Education, 12,* 121–155, 1985.

Brandt, R. "On Improving Teacher Effectiveness: A Conversation with David Berliner." *Educational Leadership, 40,* 12–15, 1982.

Brophy, J. "Teacher Praise: A Functional Analysis." *Review of Educational Research, 54,* 5–32, 1981.

Brophy, J. "Research on the Self-Fulfilling Prophecy and Teacher Expectations." *Journal of Educational Psychology, 75,* 631–661, 1983.

Brophy, J., & Evertson, C. *Learning from Teaching: A Developmental Perspective.* Boston: Allyn & Bacon, 1976.

Brophy, J., Evertson, C., Anderson, L., Baum, M., & Crawford, J. *Student Characteristics and Teaching.* White Plains, NY: Longman, 1981.

Bruner, J. S. *The Process of Education.* New York: Vintage Books, 1960.

Bruner, J. S. *Toward a Theory of Instruction.* Cambridge, MA: Harvard University Press, 1966.

Bruner, J. S., Goodman, J. J., & Austin, G. A. *A Study of Thinking.* New York: Wiley, 1956.

Caldwell, J., Huitt, W., & Graeber, A. "Time Spent in Learning: Implications from Research." *Elementary School Journal, 82,* 471–480, 1982.

Case, R., & Bereiter, C. "From Behaviorism to Cognitive Behaviorism to Cognitive Development: Steps in the Evolution of Instructional Design." *Instructional Science, 13,* 141–158, 1984.

Cassidy, E. W., & Kurfman, D. G. "Decision Making as Purpose and Promise." In D. G. Kurfman (Ed.), *Developing Decision-Making Skills.* 47th Yearbook. Washington, D.C.: National Council for the Social Studies, 1977.

Chance, P. *Thinking in the Classroom: A Survey of Programs.* New York: Basic Books, 1986.

Collins, A., & Stevens, A. "A Cognitive Theory of Inquiry Teaching." In C. Reigeluth (Ed.), *Instructional-Design Theories and Models: An Overview of Their Current Status.* Hillsdale, NJ: Lawrence Erlbaum Associates, 1983.

Condry, J., & Chambers, J. "Intrinsic Motivation and the Process of Learning." In M. Lepper & D. Greene (Eds.), *The Hidden Cost of Reward: New Perspectives on the Psychology of Human Motivation.* Hillsdale, NJ: Lawrence Erlbaum Associates, 1978.

Cooper, H., & Tom, D. "Teacher Expectation Research: A Review with Implications for Classroom Instruction." *Elementary School Journal, 85,* 77–89, 1984.

Corno, L., & Mandinach, E. "The Role of Cognitive Engagement in Classroom Learning and Motivation." *Educational Psychologist, 18,* 88–108, 1983.

Cruickshank, D. "Applying Research on Teacher Clarity." *Journal of Teacher Education, 36,* 44–48, 1985.

Cuban, L. *How Teachers Taught: Constancy and Change in American Classrooms—1890–1980.* White Plains, NY: Longman, 1984.

DeBono, E. "Critical Thinking Is Not Enough." *Educational Leadership, 42,* 16–17, 1984.

DeBono, E. "The CoRT Thinking Program." In J. W. Segal, S. F. Chipman, & R. Glaser (Eds.), *Thinking and Learning Skills* (Vol. 1). Hillsdale, NJ: Lawrence Erlbaum Associates, 1985.

Deci, E., & Ryan, R. *Intrinsic Motivation and Self-Determination in Human Behavior.* New York, Plenum, 1985.

Devin-Sheehan, L., Feldman, R., & Allen, V. "Research on Children Tutoring Children: A Critical Review." *Review of Educational Research, 46,* 355–358, 1976.

Dillon-Peterson, B. "Trusting Teachers to Know What Is Good for Them." In

K. Zumwalt (Ed.), *Improving Teaching*. Alexandria, VA: Association for Supervision and Curriculum Development Yearbook, 1986.

Doyle, W. "How Order Is Achieved in Classrooms: An Interim Report." *Journal of Curriculum Studies, 16*, 259–277, 1984.

Doyle, W. "Classroom Organization and Management." In M. Wittrock (Ed.), *Handbook of Research on Teaching* (3rd ed.). New York: Macmillan, 1986.

Doyle, W., & Rutherford, B. "Classroom Research on Matching Learning and Teaching Styles." *Theory into Practice, 23*, 20–25, 1984.

Dunkin, M., & Biddle, B. *The Study of Teaching*. New York: Holt, Rinehart & Winston, 1974.

Dunn, R. D., & Dunn, K. *Teaching Students through Their Individual Learning Styles: A Practical Approach*. Reston, VA: Reston Publishing, 1978.

Eccles, J., & Wigfield, A. "Teacher Expectations and Student Motivation." In J. B. Dusek (Ed.), *Teaching Expectations*. Hillsdale, NJ: Lawrence Erlbaum Associates, 1986.

Featherstone, J. *The Primary School Revolution in Great Britain*. New York: Pitman, 1967.

Feurstein, R., Rand, Y., Hoffman, M., & Miller, R. *Instrumental Enrichment: An Intervention Program for Cognitive Modifiability*. Baltimore: University Park Press, 1980.

Fisher, C., Filby, N., Marliave, R., Cahen, L., Dishaw, M., Moore, J., & Berliner, D. "Teaching Behaviors, Academic Learning Time, and Student Achievement." Final Report of Phase III-B, Beginning Teachers Evaluation Study. San Francisco: Far West Laboratory for Educational Research and Development, 1978.

Flanders, N. A. *Analyzing Teaching Behavior*. Reading, MA: Addison-Wesley, 1970.

Fogarty, J., & Wang, M. "An Investigation of the Cross-Age Peer Tutoring Process: Some Implications for Instructional Design and Motivation." *Elementary School Journal, 82*, 451–469, 1982.

Freedman, S., Jackson, J., & Boles, K. "Teaching: An Imperilled 'Profession.' " In L. Shulman & G. Sykes (Eds.), *Handbook of Teaching and Policy*. White Plains, NY: Longman, 1983.

Gage, N., & Berliner, D. *Educational Psychology* (3rd ed.). Boston: Houghton Mifflin, 1984.

Gagné, R. *The Conditions of Learning* (3rd ed.). New York: Holt, Rinehart & Winston, 1977.

Gagné, R., & Brigg, L. *Principles of Instructional Design* (2nd ed.). New York: Holt, Rinehart & Winston, 1979.

Gall, M. "Synthesis of Research on Teachers' Questioning." *Educational Leadership, 42*, 40–47, 1984.

Gardner, H. *Frames of Mind: The Theory of Multiple Intelligences*. New York: Basic Books, 1983.

Germano, M. C., & Peterson, P. L. "IGE and Non-IGE Teachers' Use of Student Characteristics in Making Instructional Decisions." *Elementary School Journal, 82*, 319–328, 1982.

Glaser, R. *Adaptive Education: Individual Diversity and Learning*. New York: Holt, Rinehart & Winston, 1977.

Glaser, R. "Education and Thinking: The Role of Knowledge." *American Psychologist, 39*, 93–104, 1984.

Glasser, W. "Ten Steps to Good Discipline." *Today's Education, 66,* 61–63, 1977.

Good, T., & Brophy, J. *Educational Psychology: A Realistic Approach* (3rd ed.). White Plains, NY: Longman, 1986.

Good, T., & Grouws, D. A. "The Missouri Mathematics Effectiveness Project: An Experimental Study in Fourth-Grade Classrooms." *Journal of Educational Psychology, 71,* 355–362, 1979.

Good, T., & Stipek, D. "Individual Differences in the Classroom: A Psychological Perspective." In G. Fenstermacher & J. Goodlad (Eds.), *Individual Differences and the Common Curriculum.* Part 1, 82nd Yearbook of the National Society for the Study of Education. Chicago: University of Chicago Press, 1983.

Good, T., & Weinstein, R. "Teacher Expectations: A Framework for Exploring Classrooms." In K. K. Zumwalt (Ed.), *Improving Teaching.* Alexandria, VA: Association for Supervision and Curriculum Development Yearbook, 1986.

Goodlad, J. *A Place Called School.* New York: McGraw-Hill, 1984.

Gordon, T. *T.E.T. Teacher Effectiveness Training.* New York: McKay, 1974.

Gowin, D. B. "The Structure of Knowledge." *Educational Theory, 20,* 319–328, 1970.

Griffin, G. "The School as a Workplace and the Master Teacher Concept." *Elementary School Journal, 86,* 1–16, 1985.

Grinder, R., & Nelson, E. A. "Individual Instruction in American Pedagogy: The Saga of an Educational Ideology and a Practice in the Making." In M. C. Wang & H. J. Walberg (Eds.), *Adapting Instruction to Individual Differences.* Berkeley, CA: McCutchan, 1985.

Guilford, J. P. "Creativity." *American Psychologist, 5,* 444–454, 1950.

Guilford, J. P. "Three Faces of Intellect." *American Psychologist, 14,* 469–479, 1959.

Guilford, J. P. "Creativity: Retrospect and Prospect." *Journal of Creative Behavior, 4,* 140–168, 1970.

Harns, N. C., & Yager, R. E. (Eds.). *What Research Says to the Science Teachers* (Vol. 3). Washington, DC: National Science Teachers Association, 1981.

Hayes, J. R. *The Complete Problem Solver.* Philadelphia: Franklin Institute Press, 1981.

Holt, D., & Joyce, B. "Teacher Trainee Personality and Initial Teaching Style." In B. Joyce, C. Brown, & L. Peck (Eds.), *Flexibility in Teaching.* White Plains, NY: Longman, 1981.

Holt, J. *How Children Fail.* New York: Pitman, 1964.

Inhelder, B., & Piaget, J. *The Growth of Logical Thinking from Childhood to Adolescence.* New York: Basic Books, 1958.

Johnson, D., & Johnson, R. "Cooperative Learning and Adaptive Education." In M. C. Wang & H. J. Walberg (Eds.), *Adapting Instruction to Individual Differences.* Berkeley, CA: McCutchan, 1985.

Johnson, D., & Johnson, R. "Motivational Processes in Cooperative, Competitive and Individualistic Learning Situations." In C. Ames & R. Ames (Eds.), *Research on Motivation in Education.* Vol. 2, *The Classroom Milieu.* Orlando, FL: Academic Press, 1985.

Joyce, B., & Weil, M. *Models of Teaching* (2nd ed.). Englewood Cliffs, NJ: Prentice-Hall, 1980.

Kepler, K., & Randall, J. "Individualization: The Subversion of Elementary Schooling." *Elementary School Journal, 77,* 358–363, 1977.

Kery, T. *Effective Questioning*. London: Macmillan, 1982.

Kitchener, K. S. "Cognition, Metacognition, and Epistemic Cognition: A Three-Level Model of Cognitive Processing." *Human Development, 26*, 222–232, 1983.

Klauer, K. J. "Framework for a Theory of Teaching." *Teaching and Teacher Education, 1*, 5–17, 1985.

Klausmeier, H., Rossmiller, R., & Saily, M. (Eds.). *Individually Guided Elementary Education: Concepts and Practices*. New York, Academic Press, 1977.

Koester, L., & Farley, F. "Psychological Characteristics and School Performance of Children in Open and Traditional Classrooms." *Journal of Educational Psychology, 74*, 254–263, 1982.

Krulik, S. (Ed.). *Problem Solving in School Mathematics*. Reston, VA: NCTM Yearbook, 1980.

Kubie, L. S. *Neurotic Distortion of the Creative Process*. Lawrence: University of Kansas Press, 1958.

Kuhn, T. S. *The Structure of Scientific Revolutions* (2nd ed.). Chicago: University of Chicago Press, 1970.

LeBlanc, J. F. "You Can Teach Problem Solving." *Arithmetic Teacher, 25*, 16–20, 1977.

Leiter, J. "Classroom Composition and Achievement Gains." *Sociology of Education, 56*, 126–132, 1983.

Lepper, M., & Green, D. (Eds.). *The Hidden Cost of Reward: New Perspectives on the Psychology of Human Motivation*. Hillsdale, NJ: Lawrence Erlbaum Associates, 1978.

Lochhead, J. "Research Synthesis on Problem Solving." *Educational Leadership, 39*, 68–70, 1981.

Lochhead, J. "Teaching Analytic Reasoning Skills through Pair Problem Solving." In J. W. Segal, S. F. Chipman, & R. Glaser (Eds.), *Thinking and Learning Skills* (Vol. 1). Hillsdale, NJ: Lawrence Erlbaum Associates, 1985.

Mager, R. *Preparing Instructional Objectives*. Palo Alto, CA: Fearon, 1962.

Manor, R. "Harrah's Theory of Questions." In J. T. Dillon (Ed.), *Questioning Exchange, 1*, 15–24, 1987.

Marzano, R. J., & Arredondo, D. E. "Restructuring Schools through the Teaching of Thinking Skills." *Educational Leadership, 43*, 20–26, 1986.

Maslow, A. H. *Toward a Psychology of Being*. New York: Van Nostrand, 1962.

Mayer, R. "Can Advance Organizers Influence Meaningful Learning?" *Review of Educational Research, 49*, 371–383, 1979.

McCarthy, M. "The How and Why of Learning Centers." *Elementary School Journal, 77*, 292–299, 1977.

Monk, M. "Teacher Expectations & Pupil Responses to Teacher-Mediated Classroom Climate." *British Educational Research Journal, 9*, 153–166, 1983.

Moreira, M. A. "Concept Maps as Tools for Teaching." *Journal of College Science Teaching, 8*, 283–286, 1979.

National Commission on Excellence in Education. *A Nation at Risk: The Imperative for Educational Reform*. Washington, DC: National Institute of Education, 1983.

Neil, A. S. *Summerhill*. New York: Pocket Books, 1977.

Nelson, I. D., & Kirkpatrick, "Problem Solving." In N. J. Payne (Ed.), *Mathematics Learning in Early Childhood*. 37th Yearbook. Reston, VA: NCTM Yearbook, 1975.

Nickerson, R. S. "Thoughts on Teaching Thinking." *Educational Leadership, 39,* 21–24, 1981.

Novak, J. D., & Gowin, D. B. *Learning How to Learn.* Cambridge, England: Cambridge University Press, 1984.

Okebukola, P. A. "The Relative Effectiveness of Cooperative and Competitive Interaction Techniques in Strengthening Students' Performance in Science Classes." *Science Education, 69,* 501–509, 1985.

Paolitto, D. "The Effect of Cross-Age Tutoring on Adolescence: An Inquiry into Theoretical Assumption." *Review of Educational Research, 46,* 215–238, 1976.

Paul, R. W. "Critical Thinking: Fundamental to Education for a Free Society." *Educational Leadership, 42,* 9–16, 1985.

Perkins, D. N. "Creativity by Design." *Educational Leadership, 42,* 18–25, 1984.

Perrott, E. *Effective Teaching: A Practical Guide to Improving Your Teaching.* White Plains, NY: Longman, 1982.

Peterson, P., & Swing, S. "Beyond Time on Task: Students' Report on Their Thought Processes during Classroom Instruction." *Elementary School Journal, 82,* 481–491, 1982.

Piaget, J. *The Origins of Intelligence in Children.* New York, International University Press, 1952.

Polya, G. *How to Solve It* (2nd ed.). Princeton, NJ: Princeton University Press, 1981.

Popkewitz, T., Tabachnick, R., & Wehlage, G. *The Myth of Educational Reform: A Study of School Responses to a Program of Changes.* Madison: University of Wisconsin Press, 1982.

Presseisen, B. Z. "Thinking Skills: Meanings and Models." In A. L. Costa (Ed.), *Developing Minds: A Resource Book for Teaching Thinking.* Alexandria, VA: Association for Supervision and Curriculum Development, 1985.

Reigeluth, C. M. (Ed.). *Instructional-Design Theories and Models: An Overview of Their Current Status.* Hillsdale, NJ: Lawrence Erlbaum Associates, 1983.

Resnick, L. "Changing Conception of Intelligence." Introduction to *The Nature of Intelligence.* New York: Wiley, 1976.

Resnick, L. "Toward a Cognitive Theory of Instruction." In S. Paris, G. Olson, & H. W. Stevenson (Eds.), *Learning and Motivation in the Classroom.* Hillsdale, NJ: Lawrence Erlbaum Associates, 1983.

Rogers, C. K. *Freedom to Learn.* Columbus, OH: Charles E. Merrill, 1969.

Rosenfield, I. *The Invention of Memory.* New York: Basic Books, 1988.

Rosenshine, B. "Classroom Instruction." In N. Gage (Ed.), *The Psychology of Teaching Methods.* 75th Yearbook of the National Society for the Study of Education. Chicago: University of Chicago Press, 1976.

Rosenshine, B. "Review of Teaching Styles and Pupil Progress." *American Educational Research Journal, 15,* 163–169, 1978.

Rosenshine, B. "Teaching Functions in Instructional Programs." *Elementary School Journal, 83,* 335–351, 1983.

Rosenthal, R., & Jacobson, L. *Pygmalion in the Classroom: Teacher Expectations and Pupils' Intellectual Development.* New York: Holt, Rinehart & Winston, 1968.

Rothenberg, A., & Hansman, C. R. (Eds.). *The Creativity Question.* Durham, NC: Duke University Press, 1976.

Rowan, S., & Miracle, A. "Systems of Ability Grouping and the Stratification of Achievement in Elementary Schools." *Sociology of Education, 56,* 133–144, 1983.

Rowe, M. "Pausing Phenomenon: Influence on Quality of Instruction." *Journal of Psycholinguistic Research, 3,* 203–224, 1974.

Rowe, M. "Wait Time: Slowing Down May Be a Way of Speeding Up!" *Journal of Teacher Education, 37,* 43–50, 1986.

Rubinstein, M. F. *Patterns of Problem Solving.* Englewood Cliffs, NJ: Prentice-Hall, 1975.

Sands, M., & Kerry, T. (Eds.). *Mixed Ability Teaching.* London: Croom Helm, 1982.

Schofield, H. "Teacher Effects on Cognitive and Affective Pupil Outcomes in Elementary School Mathematics." *Journal of Educational Psychology, 73,* 462–471, 1981.

Segal, J., Chipman, S. F., & Glaser, R. (Eds.), *Thinking and Learning Skills* (Vol. 1). Hillsdale, NJ: Lawrence Erlbaum Associates, 1985.

Shulman, L. "Paradigms and Research Programs in the Study of Teaching: A Contemporary Perspective." In M. Wittrock (Ed.), *Handbook of Research on Teaching* (3rd ed.). New York: Macmillan, 1986.

Sieber, R. "Classmates as Workmates: Informal Peer Activity in the Elementary School." *Anthropology and Education Quarterly, 10,* 207–235, 1979.

Silberman, C. E. *Crisis in the Classroom.* New York: Random House, 1970.

Sipe, H. C., & Farmer, W. A. "A Summary of Research in Science Education." *Science Education, 66,* 303–501, 1980.

Skinner, B. F. *Science and Human Behavior.* New York: Macmillan, 1953.

Skinner, B. F. *The Technology of Teaching.* Norwalk, CT: Appleton-Century-Crofts, 1968.

Slavin, R. *Cooperative Learning.* White Plains, NY: Longman, 1983.

Sloan, D. (Ed.). *The Computer in Education: A Critical Perspective.* New York: Teachers College Press, 1985.

Stallings, J. "Allocated Academic Learning Time Revisited; or, Beyond Time on Task." *Educational Researcher, 9,* 11–16, 1980.

Sternberg, R. J. "Intelligence as Thinking and Learning Skills." *Educational Leadership, 39,* 18–20, 1981.

Sternberg, R. J. *Beyond IQ: Triarchic Theory of Human Intelligence.* New York: Cambridge University Press, 1985.

Suydam, M. N., & Reys, R. E. (Eds.). *Developing Computational Skills.* Reston, VA: NCTM Yearbook, 1978.

Sylwester, R. "Research on Memory: Major Discoveries, Major Educational Challenges." *Educational Leadership, 42,* 69–75, 1985.

Taba, H. "The Teaching of Thinking." *Elementary English, 5,* 534–542, 1965.

Tuckman, B., & Oliver, W. "Effectiveness of Feedback to Teachers as a Function of Source." *Journal of Educational Psychology, 59,* 297–301, 1968.

Tuma, D. J., & Reif, F. (Eds.). *Problem Solving and Education: Issues in Teaching and Research.* Hillsdale, NJ: Lawrence Erlbaum Associates, 1980.

Tversky, A., & Kahneman, D. "The Framing of Decisions and the Psychology of Choice." *Science, 211,* 453–458, 1981.

Tyler, R. *Basic Principles of Curriculum and Instruction.* Chicago: University of Chicago Press, 1950.

Vernon, P. *Creativity.* Harmondsworth, England: Penguin Books, 1970.

Wales, C. E., Nardi, A. H., & Stager, R. A. "Decision Making: New Paradigm for Education." *Educational Leadership, 43,* 37–41, 1986.

Webb, N. M. "Student Interaction and Learning in Small Groups." *Review of Educational Research, 52,* 421–445, 1982.

Weinstein, C., & Mayer, R. "The Teaching of Learning Strategies." In M. Wittock (Ed.), *Handbook of Research on Teaching* (3rd ed.). New York: Macmillan, 1986.

Whimbey, A. "The Key to Higher Order Thinking Is Precise Processing." *Educational Leadership, 42,* 66–70, 1984.

Willet, J. B., Yamashita, J. J., & Anderson, R. D. "A Meta-Analysis of Instructional Systems Applied in Science Teaching." *Journal of Research in Science Teaching, 20,* 405–417, 1983.

Worsham, A., & Stockton, A. *A Model for Teaching Thinking Skills: The Inclusion Process* (Fastback No. 236). Bloomington, IN: Phi Delta Kappa, 1986.

Yager, R. E., Aldridge, B. G., & Penick, J. E. "Science Education in the United States." In F. K. Brown & D. P. Butts (Eds.), *Science Teaching: A Profession Speaks.* Washington, DC: National Science Teachers Association, 1985.

Zechmeister, E. B., & Nyberg, S. E. *Human Memory: An Introduction to Research and Memory.* Monterey, CA: Brooks/Cole, 1982.

Zumwalt, K. *Improving Teaching.* Alexandria, VA: Association for Supervision and Curriculum Development Yearbook, 1986.

Index

Ability, 152–154
Abstract ideas, 240
Academic learning time (ALT), 107, 185
Accountability, 290
Action of communication, 188, 190, 191
Adjustment decisions, 24
Advanced units, 149
Aesthetic values, 257
Algorithm, 220
Ambiguous statements, 25, 33
  asset and liability of, 182
  characteristics of, 176–177, 183
  focus of, 182–184
  identification of, 179–180
Anatomy of teaching style, 3, 4. *See also individual teaching styles; Spectrum of teaching styles*
  impact set, 20, 21, 24, 26
  postimpact set, 20, 21, 24–26
  preimpact set, 20–24, 26
Appearance, 23, 81
Ashworth, Sara, 40*n*, 144*n*, 207*n*, 252*n*, 272*n*
Aspirations, 152–154
Attire, 23, 61, 81
Audio mode of communication, 188, 190
Axiom, 4

Behavior
  deviant, 288, 292, 302
  discipline problems and, 287–288
  inappropriate, 288, 292–300, 302
  objectives for, 7. *See also objectives subentry for individual styles*
Black students, 102
Body language, 176
Boundaries, 161
Bragging, 157

Canopy. *See also* Styles A–E
  assets and liabilities of episodes and, 172–174
  concept of, 58, 168*n*
  placement analysis, 167–172
Categorization, 12, 15–16, 240–246, 266
Cheating, 157
Clarification questions, 80
Class climate, 24
Classical design, 140–143
Classroom communication model, 188–192. *See also* Communication
Closure, 62
Clusters, 4, 6
Coaching procedures, 83
Cognitive acquiescence, 18

Note: n refers to footnotes or table notes.